Ruthless Ambition

THE RISE AND FALL OF CHRIS CHRISTIE

LOUIS MICHAEL MANZO

Former New Jersey State Assemblyman

Published by:
Trine Day LLC
PO Box 577
Walterville, OR 97489
1-800-556-2012
www.TrineDay.com
publisher@TrineDay.net

Library of Congress Control Number: 2014934103

Manzo, Louis Michael
Ruthless Ambition–1st ed.
p. cm.
Includes index and references.
Epud (ISBN-13) 978-1-937584-90-0
Mobi (ISBN-13) 978-1-937584-91-7
Print (ISBN-13) 978-1-937584-89-4
1. Christie, Chris. 2. New Jersey—Politics and government 3. Cor-
ruption investigation—New Jersey—Case studies. 4. Political corrup-
tion—New Jersey—Case studies 5. Manzo, Louis Michael,—1955- . I.
Manzo, Louis Michael II. Title

First Edition
10 9 8 7 6 5 4 3 2 1

Printed in the USA
Distribution to the Trade by:
Independent Publishers Group (IPG)
814 North Franklin Street
Chicago, Illinois 60610
312.337.0747
www.ipgbook.com

For Mom

If you shut up truth and bury it under the ground,
it will but grow, and gather to itself such explosive power that the
day it bursts through it will blow up everything in its way.

Truth is on the march; nothing can stop it now.

– Emile Zola

Table of Contents

Governor Chris Christie tours a fire area with Bridget Ann Kelley at the board-walk in Seaside Heights, N.J. on Thursday, Sept. 12, 2013, the day the George Washington Bridge lane closure ended.
Kelley authored an August 13, 2013, e-mail to Wildstein: "Time for some traffic problems in Fort Lee." She was fired by Christie on January 9, 2014.

Phil Stilton/Getty Images

Beginning of the End

Listen, I'm a trained lawyer. You know what that means? I could makeup an answer at anytime that sounds convincing.
– Governor Chris Christie
Mount Laurel, NJ Town Hall Meeting
March 12, 2014

I n November of 2013, New Jersey Governor Chris Christie was on cloud nine, celebrating the pinnacle of his public service career. He had just been re-elected, trashing his Democratic opponent by more than twenty points. Christie had also been elected chairman of the Republican Governor's Association. He was the leading contender for the 2016 GOP Presidential nomination, even besting Hillary Clinton in head-to-head polling for the future contest. Christie's favorability ratings were off the charts. *Time* magazine hailed and featured Christie as the savior of the Republican Party. His celebrity was in demand – appearances on David Letterman, Jimmy Fallon, Jay Leno, and Barbara Walters' *10 Most Fascinating People* show began to stack up. By all accounts, it looked like Governor Chris Christie was well on the way to becoming the 45th President of the United States.

Then, out of the blue, fate (or karma) stepped in as it so often does: unexpectedly. In an unimaginable reversal of fortune, Governor Christie's past began to catch up with him. Truth came a-knocking at his door.

During Christie's campaign for governor, in order to secure as many Democratic defections for endorsements as possible, Christie and his campaign team might have stretched things a bit too far in the hotly contested and coveted Bergen County campaign. Surprisingly, the Mayor of the obscure town of Fort Lee, Mark Sokolich, would draw the wrath of the political gods when he failed to capitulate and endorse Christie's re-election bid. Fort Lee sits at the west end of the George Washington Bridge and is impacted by the ebbs and flows of traffic traversing the bridge.

David Wildstein, Christie supporter and high school classmate of the Governor, a former political blogger and onetime Republican mayor of Livingston, New Jersey, was a Port Authority official appointed at the behest of Governor Christie. Wildstein got the grand idea to close the Fort Lee local access traffic lanes leading onto the George Washington Bridge for four days in September 2013. The lane closures happened to coincide with the opening of Fort Lee's school year and just weeks after Mayor Sokolich declined to support Christie in the upcoming November election. Traffic jams abounded in the town, tying up everything from emergency response vehicles to school buses during rush hours.

The Port Authority's Executive Director, Patrick Foye, was kept in the dark about the lane shutdown. According to the *Huffington Post*, "other Port Authority officials said Wildstein directed them not to tell Foye about the bridge closures." When Foye finally did find out, he blew his stack, declaring that, "procedures were violated and residents' safety was put at risk." He further termed the lane closings as "dangerous" and "illegal."

Wildstein, and the man who recommended him, another Christie stalwart, Deputy Executive Director Bill Baroni, alibied that the lane closures were the result of a traffic study. Christie publically supported them, arguing that he didn't think it was fair that tiny Fort Lee had so many access lanes to the bridge. However, a New Jersey State legislative investigative committee hearing could not get any Port Authority personnel to produce a scintilla of evidence supporting the excuse of a "traffic study." Mayor Sokolich cut to the chase and alleged the actions were punitive for his failure to support Christie's re-election. The mayor would later walk back somewhat from the charge, but the accusation had been voiced. State Senator Loretta Weinberg, who represents the district, likewise suspected the closings were politically motivated and told the *Star-Ledger* that, "Wildstein has abused the agency's authority for the sake of perpetuating the governor's power."

Wildstein abruptly exited the scene, announcing that because of the distraction created by the issue, he was stepping down from his position at the Port Authority. Baroni shortly followed suit. Christie said he never bothered to question Baroni or Wildstein as to why they were making so sudden a departure; perhaps he already knew the answer. Christie called a press conference in order to feign leadership and keep an arms-distance from the matter. He later admitted to gathering certain select senior office staff together, just prior to his press conference, for the purpose of gauging their involvement in the lane closings. He said he gave them an hour to fess up to any involvement in the fiasco. No one came clean.

Confronting the badgering and accusations of reporters, Christie sarcastically commented, "I was working the cones," that were used to shutoff the traffic lanes. He scoffed at and belittled the efforts of those legislators and press investigating and reporting about the looming scandal. He insisted that neither he nor anyone on his staff had any involvement whatsoever in ordering the lane closures. He blamed the hullabaloo surrounding the controversy on partisan Democrats whom he accused of exploiting the issue to make him look bad. Christie continued to stick with the traffic study alibi that Baroni and Wildstein had floated.

The crisis was cloaked in the antics and corrupt underhandedness that seem to typify Christie's career. Yet, this fiasco, more than any other, appeared to catch traction and show signs of sticking to the otherwise teflon politico. MSNBC's Rachel Maddow categorized the event as a "rejected plotline from the Sopranos." Only time and the suspect tenacity of a usually lackluster media would tell. The ramifications could prove to be lethal for Christie's national intentions, as New Jersey Assemblyman John Wisniewski put it: "If he couldn't be trusted to run a bridge, how can he be trusted to run the country?"

Things would suddenly take the proverbial turn for the worse as the New Year of 2014 opened. The release of e-mails between senior staff in the Governor's office and Christie appointees at the Port Authority revealed the worst side of political vengeance and corruption in government. Following an August day when Christie excoriated Democrats in the legislature, including Senator Loretta Weinberg, for their failure to support his Supreme Court nominations (Christie labeled them "animals"), an e-mail from Christie's Deputy Chief of Staff, Bridget Anne Kelly, gave direction to David Wildstein at the Port Authority: "Time for some traffic problems in Fort Lee." Ironically, the town lies in Weinberg's legislative district.

"Got it," Wildstein responded, as if he knew what was meant by Kelly's cryptic message. A month later, Wildstein had all the pieces in place and he masterfully created gridlock in Fort Lee by ordering the closing of the traffic lanes leading to the bridge. The result: kids stranded in buses for hours on the first days of school and ambulances and emergency service vehicles delayed while trying to respond to calls. Fort Lee EMS workers documented the death of a 91-year-old woman from cardiac arrest. The paramedics could not reach her in time because of the traffic tie-ups.

As the massive traffic jams froze the streets of Fort Lee, Bridget Anne Kelly exchanged e-mails with Wildstein. "Is it wrong that I'm smiling?" she asked.

"No," Wildstein responded.

When Kelly expressed sympathy, "I feel badly about the kids," Wildstein retorted, "They are the children of Buono voters," referring to Christie's opponent in the gubernatorial election. Later, once the emails were revelealed, Christie fired Kelly: she had become another in a long line of scapegoats.

In a different e-mail exchange, Christie's two-time campaign manager, Bill Stepien, who had miraculously wound up on the State payroll in the Governor's office, referred to the protesting Fort Lee mayor as an "idiot." The remark and his involvement would cost Stepien a recent appointment as chairman of the New Jersey State Republican Party and a campaign position with the Republican Governor's Association. Christie sacked him from both positions – serving up more red meat to his critics.

After hiding behind closed doors for 24 hours, Christie and his team put together a statement. "I am outraged and deeply saddened to learn that not only was I misled by a member of my staff, but this completely inappropriate and unsanctioned conduct was made without my knowledge," Christie alibied. Translation: he was the victim of his staff.

At a follow-up press conference, Christie was even more vociferous. He transitioned into Ralph Kramden mode. Not the tough guy, braggadocio Kramden who vows to send his wife Alice to the moon on occasion, but the humble, puppy-dog Kramden with the sad face and sullen eyes, hamming it up for sympathy after one of his schemes falls apart. Christie pleaded for forgiveness from New Jerseyans. This was the same puppy-dog face he had put on when he claimed that he had made an honest mistake in breaking the law three times by failing to list his loan to Michele Brown, another U.S. Attorney who had worked under him, on various government disclosure forms while he was running for governor in 2009.

Christie said he was "humiliated" and that he had been "blindsided." As the *Star-Ledger's* Ted Sherman reported, "he humbly took responsibility for allowing the George Washington Bridge scandal to happen under his watch. But at the same time, he took none of the blame, as he worked to tamp down the flames of controversy that threaten to consume his administration and his national political ambitions." Christie then lashed out at Kelly, his Deputy who allegedly gave the lane closure orders all by herself. He called her a "liar."

Christie insisted that he, incredibly, knew nothing, nor bothered to learn anything more, even as the nightmare traffic jams continued to affect Fort Lee. "I had no knowledge of this – of the planning, the execution or anything about it – and that I first found out about it after it was over," Christie assured the public. In response to questions about his longstanding relationship with David Wildstein, Christie paralleled the denial of St. Peter: "We didn't travel in the same circles in high school. You know, I was the class president and athlete. I don't know what David was doing during that period of time." Then Christie quickly morphed into the role of Judas and publically announced the political executions of Kelly and Stepien.

Always demonstrating a flair for drama, Christie left the press conference and headed to Fort Lee, New Jersey. There he personally apologized to the mayor in a closed-door meeting. He extended his condolences to the residents of Fort Lee and others who had been victims of his administration's orchestrated traffic jam. While Christie was on his way to offer his apology to Fort Lee, David Wildstein was being called to testify before the state legislative committee investigating the matter. Wildstein invoked his Fifth Amendment right not to testify and incriminate himself. His lawyer followed with a request for immunity so Wildstein could tell the world what he knew.

Days after Christie's press conference, other subpoenaed e-mails released to the public revealed that when other sane Port Authority officials tried to override the lane closures, Christie's appointees at the agency resisted, using the clout of Christie's appointee on the Port Authority's Board, Chairman David Samson, to run interference. Wildstein e-mailed Kelly and informed the Governor's Office that, "The New York side gave Fort Lee back all three lanes this morning. We are appropriately going nuts. Samson helping us to retaliate."

The e-mails incriminated more of Christie's staff and appointees at the Port Authority in the brazen attempts to fight off other Port Authority brass and keep traffic clogged in Fort Lee. At the same time, they expressed concerns about having a cover story to feed to the press. Others in the Governor's office would pitch in to help out, but, despite bumping into Christie every day, they expected the public to believe that no one bothered to inform the Governor. Christie's alibi stretches credulity to the breaking point. Not one of his henchmen admitted to knowing why the action was ordered or by whom, nor did they ever endeavor to find out.

This was fast becoming a no-win situation. Even if he was telling the truth, Christie had obviously created a culture within his administration in which many of his key staff and appointees felt free to abuse power.

The repercussions of the latest e-mail revelations triggered the New Jersey legislature to cast a wider net and rain subpoenas down on Trenton, serving practically all of Christie's key inner circle and demanding even more documents, e-mails and text messages. The legislative committee ramped up and hired the former United States Attorney from Illinois, Reid Schar, who had successfully prosecuted that state's former governor, Rod Blagojevich.

The United States Attorney's Office, where other Christie allies and some of his fixers were still employed, also launched an inquiry into the matter. Some Republican legislators and Christie allies suggested that the New Jersey legislature should shut down their investigation and allow the United States Attorney's Office to run the show. That wasn't about to happen. Not to be outdone, Christie contracted a law firm to conduct an internal investigation of the matter; a smart move, in case he needed to contradict whatever the legislature or United States Attorney's Office might find.

Within days of the Christie ship of state starting to list, other torpedoes struck below the waterline. In a blockbuster allegation, Hoboken Mayor Dawn Zimmer accused the Christie administration of shaking her down to help a developer in exchange for the release of Superstorm Sandy relief funds to help her city. The development, located within three blocks of a nineteen-block redevelopment zone in Hoboken, was owned by the Rockefeller Group of New York. Coincidentally, the Rockefeller Group was being represented by Wolff & Samson, the law firm of Port Authority Chairman David Samson, a close Christie confidant. The Rockefeller Group was also a significant campaign contributor to the Governor.

Offering to help the City of Hoboken, the ex-New Jersey DCA Commissioner, Lori Grifa, leaned on the Port Authority and secured a $75,000 grant for the Hoboken Planning Board that would pay for a Port Authority redevelopment study of the area slated for rebuilding. The grant was secured with the assistance of Christie's appointee to the Port Authority, Deputy Executive Director Bill Baroni – the same Bill Baroni who was entangled in the Bridgegate scandal. Lo and behold, the Port Authority study determined that only three blocks of the nineteen-block parcel were worthy of development: the three blocks owned by – surprise! – the Rockefeller Group. How convenient.

It seemed that Chairman Samson was very busy in his role at the Port Authority. The *Bergen Record* reported that Samson was also influential in supporting and voting to approve some $256M for the Port Authority's PATH train facility in Harrison, New Jersey. This just happened to occur within months of another client of Samson's law firm proposing to convert a warehouse near the PATH facility into a luxury-housing complex. Location and timing (and clout) are everything.

Back in Hoboken, the city's Planning Board rejected the Port Authority study. Suddenly, something prompted Lieutenant Governor Kim Guadagno to visit the mile-square city to assess Hoboken's ongoing recovery following Superstorm Sandy. During Guadagno's visit, she pulled the mayor aside, and according to Mayor Zimmer, "Guadagno said ... essentially, 'you've got to move forward with the Rockefeller project, this project is really important to the governor.' And she had been with him on Friday night and this was a direct message from the Governor. 'The word is that you are against it and you need to move forward or we are not going to be able to help you. I know it's not right. These things should not be connected. But they are. If you tell anyone I said it, I will deny it.'" Zimmer told several of her Hoboken staff about the encounter and recorded the incident in her diary.

Mayor Zimmer further alleged that Lori Grifa, who had since left the DCA to work as a lobbyist for the Wolff & Samson law firm, hounded various Hoboken city officials to push the Rockefeller Group's development project forward. Months later, Zimmer was a panelist on a television program regarding Superstorm Sandy recovery efforts. Also on the panel was Grifa's replacement, the current New Jersey DCA Commissioner, Richard Constable III. According to Zimmer's diary, "We are mic'd up with other panelists all around us, and probably the sound team is listening, and he says 'I hear you're against the Rockefeller project ... If you move that forward, the money would start flowing to you.'"

Guadagno, Constable, and others of Christie's minions vociferously denied Zimmer's accusations. The Christie attack machine was in full mode. They even produced flattering comments from Mayor Zimmer praising Christie's policy initiatives from time to time. Although she was a Democrat, Zimmer liked the reforms Christie wanted to implement and she made no bones about it. She told the *Star-Ledger* that she was "emotional" about Christie. "I thought he was honest. I thought he was moral. I thought he was something very different," Zimmer wrote in her journal. "This week I find out he's cut from the same corrupt cloth that I have been fighting for the last four years."

Within days of Zimmer's revelation, the United States Attorney's Office and the FBI were interviewing witnesses who corroborated the Mayor's allegations. They seized her diary. Several days later, a federal grand jury subpoenaed the New Jersey GOP and Christie's campaign for documents relative to the lane shutdowns on the George Washington Bridge. Things were either worsening for Christie, or his friends in the United States Attorney's Office were taking care of business for him. Only time would tell. While all of it played out, there were still more than twenty-thousand New Jerseyan's who remained displaced as a result of Sandy, and were counting on the same type of relief funds as Mayor Zimmer to help restore their lives.

Unbelievably, at the very same time, Lieutenant Governor Guadagno was at the center of another political and potentially criminal scandal still evolving as word of the Hoboken scandal broke. A veteran prosecutor, ousted by Governor Christie's administration, accused the Governor's regime of corruption in court documents.

Bennett A. Barlyn, an ex-Assistant Prosecutor in the Hunterdon County Prosecutor's Office, was working an ironclad criminal case against the Hunterdon County Sheriff and two of her deputies in 2010.

The sheriff, Deborah Trout, is an acquaintance of Lieutenant Governor Kim Guadagno and played an active role in Christie's gubernatorial campaign in 2009, the court records show. Trout sent some of her Sheriff's Office deputies to assist the campaign. Guadagno personally thanked her in an e-mail. A grand jury returned a 43-count indictment in the matter. The indictment charged that Trout hired deputies without conducting background checks – a criminal offense in New Jersey. The indictment further charged that Trout's office also gave a fake police ID to a pharmaceutical executive who just happened to donate thousands of dollars to Christie's campaign. Michael Russo, the indicted undersheriff in the case, assured one of his aides at the time, "Governor Christie will have this whole thing thrown out."

Within days of the indictments, the state Attorney General's Office, under the stewardship of Paula Dow, swooped in, quashed the indictment, fired Barlyn for voicing objections, and threatened another prosecutor. The documents were cleared out of the Hunterdon County Prosecutor's Office and whisked off to the State Capitol in Trenton. Such action is almost unprecedented in New Jersey courts. Administration officials, including Attorney General Dow, have categorically denied the complaints about political retribution that were filed in the court documents. The matter is still pending.

In the meantime, Christie's presidential aspirations were taking a hit. His favorability ratings were dropping faster than the subpoenas from the agencies investigating him. He was in a virtual free-fall from his once lofty position as the leading 2016 GOP presidential prospect. He had collapsed to third place. Christie also now trailed Hillary Clinton in presidential polling by double digits.

As Super Bowl XLVIII weekend arrived in the New York-New Jersey metropolitan area, Christie was about to suffer another blow. He was blindsided on his way to a celebrity bash honoring Howard Stern's 60th birthday. David Wildstein's lawyer, Alan L. Zegas, made public a scathing letter that he had written to the Port Authority, attempting to secure fees for his client's defense as a former Port Authority employee.

The letter pulled no punches, and in a paragraph that landed like an uppercut to the jaw, Zegas dropped a bomb. "It has come to light that a person within the Christie administration communicated the Christie administration's order that certain lanes on the George Washington Bridge were to be closed, and evidence exists as well tying Mr. Christie to having knowledge of the lane closures, during the period when the lanes were closed, contrary to what the Governor stated publicly in a two-hour press conference," he wrote.

Christie, who had terminated Bridget Anne Kelly for lying to him, had apparently lied to the public.

Of course, Christie countered with another denial, but it seemed no one was buying his excuses anymore. Christie's tacticians resorted to the typical response reserved for anyone who dared challenge him – the Governor's wordsmiths pummeled Wildstein from pillar to post, assaulting his character as far back as middle school. They claimed a teacher scolded him for deceptive behavior. Oh, heavens!

The attack on Wildstein seemed petty and desperate. This routine of the Governor's henchmen had become transparent and worn out. Just weeks earlier, when Wildstein resigned from the Port Authority, the Governor's office thanked Wildstein for his "dedication" and praised him as a "tireless advocate." The *Star-Ledger* Editorial Board called for Christie's resignation, or impeachment proceedings, if the Zegas allegation could be confirmed. So did influential State Senator Raymond Lesniak. Christie was taking on too much water.

As he meandered from one Super Bowl event to the other, Christie was suddenly greeted by sounds he was unaccustomed to: jeers and booing from the public.

As more information surrounding the bridge conspiracy leaked out, Christie began massaging his original alibi. A few days following the release of Attorney Alan Zegas' letter, Christie took the opportunity to respond on his radio program, speaking in Rubik's Cube. "Christie said it's conceivable that someone might have mentioned gridlock in the city of Fort Lee, or that he might have read about it. But he said he didn't realize it was a serious issue worthy of investigation until the concerns of the Port Authority's executive director, Patrick Foye were reported publically in the press," NBC News reported. Christie's latest story now put his actions in sync with the statements in the Zegas letter that he had taken exception to just days earlier. Christie was all over the board, implementing a strategy of rolling disclosure, offering excuses to cover anything that his former staffers would charge against him.

Christie stayed on schedule with all of his previously lined-up speaking engagements around the country: opportunities for him to advance his presidential aspirations. Texas, Illinois, D.C., and Georgia were all earmarked as destinations for Christie to sell his brand. Christie was still digging in– counting on his celebrity and acerbic wit to turn the tide for him, as it had so many other times in the past.

To me, the current scandals evolving around Christie are *déjà vu*. I lived it all just a few years ago. Life as I knew it was shut down as easily as a lane of traffic on the George Washington Bridge. I too was a victim of Christie's corrupt conduct, and I still have the scars to prove it.

Day of Infamy

In the dawn of July 23, 2009, I awoke to a beautiful summer morning at the Jersey Shore. Sea-scented air drifted through my open bedroom window, reminding me that I was still on vacation at my family's summer home in Belmar, far from my Journal Square condominium in the gritty urban confines of Jersey City. Belmar melded together perfectly as a gorgeous residential ocean front community and vacation resort. I was staying on the lower floor of the split-level home, which was always my favorite place to get away from it all.

I hit the kitchen for a cup of coffee, and then began to prepare for an early morning radio interview that had been arranged earlier in the week. I was to be the guest of Jim Gearhart on radio station NJ 101.5 by telephone. As a former New Jersey state legislator, I was going to discuss issues of importance in November's upcoming gubernatorial election between incumbent Governor Jon Corzine and his challenger, former United States Attorney Chris Christie.

The dawn sunbeams streamed through the windows of the house, slowly and steadily brightening the interior of the home. Little did I know as I began scanning my notes that, in a matter of minutes, I would be plunged into a waking nightmare.

At about 6:45 am, I received a call from someone claiming to be an FBI agent, who said he was stationed outside my Jersey City home. He had been ringing the doorbell of my apartment condominium unit to no avail, not knowing that I was at my family's summer home at the Jersey Shore. In disbelief, I listened to the agent telling me that there was a warrant out for my arrest. I honestly thought someone was pulling a prank on me. He advised me to switch on the news and call him back. I flicked on the bedroom television, which blared out extensive coverage of an FBI sting just going down. I realized that this was no joke, and my heart leapt into my throat. When I managed to swallow, I muttered something along the lines that I was prepared to drive up to Jersey City to surrender to them. I had no clue what it was all about: only my certainty that it was a mistake. It would take three years, and all I had to prove that I was right.

I hardly remember the drive to Jersey City. One moment I was in my family's summer home at Belmar and the next I was pulling into the parking garage of my condominium building in Jersey City. I exited the car and took the elevator up to my unit. Disbelief still hung over my every thought.

The agents were waiting at the building's front desk, and I called down to have them sent up. When they arrived, they politely explained they were there to arrest me for extortion. I listened ... still in disbelief. They asked if they could search for weapons and I obliged their request (no, no guns). As we stood huddled around my kitchen island, one of the agents plugged in a personal computer and plopped in a disc. They played a 30-second snippet of a video showing my brother taking a FedEx envelope from someone later alleged to be a co-conspirator. I still had no clue what this was all about.

They asked me if I knew a David Esenbach. Not that I could recall. I would learn later on that I did. Esenbach had been described to me as a developer whom one of the sting's co-conspirators, Ed Cheatam, had introduced me to through my brother. Earlier in the year, I had been a candidate in the 2009 Jersey City mayoral election. Cheatam claimed that he worked for Esenbach, whom he said wanted to contribute to my mayoral campaign. The reason nothing registered was that I had never taken any contributions from Esenbach and had instructed my brother not to either. I thought he was a wise ass and wanted nothing to do with him. Esenbach vanished from my mind until an infamous day in late July.

Then the agents went through the typical routine before arresting any political figure – asking if I had information on someone else that I might want to cough up in return for some slack: the law enforcement equivalent of frequent flyer miles. I had nothing to offer, and I was promptly read my rights, formally arrested, and allowed to call a lawyer. I called my friend since high school, George Tate, but his firm had already been contracted to defend my brother. George recommended an attorney I had never heard of, John Lynch. Still in shock and unable to think for myself, I asked George if he would make the arrangements. George said he would oblige my request.

The agents told me what I could expect to be going through the rest of the day, and I adjusted my mindset accordingly. We exited my condominium, hit the elevator, and walked out the garage entrance of the building to the car waiting to transport me. I was cuffed, eased into the vehicle, and driven to the FBI building in Newark. From that point on, all color and scent left my world. I can only recall the remainder of the events of that day in the grainy black and white of an old film noir.

Arriving at the FBI building and exiting the car we had to run a gauntlet of media that had been tipped off about the sting. Someone had alerted them to where the best vantage point would be to get shots of the FBI's haul. In the building's basement there was an assortment of other defendants who had been rounded up in the sting. Because I was a late arrival, I was in the last group. Here, everyone was fingerprinted, photographed, and debriefed of personal vital information. The FBI had provided a breakfast buffet for their catch: juice, coffee, and bagels. No one seemed to have an appetite for any of it. Tagging along with me was Mayor Anthony Suarez of Ridgefield, New Jersey. He would later be acquitted of all charges.

When processing was finished, everyone was once more handcuffed and given another complementary piece of Department of Justice jewelry: leg irons. We were then led again through the gauntlet of media outside the building and loaded onto prison buses for a trip to the Federal Courthouse in Newark. Here, the formality of having the charges read and bail set was performed. However, this would not happen until the end of the day. We were unaware that the United States Attorney's Office had other ideas – they were milking the media attention to the nth degree and had press conferences and briefings planned throughout the day.

While waiting for my face time with a District Court judge, I was thrust into a holding cell with a potpourri of other defendants. I did not know it at the time, but they had also rounded up a group of alleged money launderers, mostly rabbis, who were part of a second wave of the sting. The news that night was also reporting that someone was being charged with harvesting human body parts. *I am glad I did not know that at the time.* In that holding cell, amidst the shock and mass confusion, everyone tried to make some sense of what was happening. Nobody could.

The long wait in the holding cells finally ended with an appearance before the federal magistrate, which was again conveniently scheduled right before the evening news broadcasts. The U.S. Marshalls hauled the lot of us, still in handcuffs and leg irons, into a courtroom jammed with media and family members of some of the defendants. To accommodate the overflow, two courtroom sessions were necessary. Lawyers crowded around a much too small defense table and announced their name and who they were representing for the court record. It was then that I first laid eyes on attorney John Lynch.

After the court hearing in which the terms for bail were settled, we went back to the holding cell where our shackles were removed. We were then escorted downstairs to the Office of Pretrial Intervention, assigned an officer we would be reporting to twice monthly until trial. After a short debriefing there, we were free to go home. The hallways were filled with lingering defendants, still in a daze, chatting with their attorneys. John Lynch grabbed me and drove me back to my apartment in Jersey City. He handed me a copy of my arrest warrant, but I was still too shaken up to even attempt to read it. I kept searching my mind for what this was all about and what I possibly could have done wrong. I was completely perplexed – *why was I arrested?*

Later that night I drove back down to the Jersey Shore to see my 90-year-old mother. She had been watching the events of the day as they were reported on television. I did not know if I would be able to find the words ... but I didn't need to, she had them all. "Son, I have known you your whole life. I know that you would not take a bribe from anyone." I guess Mom thought that I could use a lift. "Please … tell me you had nothing to do with the body parts," she deadpanned.

We laughed. It was the only smile I managed that day.

The travesty that was about to unfold would cost me my home, my reputation, and my business. My defense would deplete me of my entire lifesavings. On top of that, years later, Superstorm Sandy would take its toll, wrecking my family's Jersey Shore home where I had relocated. I temporarily moved into a spare bedroom in the upper floor of my brother's Belmar home a few blocks away. It would be months before I could move back in.

By the time I finally finished this book, I was practically destitute. The truth would eventually prevail, and I would be completely exonerated, but even truth extracts a great cost from us at times. When I am called to meet my maker, my tombstone should record two dates of death, with July 23, 2009 as the first. You are about to read the autopsy report.

The colors and scents of life would eventually come back, given rebirth by the indomitable spirit residing in us all – the will to survive and right ourselves from wrong. Today, against all odds, I am still trying to resurrect the semblance of a life from scratch. When I do, perhaps then I will feel the satisfaction that justice has prevailed. For now, sporadic substitute teaching is barely paying the bills.

Everything that marked what was once a lauded and exemplary life as a public servant meant nothing. People tend to believe the worst about each other, especially politicians, and I am the living proof. I wear that false arrest stigma every day. All the good deeds of my life are meaningless to many. Even some literary agents and publishing houses shunned me.

As a devout Roman Catholic, my strong faith in God has helped to carry the day for me. His blessings and handiwork are everywhere. When we were in search of case laws to support a point in our argument, they miraculously appeared. Helpful documents would arrive on my doorstep from anonymous senders. Every possible break that we needed, we got. You do not prevail as solidly as we did against the federal government without divine help. God never let us down; he answered every prayer. Moreover, anyone who helped us along the way became the benefactors of his blessings as well.

I was also blessed to make the acquaintance of John David Lynch. He appeared out of nowhere, like a guardian angel. He was the first thing that went right for me on that infamous July 23, 2009. John Lynch is not a make-a-quick-buck lawyer who would recommend a client plead out, guilty or not, to a federal prosecution. Not that you can really blame the pleading-heart attorneys. The United States Attorney's Office for the District of New Jersey had a record of 130 consecutive successful prosecutions in political corruption cases. John's grit was probably acquired from the neighborhood where he was born – New York City's Hell's Kitchen.

When John Lynch saw the depth of the depravity that engulfed the government's investigation and prosecution of the Bid Rig III cases, he did not lie down. We became a great team. He lawyered and I researched. From the day of my arrest forward, I lived and breathed the Bid Rig III investigation and each of its prosecutions. I had always been an avid investigator and a stickler for detail, whether while serving as an environmental and health professional or a state legislator. My longstanding determination to get to the heart of any matter served me well in assisting my defense. I read and researched every government guideline regulating each prosecutor and government agent that was working the cases. I read every case document, each minuscule piece of paper in the more than 14 boxes of discovery containing hundreds of thousands of pages. In the end, I knew the investigation better then the government did.

More importantly, by running a parallel timeline depicted in the government documents alongside the news reports of events leading up to and culminating in the 2009 New Jersey gubernatorial election, I would discover dark and dirty secrets.

It appeared to me that the evidence was conclusive that federal prosecutors, *including former United States Attorney Chris Christie,* broke the law and used their offices to personally and politically profit themselves, obstruct justice, and engage in what appeared to be a government orchestrated coup to disrupt the 2009 New Jersey gubernatorial election.

Christie's Way

Contriving a sting operation with a controversial confidential informant, the prosecutors used their public offices to knock out the Democratic political stronghold of Hudson County just prior to the 2009 New Jersey gubernatorial election. In so doing, as would be verified by polling and election results, the prosecutors strategically helped to tilt the election in Christie's favor.

The false charges lodged against me were subsequently dismissed by two District Court decisions and an Appellate Court decision in a case that prosecutor's intentionally dragged out until February of 2012. The Courts called my prosecution *"legal alchemy."* The initial decision snapped the prosecutors' record 130 consecutive successful prosecutions streak. The shockwave sent other fraudulent indictments from the sting into a tailspin as the underhanded tactics of prosecutors began to be exposed.

But their dirty deeds did not end there.

Little did I know it at the time, but Bid Rig III was merely one spoke in a wheel of what appeared to be contemplated and corrupt conduct on the part of numerous public officials, including Chris Christie, for the purpose of advancing a political agenda. The other spokes of the crooked Christie wheel mirror the latter day scandals that everyone seems to know about. The targeting of innocent individuals, who were regarded as mere props in his escapades, without any value other than to serve the advancing political agenda, seems to be a familiar reappearing pattern in every one of Christie's abuses.

It appears Christie's agenda began long before Bid Rig III, its targets, and an infamous confidential informant, Solomon Dwek. This agenda was given birth through an elected seat on the Morris County, New Jersey Freeholder Board, christened by a prestigious Department of Justice appointment, and confirmed by his election to the governor's seat. The next stop, Christie hoped, was the White House.

In order to present the facts without prejudice, the events depicted are gleaned from documents that Christie's office and his collaborators once tried to keep hidden, the words of Christie and other public officials, court documents, government reports and the impressions of journalists reporting the events as they occurred.

Chapter One

Born to Run:
With Help from Bush and Rove

Landing so powerful a job as United States Attorney for the District of New Jersey was not happenstance for Chris Christie. Christie's hunger for power, whether driven by ego or public service, thrust him into the foray of local politics at an early age. Bruce Springsteen, Christie's self-proclaimed rock idol, wrote the mega-hit, "Born to Run." It is his mantra.

After graduating from the University of Delaware and Seton Hall School of Law, Christie hooked up with a small law firm (Dughi, Hewit & Palatucci) in Cranford, New Jersey. Initially employed as a corporate lawyer, Chris Christie's burning political ambition would soon thrust him onto the public stage. With a powerful supporter in his friend and confidant, Bill Palatucci, the 30-year-old Christie made his entry into the world of politics in New Jersey's Morris County. It was probably no surprise to anyone who knew him.

According to Peter J. Boyer, writing for *Newsweek's* online political website, the *Daily Beast*, "Christie has never wanted for ambition. He has been running for office since he was a schoolboy, and once, when he was fourteen, he had his mother drop him at the door of a local legislator so he could ask him how to become a politician. 'I answer the door and there's this kid,' recalls former New Jersey governor Tom Kean, who was, at the time, an assemblyman. 'He said, very respectfully, "Sir, I really want to get into politics."' Kean, who was making his first run for governor, brought the kid to a political meeting that evening and became Christie's mentor."

Right out of the gate, Christie aimed high, and despite antagonizing fellow Republicans, in 1993 he launched a primary challenge to the popular State Senator and Majority Leader, John Dorsey. Christie failed to come up with the hundred signatures required to secure a spot on the ballot and embarrassingly never made it to the starting post. Undaunted, the following year, Christie ran for a seat on the Morris County Board of Freeholders. Christie teamed up with another self-styled reformer, Jack O'Keefe, to challenge the Republican incumbents in the June 1994 primary. *Salon* political writer Steve Kornacki surmised, "To Christie, the main appeal of the job was its launching pad potential."

Christie launched a good-government campaign promising an ethics code, a ban on gifts, cuts in freeholder salaries and an end to political patronage. "This is one of the major things I'm running on," he said at the time of his plan to restrict no-bid contracts. "It makes common sense. It's good government. Let the chips fall where they may, and get the best people at the best price. That's the freehold-ers' job," the *New York Times* reported.

But things would turn ugly fast and, in addition to promoting his political platform, Christie waged an aggressive negative campaign against his opponents. "Christie claimed that the GOP incumbents were 'under investigation' for their record-keeping of closed sessions – even though they weren't," *Salon* reported. The primary voters bought Christie's spiel and he secured the nomination, which in the predominantly Republican county was a virtual lock on the general election.

Following the election, Christie's opponents, Edward Tamm and Cecilia Laureys, hit him with a libel suit for his false assertion that they were under investigation. "The guy just lied!" Tamm told Gabriel Sherman, writing for *New Jersey Monthly*. "He'll do anything to get elected. He'll say anything, do anything." Christie, years later, consented to give a public apology and the case was settled.

So what about the robust ethics platform and ban on no-bid contracts candidate Christie had vowed? According to David Halbfinger of the *New York Times*, Christie "showed little persistence in pushing his proposal, which turned out to be anything but a ban: It did not apply to law firms, and freeholders would still be free to ignore bidding results and choose whomever they liked." The *Times* further reported that, in fact, "during his three-year term, Mr. Christie voted for more than *440* no-bid contracts with appraisers, architects, auditors, engineers, graphic artists, lawyers, even nurses. Some were at rates as low as $50 an hour, but dozens were worth hundreds of thousands of dollars. Records for many were not available, but 309 contracts for which costs were estimated when they were approved, totaled $10.5 million.

"Mr. Christie denied that he had abandoned the idea of a ban, saying that he 'fought very hard' for it but that 'it was very difficult as one person of seven.' He said he saw little merit in voting against other no-bid contracts merely to make a point. 'I was not a guy who was into protest votes and grandstanding,' he said."

Though not grandstanding, Christie certainly positioned himself in the cheap seats, accepting a total of $17,000 in campaign contributions from the recipients of more than 50 no-bid contracts.

Emboldened by his successful election to freeholder, Christie wasted little time in trying to further ascend the political ladder. Within months of his swearing in, Christie announced his candidacy for the State Assembly. Challenging well liked incumbent Republicans Anthony Bucco and Michael P. Carroll, Christie went on the attack again. This time, however, the results were disastrous – Republican voters eyed Christie as "a young man in too much of a hurry." Hanging the defamation suit around his neck, Republicans he had alienated were more than happy to pile on. Christie and his running mate were trounced at the polls by a 2-to-1 margin.

The sting of that beating would linger, and when Christie stood re-election for his Freeholder seat, still beset by the defamation lawsuit and his inability to deliver reform, he was trounced in the primary, finishing dead last. Christie exited from the elective office scene and soon resurrected himself as a registered lobbyist, representing some dozen corporate clients. Christie's appetite for politics was temporarily satisfied as a supporter and fundraiser of other candidates, mostly Republicans.

The Pioneer

A prominent supporter of George H.W. Bush's 1988 presidential campaign, Christie's confidant, Bill Palatucci, had developed a friendship with future President George W. Bush Jr. It was through Palatucci that Christie gained entrée into the Bush political world. "In January 1999, Christie boarded a Continental flight in Newark and flew down to Austin with Palatucci and eight top New Jersey Republicans to meet Bush for a private lunch at the Governor's Mansion with Karl Rove, during which Bush discussed his possible run for president. Christie made a total of three trips to Texas to meet Bush and signed on as the campaign's New Jersey lawyer," Gabriel Sherman reported for *New Jersey Monthly.*

Christie and Palatucci raised approximately $350,000 for Bush's campaign – qualifying them for membership in the Pioneer Club, reserved for the campaign's elite fundraisers. He soon developed a relationship with the Bush upper echelon: Karl Rove affectionately called him "Big Boy." Sherman reported: "After the election, Palatucci recommended Christie for U.S. Attorney and personally sent his resumé with a cover letter to Rove." Christie, however, has always downplayed his relationships with the Bush inner core.

Suddenly, a lobbyist lawyer, who had never handled criminal law, became the new President's nominee to become the United State Attorney for the District of New Jersey. The news went over about as well as Christie's initial foray into state politics. The opposition to Christie's nomination began to mount. The Association of the Federal Bar of the State of New Jersey adopted a resolution deploring political influence in the selection of a federal prosecutor. The resolution called upon President Bush to make a selection based strictly on merit.

In an editorial captioned, "Try again on U.S. Attorney," the *Star-Ledger* savaged Christie's nomination and the circumstances surrounding it: "Christie is a smart attorney by all accounts and a man of some charm.... But he is not yet qualified for the job of U.S. Attorney. He has never tried a criminal case. He has no substantial experience in federal court. He has never directed a corruption investigation or even participated in one. He is 39, can claim no distinguished academic or legal accomplishment and works primarily as a lobbyist and mediator."

The pummeling continued. "What Christie brings to the table is excellent political connections. He has energetically raised money for various candidates, including George W. Bush in 2000, and his mentor and law partner is William Palatucci, a friend of the President and a powerful figure in the state GOP. Christie's history as a partisan rainmaker not only fails to qualify him, it could undermine trust in the office."

The newspaper editorial was prophetic. "His motives will inevitably be questioned if he indicts Democratic office holders or fails to indict important Republican donors who are under investigation. It is common for U.S. attorneys to have political ties, but Christie's party links are closer than most."

At the end of the day, the entire hullabaloo was ignored. The President eventually got his man with the help of New Jersey's two Democratic U.S. Senators, Robert Torricelli and Jon Corzine, who fully supported Christie's nomination. After all, President George W. Bush was blazing new trails and Chris Christie was a "Pioneer."

"This is a patronage appointment, plain and simple," moaned the *Star-Ledger*.

On January 17, 2002, Chris Christie ushered in a new era for the United States Attorney's Office for the District of New Jersey. He was not much for learning the ropes or following the established protocols of his predecessors. Christie implemented a wholesale reorganization of the office. Two previously stand-alone divisions in the office were merged into the Criminal Division, which was then organized into eight units. Unit Chiefs would meet with Christie and his senior staff every ten days to report in and receive policy directives concerning the units they oversaw.

The Special Prosecutions Division would handle political corruption, Christie's pet peeve. Special Prosecutions would have no mid-level management between its division and the United States Attorney – it would report directly to Christie and his senior staff.

Christie also appointed Camden County Prosecutor Lee A. Solomon as Deputy United States Attorney to handle South Jersey. There had historically been an imbalance of resources covering the lower part of the state, so Solomon was provided with a bump in staffing to operate the South Jersey office.

Each year after the reorganization, Christie brought more federal cases forward than the year before. In the post 9/11 era, Christie also focused on terrorism and brought forth two prominent cases which garnered national attention: the Fort Dix Six and the Hemant Lakhani illegal arms sale sting. Christie's bread and butter, though, was public corruption. He triumphantly presided over a majority of the 130 consecutive prosecutions of elected or appointed public officials without an acquittal.

Christie also focused his efforts on white-collar crimes; charging firms and institutions as well as the CEOs running them. Among the notable prosecutions were Bristol Myers Squibb for defrauding shareholders, the University of Medicine and Dentistry of New

Jersey for illegal business practices, and the artificial knee and hip replacement industry for kickbacks and Medicare fraud. Christie utilized a unique tool to resolve many of the white-collar cases: deferred-prosecution agreements. Through an arrangement with the government, a corporation or individual could avoid prosecution by making reparations to the victim of the alleged crime and agreeing to pay for a monitor appointed by the United States Attorney's Office to oversee the arrangement. This later became a source of much consternation for Christie; many of those who benefitted from the deferred compensation contracts were friends and future campaign contributors.

To preserve the record of his office, Christie heralded his achievements in a report that he co-authored, which summarized his view of his six-year stint as United States Attorney. Christie stalwarts Ralph Marra, Michele Brown, Jeffrey Chiesa and Charles McKenna signed off on the document, which was a nice promo piece for Christie's exit from office and entry into the race for Governor of New Jersey.

Chapter Two

Persecuting a U.S.
Senator and Other Democrats

In the narrative documenting his tenure Christie echoed the words that he had spoken seven years prior upon taking charge of the U.S. Attorney's office. He fired shots across the bow of every New Jersey politician. These words, spoken nearly seven years ago, seem to be prescient given the performance of his office in fighting political corruption: "As I begin my time on this watch, I have a simple message for New Jersey's public officials.... If you break your oath, if you choose to lie, to cheat and steal from those who you were sworn to serve, you will have no greater enemy. There is no more simple test of right versus wrong and this United States Attorney will make sure that those who violate the public trust will pay for that betrayal, and they will pay with their freedom," he warned.

The Giant Killer

The politicians did not have to wait long for the first ship to sink. Picking up on a political corruption investigation that had been initiated by his predecessor, United States Attorney Robert Cleary, Christie arrested, indicted, and successfully prosecuted former Essex County Executive James Treffinger, a popular Republican. Treffinger, at the time, was about to launch a campaign for the United States Senate. Writing for the *New York Times*, Correspondent David Kocieniewski reported that Treffinger was not allowed to surrender as most elected officials in similar circumstances had been permitted to do. Treffinger was "arrested and spent more than six hours in handcuffs."

Christie's aides claimed that the decision to shackle Treffinger was made by the United States Marshall Service, which was concerned, they said, about Treffinger's access to a gun. The *Times* further reported that there might have been a little bit of score settling involved: "Politicians and lawyers involved in the corruption case say that they knew that an informant had secretly recorded Mr. Treffinger making a vulgar derogatory comment about Mr. Christie's hulking frame, and some former Treffinger aides contend that his harsh treatment was a payback."

Treffinger represented the most prominent Republican official initially indicted by Christie; thereafter, his targets were predominantly Democrats. Whether they were targeted and prosecuted as part of a sting operation, or as part of an isolated investigation of criminal activity focused on a specific individual, the investigations or prosecutions seemed to fit a pattern. First, they tended to precede and have impact upon an upcoming election, no matter how far in advance of the election the news about the investigations, arrests, or indictments were hyped. Second, they tended to focus on major Democrat political powerbrokers who were vital to the New Jersey Democratic Party apparatchiks for statewide elections: like a governor's race.

It is important to note that New Jersey has elected predominantly Democrat officials to its statewide offices since the latter half of the last century. Democrats prevailed 15 to 5 in United States Senate elections commencing with Republican Howard Alexander Smith in 1952, and prevailed 9 to 6 in gubernatorial elections commencing with Democrat Robert Meyner in 1953. In later elections, the statewide Democratic victories have been delivered from strongholds such as Middlesex and Hudson Counties. Whereas, Monmouth, Ocean, and Morris Counties could be typically counted on to deliver for Republicans. Large black populations in Newark and Camden have also tipped the scales significantly for Democrats. Bergen County was independent and could tilt either way. Both parties waged intense campaigns in Bergen. For a time, without carrying Bergen, a candidate could not prevail in a New Jersey statewide election.

In the fall of 2006, Christie served subpoenas and expanded what had already been a much-publicized investigation of Camden County's prominent Democratic icon, Senator Wayne Bryant. Bryant was eventually indicted early in 2007 and subsequently convicted, dealing South Jersey Democrats a significant blow. Christie also heated things up in the summer of 2007, targeting and indicting Newark's Mayor and State Senator Sharpe James in mid July. Later that fall, leading into the high stakes New Jersey legislative elections, with every Assembly and Senate seat up for grabs, Christie's office moved into action again. As the Democrats were huddled in their party's pre-election convention, the arrests of eleven public officials for bribery in a government sting operation were announced on September 6th. Ten of the eleven public officials were Democrats and two were prominent State Assemblymen.

As 2008 kicked off, the year preceding New Jersey's gubernatorial election, Christie's office focused on Bergen County public officials – all Democrats. In February, State Senator Joseph Coniglio was indicted in an influence-peddling scheme. Then came the blow of blows. Preceding the fall presidential election, Christie kyboshed the entire newly-rebuilt Bergen County Democratic Party by sacking its leader, County Democratic Chairman Joseph Ferriero. Ferriero was indicted for honest services fraud, a questionable charge, and his eventual conviction would later be overturned by the federal courts. But the damage was already done, and it would take years for the Democrats in Bergen to regroup.

Conveniently, the majority of Christie's prominent arrests since the 2005 New Jersey gubernatorial election had struck at the heart of Democrat strongholds and chipped away at the formula necessary for the Party to prevail in statewide elections.

The Senator Menendez Matter

The Department of Justices's darkest hour, the Congressional investigation of the U.S. Attorney scandal, touched off an inquiry regarding Christie, who was serving as the U.S. Attorney of New Jersey when the crisis erupted. The Congressional record indicates that the query focused on Christie's issue of subpoenas for records concerning United States Senator Robert Menendez of New Jersey and his acquisition of federal grants for a Federally Qualified Healthcare Center that leased office space in one of Menendez's real estate holdings.

The subpoenas were issued in the heat of the 2006 New Jersey campaign for Menendez's United States Senate seat, sixty-one days prior to the actual election. The news of the subpoenas was leaked to the media, citing unnamed officials in the Department of Justice as a source.

Menendez's Republican opponent in the race was then-New Jersey Senator Thomas Kean Jr., who had once benefitted from a Christie financial donation when he ran for a 2000 Congressional seat. Obviously, Menendez and his campaign cried foul.

"Suddenly, 61 days before an election, a prosecutor appointed by George Bush decides to take an interest, and not coincidentally, leaks to the press follow immediately. There are serious questions about the timing of this inquiry and I will not allow an orchestrated concerted effort to smear and personally destroy those who oppose this administration," Menendez charged at the time.

Already excoriated for his persecution of former Governor James McGreevey while he, himself, pondered running for Governor in 2005, the actions of Christie's office in issuing the subpoenas were considered suspect by the media, again raising questions about his partisanship. Christie dug in, defending his position. "I just stand by my record. I don't worry about that. I don't get involved in politics, the silly season – that's for politicians, not for prosecutors," he rebutted.

The *New York Observer* had another take: "But here's the thing: Whether by design or not, Mr. Christie is involved. His investigation – dealing with allegations that Mr. Menendez steered federal grants to a nonprofit that was paying him rent – has become the central focus of the Kean campaign. Recent polls have shown Mr. Menendez hanging onto a lead of several points," reported Jason Horowitz. "In one of Mr. Kean's radio ads, a narrator repeats four times the phrase 'Bob Menendez, under federal criminal investigation.' His first television ad asserts that Mr. Menendez is 'just one scandal away from becoming the next Bob Torricelli,' referring to the former U.S. Senator who was driven from his re-election campaign in 2002 amid questions about his ethics."

Christie's investigation of the Senator never went anywhere, but the subpoenas had tightened the election contest, and nearly cost Menendez the race. Nearly a year later Christie's actions were finally examined, but through a different prism – the Congressional investigation of the U.S. Attorney scandal. Amidst the investigation of the firing of federal prosecutors for failing to initiate partisan prosecutions, it was disclosed that Christie had been on two lists of U.S. Attorneys suggested for firing. His name had been removed from the list shortly after the United States Senate election in New Jersey.

The Christie incident and the U.S. Attorney scandal would have been a small ripple on a large pond had the lies not piled up before Congress. Most of the media was ready to give the Bush Administration a pass, because it is the prerogative of the President to hire or fire United States Attorneys at his pleasure. However, when the first political appointees at Justice lied about *why* the prosecutors were fired, and then the prosecutors fought back with facts and accusations of political interference in their jobs, all hell broke loose.

Christie gave conflicting accounts to the media concerning how and when he learned of his proposed firing. In May of 2007, Christie told *Washington Post* Staff Writers Dan Eggen and Amy Goldstein that he had first learned he was on a termination list in Mid-March of 2007. Christie claimed that Chief of Staff to the Deputy Attorney General, Michael J. Elston, called to give him the heads up, so he would not be surprised by the Congressional inquiry. "I was completely shocked. No one had ever told me that my performance had been anything but good," Christie said. "I specifically asked him why he put my name on the list. He said he couldn't give me an explanation."

In August of 2007, the *Daily Record* of New Jersey reported, "Christie said he was told in December that he was on the list of U.S. Attorneys to be fired, but in January was told his name had been taken off the list." Christie commented, "I was speechless. I just could not believe I was someone who was actively considered for being fired. It makes you search yourself and ask: 'Was I doing my job well?'"

The significance of Christie offering two different timelines allowed the media to speculate if there possibly could have been a third; did Christie know he was on the initial firing list *before* he launched the probe of Menendez, and was he taken off the list for doing so?

Reporting in the August 12, 2009 *New York Observer,* Steve Kornacki wrote, "But, try to put yourself in Christie's shoes: He had strong political ambitions, and the U.S. attorney's job had been a gold mine for him. His high-profile corruption busts had helped him build a sterling reputation – the kind that made him a natural candidate for statewide office. So he had strong incentive to hold on to his job: without it, he'd lose an invaluable P.R. machine. And if Christie had an inkling that he'd be in trouble – maybe he heard about the January '06 memo, maybe he just heard rumblings that "uncooperative" U.S. attorneys might face termination – going after Menendez would have been a very logical response.

"After all, the G.O.P. was clinging to its Senate majority in '06, and Menendez, appointed to the Senate by Governor Jon Corzine in January '06, was easily the most vulnerable Democratic incumbent in the nation. If Republicans could knock off Menendez, their majority would almost certainly be safe. And what better way to go after Menendez – whose ethical standing was already questionable to many voters because of his roots in the machine politics of Hudson County – than with charges of corruption from Mr. Clean, a.k.a. U.S. Attorney Christopher J. Christie?"

Christie's rapport with Karl Rove certainly lends more credence to the speculation that he knew he was on a termination list. Rove testified before Congress that he had spoken to Christie on occasion, but only concerning Christie running for New Jersey Governor. It seems only logical that if Rove and Christie's relationship was so congenial, Rove would have somehow, some way, reached out to alert Christie.

Five years later, almost begrudgingly, the Department of Justice exonerated Menendez of any implied wrongdoing and closed its investigation. Menendez, not wanting to see unsubstantiated innuendo being used again as political fodder for attacks on him in his 2012 re-election bid, had his attorney beating down the doors of the Department of Justice to clear his name. The New Jersey District United States Attorney Paul Fishman had recused himself from the case because Menendez had been one of the sponsors of his nomination.

The matter was kicked over to the United States Attorney's Office in Pennsylvania's eastern district. Writing for the *Star-Ledger*, Mark Mueller reported in October of 2011, "In a letter sent to Menendez's lawyer, the U.S. attorney for the eastern district of Pennsylvania said the case has been quietly closed.... It's highly unusual for federal prosecutors to issue letters clearing targets of investigations. 'It's very rare,' said Jay Fahy, who headed the corruption unit at the U.S. Attorney's Office in Newark and who later served as Bergen County prosecutor."

Christie, asked for a comment, simply acknowledged that he stood by his actions and the investigation. In response, Menendez offered a more tersely worded statement, "As I said almost five years ago, during the height of my first campaign for United States Senate, there was no merit to this investigation and there never was. This official letter – though long delayed – finally confirms this fact."

The *Star-Ledger* editorial board, which had defended Christie's inquiry back in 2006, suddenly found religion. In an October 24, 2011 editorial, the *Ledger* commented, "It is chilling to think that Menendez might have lost that election based on an allegation we now know is unfounded.... Our own view at the time was that then-U.S. Attorney Chris Christie was justified in doing so.... But with the passage of time, we've changed our guess – based on two reasons. One, the investigation turned up nothing. We know now that this case was not so compelling that it justified warping the outcomes of a race for Senate.

"And two, we have learned more about Christie. His ethics are selective. As governor, he has solicited secret donations from state contractors, a practice he used to consider a form of legalized bribery.... Yes, this is all guesswork, peering into Christie's heart to judge his motive. But for the record, our guess has changed."

Chapter Three

Helping John Ashcroft
and Company

As United States Attorney, Christie often expressed outrage at government awarded no-bid contracts. He once categorized them as "the biggest problem in corruption in New Jersey." In an interesting paradox, what Christie considered New Jersey's biggest corruption problem turned out to be one of his greatest tools for rewarding friends, colleagues, and future campaign donors. The aforementioned, which include deferred prosecution agreements, (whereby a corporation or individual could avoid prosecution by making reparation to the victim of the alleged crime) became an instrument for Christie to play Santa Claus all the year round.

These settlement agreements often called for outside lawyers to be retained by the individual or corporation in order to monitor the agreements struck by the prosecutors. The resulting contracts specified that the lawyers were to monitor the company's compliance with the settlements through financial audits and other types of internal investigations. The monitoring was typically outsourced to private sector law firms and attorneys who, although being compensated by the individuals or corporations granted the deferred prosecution agreement, were chosen by the United States Attorney's Office. Can you see what's wrong with this picture?

The Rainmaker

John Ashcroft, the former United States Attorney General who once supervised Christie, was fortunate enough to have his lobbying firm awarded one such monitoring agreement to oversee a deferred prosecution agreement granted Zimmer Holdings, one of several medical device manufacturers accused of giving kickbacks to surgeons who used their replacement hips and knees. Ashcroft, a former U.S. Senator from Missouri, took the reins of the Justice

Department in 2001, the same year President Bush nominated Christie to be the top federal law enforcement officer in New Jersey. Three years later, the Attorney General tapped Christie to be one of 17 U.S. Attorneys on an advisory panel he regularly consulted.

Describing the Zimmer Holdings monitoring arrangement contract with Ashcroft, the *New York Times* wrote, "with no public notice and no bidding, the company awarded Mr. Ashcroft an 18-month contract worth $28 million to $52 million." In its filing with the Securities and Exchange Commission, Zimmer Holdings claimed it had agreed to pay the Ashcroft firm a monthly fee of $750,000, and reimburse it for expenses that were expected to total $150,000 to $250,000 a month. As *New York Times* correspondent Philip Shenon further reported, "The firm said Mr. Christie had directed it to hire Mr. Ashcroft. Mr. Christie has acknowledged that he chose Mr. Ashcroft for the assignment."

Another monitoring contract that was cut courtesy of Christie went to a colleague, David Kelley, a former U.S. attorney for the Southern District of New York. Kelley was picked in 2007 to monitor Biomet Orthopedics Inc., another of the five medical manufacturing companies accused of giving kickbacks to doctors for using their products. Two years earlier, Kelley had investigated Christie's younger brother, Todd, on stock fraud charges, but ultimately decided not to prosecute him.

Todd Christie was one of 20 stock traders accused by the Securities and Exchange Commission of cheating customers for financial gain, and charged with civil fraud. Fourteen of them – but not Todd Christie – were also indicted on criminal fraud charges by Kelley's office. Todd Christie and the S.E.C. reached a settlement in 2008 in which he agreed not to conduct improper trading, but admitted no wrongdoing. At the time, the *New York Times* criticized the decision on its editorial pages, stating, "We can't help but note that Todd Christie, the brother of Christopher Christie, the United States attorney for New Jersey, was among the twenty stock traders charged. But while fourteen of the traders were charged with criminal fraud, Mr. Christie, a major donor to Republicans and the youngest brother of a prosecutor who has specialized in rooting out political corruption, faced only civil penalties and fines.

The S.E.C. said Mr. Christie's firm had earned $1.59 million for its own account in trading maneuvers that cost customers $1.4

million in extra expenses. Mr. Christie ranked fourth in the S.E.C. complaint among the twenty traders who earned the biggest profits at customers' expense. The top three were indicted, as were eleven traders lower down. We don't know whether this is a case of how nice it is to have big brothers in high places. But it doesn't look good."

Further, FactCheck.org reported, "Kelley has maintained that his involvement in Chris Christie's brother's case had nothing to do with his selection as a monitor in 2007. According to an Associated Press report, Kelley has said that the 'stock trading case was prosecuted on its merits;' he 'denied any conflict of interest in his later work as a monitor." The same source reported that when the matter came up at a press conference in April 2009, Gubernatorial candidate Christie, "lashed out at critics for 'impugning' his reputation and dragging his family into the campaign. Christie said he chose Kelley for no other reason than his prior record as a U.S. attorney and added that he and Kelley had never discussed his brother's case."

A New Jersey State Assemblyman and then New Jersey Democratic State Committee Chairman, Joseph Cryan, had a different take on Kelley's and Christie's defense of the monitoring agreement: "Chris Christie wants us to believe that in a country with more than one million lawyers, the one most qualified to receive this no-bid work is the same one who let his brother off the hook for stock fraud," he said, as quoted by FactCheck.org.

One of the entities that Christie's office had determined to be rife with abuse was the University of Medicine and Dentistry of New Jersey. The institution was accused of Medicaid fraud, along with patronage and financial abuses. Reporting on the work of the monitor appointed by Christie to handle the matter, *New York Times* journalist David Kocieniewski wrote, "The school reformed many of its bookkeeping procedures and ended its practice of awarding no-bid contracts. Yet one of the biggest no-bid contracts to come out of the investigation was for the monitor itself: Mr. Christie appointed the law firm of John Inglesino, a Republican who served as a Morris County freeholder from 2001 to 2007, and Herbert Stern, a former United States attorney, whom he has described as a mentor. Mr. Christie was also a freeholder, from 1995 to 1997. Their firm ultimately billed the state for more than $10 million."

Not only were the monitors helpful in putting the University of Medicine and Dentistry of New Jersey back on the straight and narrow, they also made sure that the coffers of Christie's gubernatorial campaign remained flush with money. Stern and Inglesino's firm, inclusive of their employees, was one of the biggest contributors to Christie's election fund. Inglesino actually acted as an intermediary for Christie's campaign, according to news sources, by attempting to lure Christie's primary opponent, Assemblyman Rick Merkt, out of the race with the promise of a job.

Another prominent monitor Christie selected to oversee deferred prosecution agreements was David Samson, a former Republican New Jersey Attorney General and party fundraiser. He was chosen to monitor Smith & Nephew Inc., a medical device maker. Samson's law firm was also on the payroll of Christie's campaign for legal work and rent, according to New Jersey Election Law Enforcement Commission reports. Governor Christie nominated David Samson to the Board of Commissioners of the Port Authority of New York and New Jersey on September 30, 2010. He was confirmed by the New Jersey State Senate on January 25, 2011 and was elected as the agency's Chairman on February 3, 2011.

Former Christie colleague Debra Wong Carr, a former United States Attorney for the Los Angeles California district, was chosen as a monitor for another medical device company: Deputy Orthopedics Inc. Yet another corporate entity under the scrutiny and prosecution of Christie's office was Bristol-Myers Squibb, one of New Jersey's and the nation's most prominent businesses. The drug manufacturing company was accused of defrauding its shareholders, and was quick to enter into a deferred prosecution agreement. Part of that agreement had a bizarre stipulation – that the company would endow a chair in business ethics at Seton Hall University, Christie's alma mater.

Not only were some of the Christie-appointed monitors benefitting his gubernatorial campaign, so were, in certain instances, other potential criminal targets that had escaped prosecution. News blogger and award winning investigative journalist Lucy Kosimar reported in October 2009 that IDT Corporation, a New Jersey based global telecommunications company that had been involved in a case of international bribery, had come under Christie's scrutiny. A former Republican Congressman, James Courter, who was also a prominent New Jersey GOP figure, headed the company. Despite successful prosecutions of IDT-like conduct brought against other entities by the United States Attorney's Office of Southern Florida, under Christie's and a Republican appointed Attorney General's stewardship, the IDT matter was treated differently.

The allegations against IDT became known in a wrongful termination suit brought by a former IDT executive, J. Michael Jewett. Jewett claimed he was fired for refusing to be the conduit for bribes intended for a Haitian telecommunications company – Haiti Teleco – and the Haitian President. As reported by Kosimar, "According to the contract between Haiti Teleco and IDT, the Haitian phone company directed IDT to send payments that were made for U.S.-Haiti phone calls not to Haiti, but to a shell company, Mont Salem, in the offshore Turks & Caicos Islands, a bank and corporate secrecy haven.... The arrangement included potentially hundreds of thousands of dollars in kickbacks to Haiti's president at the time, Jean-Bertrand Aristide, in exchange for a sweetheart deal to supply long-distance phone service to Haiti, according to claims made in both Jewett's lawsuit and a separate suit filed by the Haitian government after Aristide was forced from office." As previously indicated, other charges involving these entities and another Florida-based telecommunications company were successfully prosecuted by the United States Attorney's Office for the District of Southern Florida – with the exception of IDT.

Jewett's attorney, William Perniciaro, claimed that initially Christie's office had expressed an interest in the matter over the course of a series of meetings that began in 2004. This was over the same time period that Perniciaro brought Jewett's case to the attention of the Department of Justice. Alice Fisher, a partner at Latham & Watkins, IDT's law firm, conducted an internal investigation of the matter. Not surprisingly, as an advocate for the accused, she concluded that IDT's dealings with Haiti Teleco were legal. Shortly afterward, Perniciaro told Kosimar that he'd stopped hearing from federal officials. The matter was dropped. According to Kosimar, "As the U.S. Attorney cooperating in the subsequent Department of Justice investigation – in which his staff participated for several years – Christie would have been involved in advising on the final decision about whether or not to prosecute."

The Department of Justice, Christie, and IDT refused to answer Kosimar's inquiries, especially in light of some interesting coincidences, not to mention the fairy tale ending of the escapade.

Kosimar points out that the matter might have drawn the attention of the alleged architect of the national United States Attorney's scandal, President Bush's right-hand man, Karl Rove, the man who also handled Christie's resumé for United States Attorney. "Rove would have also been concerned that the IDT board of directors was stacked with high-level Republicans, including Rudy Boschwitz, former senator from Minnesota; James S. Gilmore III, former Virginia Governor; Thomas Slade Gorton III, former senator from Washington State; Jack Kemp, former congressman from New York and 1996 vice presidential nominee; and Jeanne Kirkpatrick, U.S. ambassador to the U.N. under President Ronald Reagan."

It also happened that the IDT Corporation head, James Courter, had a good friend, at the time, in Vice President Dick Cheney. "When Net2Phone, an IDT Internet phone company, went public in 1999, Cheney was invited to buy 1,000 initial shares at the insider price of $15,000. He sold them the same day for $26,574, a neat profit of 77.2 percent," Kosimar reported. The investigative journalist also noted that Courter had been one of presidential nominee John McCain's 20 national finance co-chairs.

The fallout from this situation would be of great benefit to Christie's campaign for Governor. "Courter donated the legal limit of $3,400 to Christie's gubernatorial primary campaign. Besides Courter, the 17 IDT employees who gave to Christie's campaign contributed between $100 and $500 each, either for the primary or the general election. A political action committee identified with IDT gave the $3,400 limit for Christie's primary campaign. Most of the contributions, including those from Courter and the PAC, were made on May 13, which indicates they might have been bundled." In total, Kosimar reported that there were as many as 27 individuals who contributed to Christie's campaign that might have had a direct interest in the IDT matter. That represented a total of "$26,800 in campaign contributions – earning him a total of $80,400 including state matching funds."

IDT attorney Alice Fisher had a Cinderella experience herself. Her prowess had apparently so impressed the government that she was offered a stint of work at the Department of Justice from 2006 through 2008; after which she returned to Latham & Watkins. Not wanting to feel left out, Fisher also contributed to Christie's campaign.

The United States Attorney's Office for the District of New Jersey did not have to worry about a shortage of prosecution targets by giving a pass to IDT. There would be more than enough to make up for that number with the 44 defendants rounded up in the Bid Rig III sting – not one of whom had any of the political connections or influence of IDT and Courter. Yet all of these instances may have served to prove Christie right about one thing: his sentiment that government awarded no-bid contracts are "the biggest problem in corruption in New Jersey."

A Day at the Circus

Christie's abuses of the deferred prosecution process drew the concern and ire of Democrat lawmakers, who suspected "foul play." U.S. Representative Frank Pallone of New Jersey, a Democrat and one of Christie's most vocal critics on the subject, wrote a letter to the Department of Justice in 2007, saying that, in particular, the contract awarded to Ashcroft "invites the very sort of favoritism, political interference, and back-room dealing that your office has been so successful in combating throughout New Jersey." Pallone further stated that he was particularly troubled by the "increased use of deferred prosecution agreements generally and the lack of any apparent safeguards to protect against their abuse, particularly with regard to the way federal monitors are chosen." He also called upon Congress to investigate all of the contracts that had been doled out by Christie.

Pallone's initiative led to a 2008 hearing before the Commercial and Administrative Law Subcommittee of the House Judiciary Committee, at which Ashcroft was called to testify. The former Attorney General asserted that his firm's selection did not represent a conflict of interest. According to FactCheck.org, when Representative Linda Sánchez of California, a Democrat, pressed further, Ashcroft insisted, "There is not a conflict. There is not an appearance of a conflict." Sánchez responded to Ashcroft that she was "troubled to learn of what appeared to be a backroom sweetheart deal."

The Department of Justice attempted to preempt the Congressional inquiries by making an effort to clean up the mess. They did this by issuing a report based on their own internal inquiry. As was done in the national scandal in 2007 when United States Attorneys were pressured by White House operatives, allegedly including Karl

Rove, to prosecute selected Democrats throughout the country, and then were fired for refusing to carry out these political hatchet jobs, the Department of Justice was more interested in making sure abuses of the Justice system did not happen again rather than holding anyone accountable for past transgressions.

In March of 2008, in anticipation of a Congressional query, Acting Deputy Attorney General Craig S. Morford issued a memorandum for United States Attorneys that established new criteria for the "selection and use of monitors in deferred prosecution agreements and non-prosecution agreements with corporations." Morford's directive stated that monitors are to be chosen by a selection committee and that the deputy attorney general must approve of the selection.

The mild Department of Justice reforms did not quell congressional dissatisfaction. The General Accounting Office acknowledged the DOJ's new guidelines, but found that "more could be done to avoid the appearance of favoritism," such as "requiring that the process and reasons for selecting a specific monitor be documented." Congressman Pallone called the department's new guidelines "far too weak."

When Christie announced his candidacy for Governor, and some of the monitors that he had selected turned up as donors to his campaign, all hell broke loose. "This was the concern we've had all along.... He chooses his friends to be the monitors with the idea he would run for Governor and go back to his political friends to raise money for his campaign," Pallone told the Associated Press.

Pallone was describing conduct that is typically prosecuted as criminal by the Department of Justice, that is, when the conduct can be attributed to the Average Joe or countless public officials at the lower local and state echelons. Christie was fortunate; he, along with a long line of other federal prosecutors who had abused their offices and stripped countless defendants of due process, had golden parachutes and would never be held accountable by the Department of Justice. After all, they were United States Attorneys and above the law. Cover-up is a time-honored tradition at the venerable Department of Justice, which is sworn to uphold the law for all of us, not just a favored few.

The matter was still far from over, and another round of congressional hearings was called for to revisit the issue. This time,

Christie was called upon to testify before Congress by Representative John Conyers (D-Michigan), the chairman of the judiciary committee in the House of Representatives. Believe it or not, the fact that Christie was enmeshed in the middle of a gubernatorial election would help serve his purpose. He played the political victim, intimating that Democrats were assailing him in order to aid and abet the campaign of his opponent, Governor Jon Corzine.

The subcommittee was split along party lines in its assessment of Christie, with Democrats portraying him as a poster-boy for "pay-to-play" reform, and his fellow Republicans praising him as a "hero."

Christie attempted a robust defense of his actions. He did not shy away from the intimidating power of the congressional committee, but rather went right at them. Reporting for the *New York Times*, correspondent David Kocieniewski wrote, "All seven of the contracts Mr. Christie awarded during his seven years in office had a single goal, he asserted: 'to achieve results of justice for the public.' But under tense questioning, he acknowledged that one of the law firms that he had given a contract has since made substantial donations to his campaign for Governor. He also found himself on the defensive over newly released e-mail messages indicating that he refused to intervene on behalf of a company that had objected to the high fees Mr. Ashcroft's firm was charging, including $750,000 a month solely to pay Mr. Ashcroft and two other executives."

When asked about the Ashcroft contract, and why he refused to intercede for the firm that felt they were being gouged by Ashcroft's excessive billing, Christie defiantly replied that his office was too busy to regulate every aspect of an agreement, and that news reports indicated that Mr. Ashcroft's fees were in line with what other firms charged to act as a monitor. "I was not in the least bit shocked to receive e-mails from high-priced lawyers arguing about fees," he testified. He also brushed off inquiries concerning his stipulations that another firm endow a chair for his former alma mater. "The company initiated the proposal to pay for ethics training at Rutgers, which already had a program, and switched to Seton Hall because it was New Jersey's only other law school, Mr. Christie said," reported the *New York Times*.

Congressman Pallone had a much different opinion from that of Chris Christie. During a conference call with reporters concerning the Christie congressional committee appearance, the New Jersey representative was rather blunt: "I think Christie was probably the worst example of how this system was abused. He just basically could hire his friends to be the monitors regardless of what expertise they had. And it's just a very political, and in my opinion, corrupt system. And it shouldn't be allowed to continue."

Representative Steve Cohen (D-Tennessee) was also not buying the explanations that Christie was selling. "You made them an offer they couldn't refuse," making the point that companies entering these agreements have little leverage and simply accept the recommendations made by the prosecutors. "The fact is none of them turned them down because they couldn't afford to because otherwise they'd be prosecuted," Cohen said, as reported by Fact-Check.org. Christie took umbrage at the Congressman's use of the line from *The Godfather*, and in an attempt to garner sympathy, he portrayed the remark as a slur on his Italian-American lineage.

When the questioning turned to David Kelley's no-bid monitoring agreement (the prosecutor who had let Christie's brother, Todd, off the hook in the insider trading scandal), the tension mounted. Now it was personal. Christie seemed incensed. "My brother committed no wrongdoing," he insisted, pointing out that neither the Department of Justice nor the Securities and Exchange Commission decided to pursue a case against his brother. The Democrats persisted. Would they have desisted if he were not the brother of a politically well-connected United States Attorney? Christie decided that he'd had enough.

"Mr. Christie's testimony ended in politically charged bedlam. After two and a half hours, he told the panel chairman that, as he had previously informed the subcommittee, he had to leave to catch a train and attend to 'pressing business' in New Jersey. When Democrats urged him to stay anyway and continued peppering him with questions, Mr. Christie and his entourage stood and marched out. 'This should be the end of it, but it won't be,' he said, as he and his aides hurried from the Capitol. 'It's all politics.' Mr. Christie said it was unfortunate that the hearing had been turned into 'a political circus,' and added that his answers were thorough enough to put the matter to rest," reported the *New York Times*.

Assemblyman Joseph Cryan, a New Jersey state lawmaker and also the state's Democratic Party chairman, had a different take on

Christie's bringing down the tent on the congressional committee. "It is very telling that Christie got up and walked out as he began to be questioned about the multimillion-dollar, no-bid contract given to the former U.S. Attorney that refused to charge his brother," said Assemblyman Cryan. "If Christie tried to answer for all the other multimillion-dollar, no-bid contracts he gave out to friends, he would have been testifying until Election Day, and none of his statements would have matched," he added.

And to think, again, that at one time the United States Attorney had called no-bid contracts "the biggest problem in corruption in New Jersey." At least Christie has had *some* positive impact in this travesty. While he seemingly got away with his various transgressions, his conduct has resulted in reforms to the Department of Justice's system meant to ensure that any attempts at similar conduct will not re-occur. Nonetheless, the Department of Justice chose not to punish Christie. It seems as though the Department is content to let sleeping dogs lie, and simply stifle the ambitions of the *next* prosecutor who decides to pad his future campaign coffers with donations from friends to whom he handed out contracts.

New Jersey Governor Jim McGreevey

Chapter Four

From U.S. Attorney
to Almost Governor

In 2001, as the administration of the newly-elected New Jersey Governor, James McGreevey, began to rapidly unravel, Christie, then United States Attorney for New Jersey, positioned himself as a stark contrast to the Governor. McGreevey's staff and financial supporters had become enmeshed in a series of ethics scandals. Christie's public relations machine was fast gaining him a reputation as the proverbial knight in shining armor. He launched corruption probes of McGreevey's Administration several times during his tenure. The ethics lapses and the sustained probes began to extract a political toll on McGreevey and he was soon seen as vulnerable to defeat in the 2005 election. With few prominent Republican politicians capable of mounting a challenge, Christie's name surfaced as a potential candidate.

The Almost Governor 2005: Christie's Trial Run

Christie would be up for reappointment as United States Attorney after the 2004 Presidential race, and at the time, it was not a safe bet that George W. Bush was going to be able to hold onto the White House. Christie had to be careful about venturing into politics while serving as United States Attorney, but with the media providing all the speculation about a race for governor, Christie could play it cute: able to avoid talking about a running, while all the time looking like a candidate.

However, this strategy soon drew the criticism of McGreevey Democrats, who saw Christie's actions as a conflict of interest.

From January through March of 2004, the *New York Times* covered the high-stakes poker game. Correspondent David Kocieniewski reported, "A widening federal investigation into one of Gov. James E. McGreevey's fundraisers has forced leaders of both parties to brace for a legal showdown pitting Democratic insiders against the United States Attorney for New Jersey, who is considered a Republican contender to run against Mr. McGreevey in 2005.... In recent weeks, the United States Attorney Christopher J. Christie has directed federal agents to subpoena records from the Democratic State Committee, two state agencies and the Governor's office, in an effort to determine whether the McGreevey administration granted political favors to contributors in exchange for tens of thousands of dollars in donations.

"... Although none of the information that has thus far become public indicates any wrongdoing by the administration.... As the investigation progresses there have been increasing calls for Mr. Christie to either rule himself out as a candidate for Governor or declare his candidacy and recuse himself from the case."

Christie eventually wound up prosecuting David M. D'Amiano, a Democratic Party fundraiser, and then Charles Kushner, whom the *New York Times* referred to as one of McGreevey's "top contributors." Kushner's indictment mentioned a "Public Official One," which the whole world knew was McGreevey. It charged that McGreevey had invented a code word, "Machiavelli," that was established to extort campaign contributions in exchange for official help in a land dispute.

The indictment was a scathing document. On July 14, 2004, *New York Times* Correspondent Ronald Smothers wrote, "In a criminal complaint that reads like a plot line from an Elmore Leonard novel, Charles Kushner, a New Jersey landowner and businessman with close ties to many religious and political figures, was charged with hiring prostitutes to entice his brother-in-law and his accountant into sexually compromising situations."

An angry McGreevey termed the indictment a "politically motivated smear."

In a July 9, 2004, *New York Times* news item, Correspondent David Kocieniewski reported Christie's pushing of the ethics envelope – his actions appeared to be motivated by his political agenda. "Mr. Christie has made himself particularly susceptible to charges of prosecutorial grandstanding. In addition to his coyness about a possible run for governor, he has cut an uncharacteristically conspicuous profile in New Jersey political circles: on the day Mr. McGreevey unveiled his budget address, Mr. Christie met with Republican Party leaders in Trenton; his office is in Newark. A few days after he issued subpoenas to seize records at the Governor's office, Mr. Christie was seen in one of the capitol's most popular restaurants, having lunch with Rich Bond, former chairman of the Republican National Committee. (A Republican fund-raiser who also attended the lunch later explained that Mr. Christie and Mr. Bond were old friends.)"

In a scathing thirteen-page white paper report examining the entire sordid episode, Sandra Caron George, writing for the *Georgetown Journal of Legal Ethics*, excoriated the actions of Christie as United States Attorney. George took issue with the fact that once Christie had implicated McGreevey in the Kushner fundraising scandal, by referencing him in the indictment, it raised considerable concerns. She pointed out that the media and the public had been led to wonder whether McGreevey was involved based on the indictment references, and that it seemed incumbent upon Christie to either investigate McGreevey or dispel any question surrounding his involvement. "The role of the prosecutor, though, is to seek justice, not merely raise inferences about an individual's guilt. Christie's decision, thus far, not to investigate or prosecute McGreevey simply furthers suspicions that Christie lacks a case against him and that his motives are political," George concluded.

As a member of the New Jersey legislature at the time, I recall the overwhelming sentiment of our Democratic Assembly Caucus. We felt Christie's actions were purely politically motivated. The public meetings Christie was having with Republican Party political operatives all across New Jersey helped to solidify the opinions of the Democratic lawmakers.

Five years later, in its coverage of the 2009 New Jersey Gubernatorial election, the *Star-Ledger* would reflect on Christie's actions as United States Attorney in 2004. "During his years as a federal prosecutor, Christie, a former Morris County freeholder, attracted buzz from GOP leaders as a potential future candidate for governor. Christie downplayed the speculation and maintained he was focused on the U.S. Attorney's Office," Correspondent Michael Rispoli reported.

Besides criticizing Christie for his political meetings with Karl Rove, while he continued to prosecute his soon-to-be opposition, the 2009 Corzine gubentorial campaign also slammed Christie for his improper meetings in 2004 with former Republican National Chair Rich Bond, Somerset County GOP Chair Dale Florio and former Sussex GOP Chair Rich Zeoli during his investigation of McGreevey's Administration. "The Hatch Act is very clear in saying political activities are off limits," Governor Jon Corzine commented. "It is very hard to understand how someone who is responsible and mission is law enforcement should be violating – potentially violating – laws like the Hatch Act."

In 2004, the U.S. Attorney's Office's continued bludgeoning of McGreevey made it more and more appetizing for Christie to take the weakened incumbent Governor on at the polls. Fate then dealt a fortuitous wildcard when a scandal erupted in McGreevey's Administration concerning an Israeli national, who had been hired as a Counselor to the Governor, Golan Cipel. Cipel had made known his intention to file a sexual harassment lawsuit against McGreevey. McGreevey declared that he would not allow his office to be blackmailed and then shocked the country by outing himself on national television as a gay American. The next words out of his mouth were just as shocking. He announced that he would be resigning his office.

The incident sent the Democratic Party into free-fall with no ground in sight. Under the provisions of the New Jersey Constitution, State Senate President Dick Codey should assume the role of Governor. Codey was a remarkably popular political figure across New Jersey, but his independence troubled many of the powerbrokers in the Democratic Party hierarchy, who pushed him aside, and opted instead to run the well-financed U.S. Senator Jon Corzine as their 2005 nominee. Corzine was considered the eight hundred-pound gorilla of the day and his candidacy ended any further illusions that Chris Christie might have harbored of running for Governor in 2005. It also ended any further persecution of former Governor James McGreevey.

Chapter Five

The Infamous Solomon Dwek

History teaches us that politics makes strange bedfellows. So do prosecutions.

The two central figures in the Bid Rig III investigations were an unlikely pair: Chris Christie, the former United States Attorney who became New Jersey Governor, and Bid Rig III informant Solomon Dwek. To understand the sting that would catapult Christie to the Governorship, you must come to understand these two men: the events, yes, but especially the motivations that drove each of the perpetrators.

An Unholy Alliance

When Solomon Dwek was arrested for bank fraud in 2006, the two men's destinies collided. In fact, there is no one individual who had a more di-
rect impact on Chris Christie's career than the notorious confidential informant Solomon Dwek. Likewise, there was no one  individual who would have more of an impact on Solomon Dwek's life after his criminal escapades than Chris Christie. Without Dwek there would have been no Bid Rig III to turn the tide of the 2009 gubernatorial election towards Christie. Without Christie, Dwek would have been without a plea deal or the role he then took on as a confidential informant. Had that not happened, he might very well be serving out a 20-year or more prison sentence, or possibly (as he feared) left to die in jail.

In their book *The Jersey Sting*, authors Ted Sherman and Josh Margolin, both respected journalists, established the definitive narrative on Solomon Dwek – capturing his sordid life story in vivid detail. As the authors researched, interviewed, and wrote, prosecutors lined up to spout their personal war stories about the sting. Reading *The Jersey Sting,* one could sense just how loose lipped the prosecutors were – not realizing that investigation documents not intended to see the light of day would suddenly be open to scrutiny.

The same prosecutors left a trail of dots that the once hidden documents would help to connect. Those connections further explained the mystery that was Solomon Dwek, a criminal whose emissaries got him the plea deal of the century through Christie. That deal meant the chance for Dwek to see daylight as a free man, after a relatively shorter prison sentence, had he not agreed to cooperate in entrapping innocent men and women on Christie's behalf.

A Scam for All Seasons

"I was hungry to make money," Solomon Dwek told his sentencing judge, trying to explain the lifestyle that ruined countless lives and institutions. It came with a price tag estimated in the hundreds of millions of dollars.

Solomon Dwek was raised in the Syrian Sephardic community of Deal, New Jersey. The son of Rabbi Isaac Dwek, Solomon was brought up in a strict Orthodox home. As part of that upbringing, Dwek attended a Yeshiva in Riverdale, New York, followed by rabbinical college, where learning was focused on understanding and mastering the Torah. However, along the way a man named Jack Adjmi, a close friend of Dwek's family, would plant the seeds of real estate entrepreneurship in young Solomon. Adjmi's daughter Terry was married to Joey Dwek, Solomon's uncle, so there was an element of trust, however misplaced, that Adjmi initially felt for Dwek.

Adjmi fronted the purchase of a real estate parcel, and cut Solomon Dwek in. Dwek, in return, would manage the properties. The profits were split 50/50, and Dwek would remit a stipend back to Adjmi until he paid back the money that he had been fronted for his "sweat equity" share. But it did not take long for Dwek to forget his religious studies; especially "Thou shall not steal." The benevolent Jack Adjmi, who put Solomon Dwek into business, would become his young apprentice's first victim. Dwek robbed him blind.

So began Solomon Dwek's career in crime, creating an elaborate real estate Ponzi scheme in which he sucked in investors for partnerships and simply pocketed their money. Whenever they wanted a return on their money Dwek would flip their shares to another investor, or find someone else to front a new property purchase, and then funnel that money back to cover the person looking to get out.

Dwek's robbing-Peter-to-pay-Paul routine was not limited to investors only; he defrauded banks as well. He loved regaling juries with his stories about how easy the banks were to scam. He made it sound as though they were desperate to loan him money. He even got loans for properties that did not exist, providing make-believe block and lot numbers. According to Dwek, the banks never checked.

Like all Ponzi schemes, it couldn't last forever. Soon enough, Dwek's swindles could not keep pace with those investors looking for their capital back. Dwek was putting deals together in the tens of millions of dollars. Higher amounts only insured a higher fall. Dwek had racked up more than $20 million dollars in loans from HSBC bank in New York. The bank sensed something was wrong and called in the loans. As Dwek scrambled for the funds to cover the loans, he had the gall to reach out to his various partners, the very people he swindled, to help bail him out. At this point Dwek's partners realized they were not really partners but actually Dwek's victims, having been collectively conned out of millions of dollars. Dwek's Uncle Joey was taken for $60 million himself – money used by his nephew to guarantee tens of millions of dollars in loans for properties that never existed.

Desperate, Dwek tried one last ploy. He pulled into the drive-in teller's window of PNC bank in Eatontown, New Jersey. The bank knew him well. Dwek wrote a check for $25 million dollars from a defunct account into another of his accounts. The teller informed him that the account he was drawing down on was closed. As cool as a cucumber, Dwek told the teller, "Corporate is reopening the account for me.... It's okay." He might as well have been at the McDonald's drive-thru ordering a Happy Meal; within seconds the teller credited Dwek's account with the $25 million.

Where are these sorts of tellers when *I* go to the bank to cash a check? I'm usually barraged with requests for various forms of identification. They chain up their counter pens, but then hand over $25 million through the drive-in teller's window?

Dwek sped off and made one more go-around with his shell-shocked partners, who were still dazed by their sudden reversals of fortune. Dwek pleaded for money to help dig his way out. He knew the transaction at PNC had just raised the stakes – without the dough to pay back the bank, he could be facing a bank fraud charge. Uncle Joey expressed the sentiment of everyone Dwek had defrauded: "Go fuck yourself!" he told his nephew.

The next afternoon, still desperately trying to get out of the woods, Dwek drove up to the drive-in window at PNC bank in North Asbury Park. He tried cashing another $25 million check, using the same routine. For a few moments it worked; they credited Dwek's account with the money. But the bank's corporate office was on alert. Realizing that they had been duped the day before at another branch, the bank reversed the transaction and called the Feds. Solomon Dwek was soon arrested for bank fraud.

Of course, bank fraud was just the tip of the iceberg. When Dwek was arraigned for the state charges he also faced, one had only to see the hundreds of investors and creditors who piled into a Monmouth County courtroom to understand the immense scope and ramifications of Dwek's con. Behind each type of fraud were various stories of outrageous moral depravity that depicted not only a cunning con artist but also a truly diabolical madman.

Here is a perfect example of how this man's immorality knew no bounds. Dwek conveniently worked at the Deal Yeshiva, a temple that had been founded by his parents. Although he was mostly doing fundraising, he set his own salary at $200,000. Soon the Yeshiva became a tool for Dwek's money laundering. He would accept and report exaggerated donations from wealthy individuals looking for tax write-offs, give back as much as ninety percent to the tax cheats, and keep the other ten percent for the Yeshiva. The only exception was when Dwek would pocket the actual contribution, or a portion of it, for himself.

During the trial of Mayor Anthony Suarez, another Bid Rig III defendant who was found innocent, Suarez's defense attorney Michael Critchley exposed Dwek for what he was. Under questioning, Dwek explained his corruption of the Yeshiva. Critchley asked, "This was a school that had the noble purpose of providing a religious education to certain people, correct? I don't mean certain people. It was a school designed to provide a religious education and a secular education, correct?" The purpose of the question was to establish a lead-in for his overall questioning of the government's star witness. Dwek acknowledged the noble purpose of the Yeshiva, and then Critchley moved in for the kill. "You corrupted that institution?"

"I did," admitted Dwek.

"You basically made Deal Yeshiva, which was a school of education, into a crime scene?" Critchley continued.

"Correct," Dwek confirmed, then further acknowledged that his actions had caused the religious school to close.

"So you basically destroyed that institution?" Critchley surmised.

"Unfortunately," reflected Dwek.

The Deal Yeshiva was not the only religious school that fell victim to Dwek: the Torah Academy of Monmouth County was another. In order to hinder creditors hunting down Dwek's assets, he dumped a cool $1.2 million of his criminal proceeds into the academy. This had his creditors lined up to file claims for the academy's assets.

Later in the same Suarez trial, Dwek spun another tale of woe. Without the Torah Academy's knowledge, Dwek had loaned himself approximately $2 million dollars from the religious institution to buy a partnership in a casino boat that operated off the coast of Florida, in international waters. Under Captain Dwek the floating crap game quickly moved from dice to vice: along with gambling it also served as a floating brothel, providing prostitution services for its voyagers. Astonishingly, Dwek claimed both the gambling and the prostitution *lost money*. What are the odds that a floating casino-brothel would go into the red?

Dwek had even figured out a way to turn a profit in death, but he needed the services of an amoral life insurance salesperson to carry out this caper. Enter Chaskie Rosenberg, a character out of a Damon Runyan tale. Rosenberg would have leads to people who were in ill health or dying and in desperate financial straits, about to default on their life insurance premiums. Dwek and Rosenberg would then invest in the deaths of the soon-to-be dearly departed. Critchley described this con as "sleazy," which as in all things Dwek was an understatement.

As Dwek related, "The way it happened was that the family already had a policy in place for either the person or the father or grandfather, and at some point the family couldn't afford to pay the premium any more. The policies usually were two-year-old, five-year-old or 15-year-old policies. The families didn't want to lose the policies, and we offered, me and Rosenberg – or Rosenberg offered the families, instead of the families losing the policy, we said, 'sign the policy over to Rosenberg and the Yeshiva, and we will continue paying the premiums, and we will give you ten percent of the proceeds after the death of your beloved one.'... Mr. Rosenberg paid a portion of the premium, and then the older person or their family paid a portion of the premium. Then when that person died, the family got ten percent, Rosenberg got 45 percent, and Deal Yeshiva, the charity, would get the other 45 percent. We shared in the premiums." A full ten percent for the bereaved and needy families – what a sport!

Perhaps the *crème de la crème* of all of Dwek's frauds involved Dwek's former secretary Susan Wagner and her husband. As defense attorney Michael Critchley stated, Susan Wagner did something that was "very dangerous" when it came to Solomon Dwek – she trusted him. In 2006 the Wagners had recently retired and purchased a retirement home in North Carolina. They were desperate to unload their Jackson, New Jersey home. Understandably, Susan Wagner turned to her real estate guru boss for help. Dwek told her he would help take the property off her hands, and he did, but in a way that the Wagners never expected.

Initially, Dwek co-opted an associate with ties to an appraisal company to deflate the value of the property in order to lower the Wagners' asking price. When the Wagners moved down to North Carolina, Dwek moved in to swindle the couple out of their life savings and purchased the home. The Wagners had a purchase agreement prepared, but Dwek had also drafted another set of sales documents. The couple only executed the sales document they prepared, but magically their signatures appeared on the sales document that Dwek's associate had prepared. The Wagners' document provided for the payoff on two mortgages still owed by the couple. The sales document filed by Dwek made no provision to pay off the mortgages, so when they defaulted on the payments to the bank the couple lost everything, including their credit rating.

One would think that Dwek's sordid portfolio of crimes would earn him harsh treatment from federal law enforcement officials. Interestingly, it did not. In fact, the most outrageous crime in all of this might have been the kid gloves treatment that Dwek received from the United States Attorney's Office, which was headed by "corruption-busting" prosecutor Chris Christie.

The Plea Deal of the Century

The feds had Solomon Dwek dead to rights when they arrested him in May of 2006 for bank fraud. Dwek was the perfect ham sandwich – easy to prosecute. As stated by the authors of *The Jersey Sting*, who, as noted earlier, had access to the prosecutors working behind the scenes: "Dwek was easily facing 30 years or more in prison and a $1 million fine. It had been a $50 million bank fraud, and there was absolutely nowhere to go with it.... To the front office, it was an already an open-and-shut fraud case. Dwek was going to jail." Given the broad spectrum of frauds that Dwek had perpetrated on so many unsuspecting victims and institutions, the need to negotiate a co-operation agreement, in a case that was a slam-dunk, seemed unreasonable. Yet that is exactly what Christie's office did!

With the aid of perfect hindsight, Dwek's testimony in the trial of Mayor Anthony Suarez, and the portrayal by prosecutors of the events that led to his plea deal now raise serious questions about whether Dwek pulled some political strings to get himself off the hook. The question is, how, and why did the prosecutors give him the plea deal? It was no secret that Solomon Dwek was a major donor to political campaigns. When Chris Christie and Bill Palatucci were heading George W. Bush's New Jersey fundraising for the 2000 presidential campaign, Dwek contributed $50,000 to the Texas Governor's campaign. Dwek, at trial, admitted there had been a plan to influence a plea bargain, courtesy of the hefty campaign contribution. Again, while he was testifying in the Suarez trial, Dwek acknowledged a plot to seek a Presidential pardon for his crimes from George Bush.

Defense attorney Michael Critchley asked Dwek, "And do you ever recall attempting, at least beginning efforts, to get a pardon from the President of the United States?" .

"There was talk about that, yes," Dwek acknowledged, and then further elaborated.

"I believe my father spoke to an attorney in Lakewood ... Larry Bathgate, B-a-t-h-g-a-t-e ... I believe he was a fund raiser at one time in New Jersey for the Republican Party."

Critchley then zeroed in. "This was an attempt to get a presidential pardon from President Bush."

"It was at the time, yes," Dwek confirmed.

"You had contributed $50,000 to President Bush's campaign?" Critchley followed.

"I believe I did, yes," Dwek again confirmed. He then focused the time frame of his father's actions after his arrest in May of 2006.

If you do not think money plays a role in the pardon process, think again. As the authors of *The Jersey Sting* acknowledge, it has happened before. They even cite the matter of Isaac Toussie, a Brooklyn developer facing prison in another real estate swindle, who was granted a presidential pardon following his father's $28,500 contribution to the Republican National Committee. In that case, however, thanks to tremendous criticism concerning the pardon, it was withdrawn within days of its having been issued.

There is a bit of contradiction between the prosecutors' recollections, as depicted in *The Jersey Sting,* and Dwek's trial testimony, with regard to the date or dates that Dwek's father spoke to Bathgate about the pardon. The prosecutors contend the incident occurred in late August of 2008, and not close to Dwek's arrest in May of 2006, as the confidential informant himself testified. What is known is that Dwek's lawyer, Mike Himmel, was hot on the idea of a plea deal immediately following Dwek's arrest. Himmel was trying to get traction and right after the arrest would have been the appropriate time for requesting a political fix. The question remains: Did Dwek's father petition the government right after his son's arrest and then get turned down or was 2008 the first time the pardon issue came up?

Evidence may support the fact that a pardon had been sought on both occasions, although each time for entirely different purposes: Once, to force a softer landing for Dwek; and later, to entrap a target in a crime in order to support Dwek's quest to knock time off any eventual sentence. Dwek's team was not going to wait while their circumstances steadily got worse. They were going to move for help as quickly as possible. Common sense also dictates that on the heels of Dwek's bank fraud arrest, along with the pure heinousness of the crimes he committed in defrauding his endless list of victims, a Presidential pardon was just not happening. However, if someone still wanted to help Dwek, then a possible compromise would be a co-operation agreement exactly like the one that Dwek did eventually receive, which, given the circumstances, was the next best thing to a pardon.

This could explain the bizarre decision to allow a slam-dunk prosecution to go by the wayside, and why, instead, the United States Attorney's Office caved in and negotiated for the use of Dwek as a confidential informant.

This would also explain why Dwek's prosecution was uncharacteristically maneuvered within the federal prosecutors' offices. James Nobile, the head of Special Prosecutions in the United States Attorney's Office, was the one assigned to do the maneuvering. "He wanted Dwek for special prosecutions but refused to say exactly why," *The Jersey Sting* noted. "Typically a bank fraud would have immediately been sent to the commercial crimes division of the U.S. Attorney's office. This seemed like an open-and-shut-case of check kiting, and some of the front office questioned why Jimmy (Nobile) would want any part of it. Nobile insisted that Dwek 'is a name I'm interested in.' That was all Jimmy would say."

The negotiations that hammered out the parameters of Dwek's co-operation agreement lasted approximately six months, and culminated with the deal being inked in early January 2007. When the dust settled, Christie's office had rescued Dwek by offering him a plea deal and agreeing not to seek prosecution on any of the "thousands of crimes" that Dwek admitted to under oath, at an estimated cost to his victims of hundreds of millions of dollars. Christie's office agreed to recommend a substantial reduction of Dwek's potential sentence for the bank fraud charges in return for his participating as the confidential informant in the Bid Rig III investigation. Dwek actually testified on the stand that he thought his cooperation could lead to *no* time in jail!

As if the plea deal was not enough, further evidence would later surface that Dwek had friends in high places. When Charles Stanziale, the trustee assigned to Dwek's bankruptcy, saw that he would need Dwek's help in order to unravel the complex frauds, Dwek was actually offered a job to assist Stanziale while he worked as the government's informant. Christie's office did not object to this irony of paying a criminal to detail his crimes, even though Dwek could and should have been told that he had to co-operate with the bankruptcy court as a contingency of his plea deal. He was not. Unbelievable as it may seem, this allowed Dwek to negotiate a salary for his help.

For his services in assisting the bankruptcy trustee, Dwek was paid an approximate average of $12,000 per month, drawn by depleting the solvency fund reserved for the victims of his fraud. So, in effect, Dwek was defrauding them a second time—with help from the government. When Christie's prosecutors then petitioned Bankruptcy Court Judge Kathryn Ferguson several times to prolong Dwek's bankruptcy case for the sake of the Bid Rig III sting, the prosecutors were essentially putting money into Dwek's pocket. This benefit to Dwek was above and beyond the terms spelled out in his co-operation agreement.

In the trial of Mayor Anthony Suarez, defense attorney Michael Critchley emphasized the details of Dwek's compensation package. "OK. Now, you indicated that you were compensated by the bankruptcy court as working with the trustee. How much did you receive in compensation and expenses to date?" Critchley asked.

"Over the last three and a half years, hmm, over a million dollars," Dwek answered, to the astonishment of the Court.

"Not bad. You caused all of this fraud, and you get paid a million dollars to unravel it. It is a great country, isn't it, Mr. Dwek?" Critchley snapped sarcastically – and with good reason.

Christie's office then decided to pile whipped cream and cherries on top of the already generous plea deal. To make sure Dwek could keep his appointments with the bankruptcy court and earn his twelve grand per month, the government provided him a brand new, mint condition Lexus, including the lease, insurance, gas and parking tolls.

One would think the government would at least get a stipend back from the fortune they were allowing Dwek to collect and for the Lexus they provided to their confidential informant. This return could have come through the income taxes Dwek would have to pay. Alas, the government relaxed the law even more for Solomon Dwek. While other honest Americans scrimp and save to pay their federal taxes each year, this criminal was given a tax holiday. Dwek never filed his taxes during the entire approximately three-year Bid Rig III sting. "I did not file my tax returns because the FBI told me not to because it would blow the cover off the investigation," Dwek told the Court.

Given the circumstances, Solomon Dwek received the gift of a lifetime when he was handed that plea deal, and the man ultimately responsible for it was none other than U.S. District Attorney Chris Christie.

"Dwek, Seen as Loose Cannon, Angers Christie."

The reference to the second reported attempt at a Presidential pardon for Dwek, as depicted by prosecutors recalling war stories for the authors of *The Jersey Sting*, occurred after the summer of 2008. The true motivation behind that instance was not as clear-cut and it angered Christie, who thought Dwek was trying to set up prominent Republican Party fundraiser Larry Bathgate. Thanks to Christie's generous plea deal, Dwek, who had professed that he was expecting to serve no jail time, had little need for a pardon at this point. Common sense would dictate that Dwek, now intent on working time off his sentence by drawing others into crimes, was actually using the pardon routine as a ruse, trying to snag Bathgate in his web.

Christie's instincts may have proved right about Dwek targeting Bathgate, which is why he lowered the boom and ordered his office and Dwek's attorney to yank the choke chain around his neck. *The Jersey Sting* described it this way: "No matter what angle Dwek thought he was playing, Christie just flat out hit the roof.... 'Get this guy under control,' Christie thundered."

We know from Karl Rove's testimony to Congress that Christie was already pondering a run for the Governor's office at this point, and Dwek was now potentially putting that run at risk if he was targeting Bathgate. The perceptive reporters who later authored *The Jersey Sting* knew the implications immediately: "Bathgate was a pillar of New Jersey's public life and a figure that could single-handedly make or break a Republican's chances to win the Governorship."

Of course, the Democratic targets of Bid Rig III from Hudson County would never be afforded such prosecutorial courtesy from a U.S. Attorney seeking the Republican nomination for New Jersey's Governorship – a man who badly needed Larry Bathgate's help.

Prosecution Passover

Potentially targeting Larry Bathgate was not Solomon Dwek's only misstep. As Chris Christie seemingly started to think less from a federal prosecutor's perspective and more from the perspective of a gubernatorial candidate, Dwek was becoming a problem. In fact, Dwek was becoming too good at the job he was given to root out corruption (Are you seeing the irony?), putting the confidential informant on a collision course with the evolving but still unannounced Christie campaign for Governor.

Two of the early operatives tasked with laying the groundwork for Christie's campaign were Bill Palatucci, his key advisor, and Christie's brother Todd. In order to win the Governorship, Christie would first have to win the Republican Party's primary election. The key to winning the primary was support from as many Republican Party County Chairpersons as soon as possible; especially those representing large Republican voting populaces such as Morris, Ocean and Monmouth counties. The usual winner of the primary was the candidate who rounded up the majority of chairperson support – and did so earlier than anyone else.

The 2009 Republican Party primary for Governor would be contested between Christie, Assemblyman Rick Merkt, and former Bogota Mayor Steve Lonegan. By his choice of political targets, one might have thought that Dwek himself was running for Governor. Dwek had in fact compromised two prominent county chairpersons around the same time that Christie's campaign emissaries could have been courting them for support: Monmouth County Republican Party Chairman and former Sheriff Joe Oxley, and Ocean County Republican Party Chairman George Gilmore.

Gilmore became enmeshed with Dwek because of the confidential informant's sting run on Daniel Van Pelt, a South Jersey Assembly member, and Al Santoro, the Ocean County Democratic Chairman. The gist of Dwek's con was his story that he was seeking to acquire official influence that would lead to approval for a development project in Ocean County, and that he could do this in exchange for money. Dwek informed jurors in the trial of Assemblyman Van Pelt that he told Santoro, "I would like him to introduce me to people that were like him, that were takers, people that would accept cash; in return they would help me with getting my approval process expedited and items of that nature."

Dwek's statement drew further inquiry from the prosecutor conducting the direct examination. "Without telling me or telling us what he said to you, what did he do in response to your request for assistance?"

"He set up an appointment for me to meet with George Gilmore in Mr. Gilmore's law offices," Dwek responded.

As Dwek explained, Gilmore was offering to help grease the skids for acquiring Van Pelt's much needed influence. "Mr. Gilmore brought up the fact that Mr. Van Pelt's wife was an attorney and a judge in some smaller towns and she was looking to become a New Jersey court judge."

"Do you have an understanding as to why that was raised at this meeting?" the federal prosecutor pressed.

"Well, because Mr. Santoro, in his capacity as Chairman of the Democratic Party, in order for a person to become that type of judge, you need the votes of both leaders of the Democratic party and the Republican party and Mr. Santoro being the Democratic party in Ocean County, they would need his vote in order to make her a judge," Dwek explained.

Dwek was getting Gilmore in deeper. Around this same time, according to *The Jersey Sting*, "Gilmore had been one of the chief New Jersey delegates to the Republican National Convention in Minnesota, where Christie's brother Todd and best friend, Bill Palatucci, were quietly pushing Chris' political agenda." This was bad news for candidate Christie; Gilmore's political prowess in delivering votes made him indispensable. "George Gilmore was the unquestioned political overlord in the usually quiet county along the Shore. The chairman of the Ocean County GOP, Gilmore was a player and a critical cog in the wheel of the state's Republican Party – one of the most important and powerful leaders," the authors of *The Jersey Sting* explained.

James Nobile, the head of special investigations and the apparent fixer for the United States Attorney's Office, sensed a predicament for Christie. According to what law enforcement officials told the authors of *The Jersey Sting*, Nobile pressed Christie to recuse himself from the Gilmore matter: "'Listen; let's talk through recusal,' Nobile told Christie. 'You know Gilmore, you've met with Gilmore,' Nobile said to his boss. Was this a problem? Could Christie separate the Gilmore he knew from the man they were seriously thinking of arresting?"

What actually prompted Nobile to raise recusal, even if Christie had just met with Gilmore? What was Christie's stake in the matter? Would there be a conflict posed by Christie looking for Gilmore's support in the gubernatorial election, which would mean that

Christie was actually breaking the law, primarily the Hatch Act, by remaining in his job as United States Attorney while manipulating his intended run for political office? If so, that also meant that Nobile knew his boss was breaking the law. Ironically, Christie asked Ralph Marra and Michele Brown to determine if he had a conflict because of the Gilmore matter – two individuals who were central to a misconduct, recusal and conflict argument in the *United States v. Manzo*.

After Christie was notified that the Ocean County Republican Party Chairman was a potential target, in a miraculous stroke of good timing, George Gilmore suddenly decided not to take any subsequent meetings with Dwek. He dropped completely off the investigation's radar screen. However, Gilmore's name and his implication in potential criminal activity remained all over the non-public FBI 302 reports regarding Van Pelt and Santoro. As the cases proceeded against Van Pelt and Santoro, once the arrests had been made prior to the November gubernatorial election, it would have been difficult to exculpate Gilmore from the matter without referencing his presence at some of the key meetings he attended.

As luck would have it for the Christie campaign, George Gilmore decided to support Christie in the 2009 Republican primary election. When the Bid Rig III arrests went down shortly after the primary election, Christie had a second stroke of good luck. Despite Gilmore's pivotal meetings with Dwek, Van Pelt, and Al Santoro – which served as the catalyst for the sting that was run on Van Pelt – not a peep was heard about Gilmore, neither in Van Pelt's criminal complaint or indictment, nor in Santoro's "Information" supporting his guilty plea.

The Van Pelt matter was publically depicted, without mention of Gilmore, in the "Information" pleaded to by Santoro in December of 2009, after the New Jersey gubernatorial election. The United States Attorney's Office prepares those documents. The fingerprints of a fixer were all over these incredible coincidences. Someone seemingly had a hand in exculpating Gilmore's involvement in the Bid Rig III investigations and prosecutions. Then again, George Gilmore was not a Hudson County Democratic politician supporting Jon Corzine: he was supporting Chris Christie. Gilmore went on to deliver a record 70,000-vote plurality to Christie over Corzine in Ocean County on election night. Besides his propensity for good fortune, Gilmore also demonstrated an uncanny knack for clairvoyance. In one of Ocean County Democratic Chairman Al Santoro's FBI 302 reports, the agents write, "SANTORO advised that approximately one week prior to the July 23, 2009 FEDERAL BUREAU OF INVESTIGATION raids, he was told by GILMORE that there was going to be a lot of arrests north of the Raritan. GILMORE did not provide any more details and did not say who told him about the upcoming arrests."

Here Comes the Judge

Another apparently charmed target of Dwek was Joseph Oxley, a former assistant prosecutor from Monmouth County, who had served as Monmouth County Sheriff from 1996 through 2007. He also served as Chairman of the Monmouth County Republican Committee since 2008. Oxley was Chairman during Chris Christie's campaign for Governor.

In statements made to the FBI concerning Oxley's alleged criminal activity, and documented in an FBI 302 report, Dwek alleges that in exchange for political contributions Oxley gave him tips on real estate foreclosure opportunities handled by the Sheriff's Office which had not yet been made public. The conduct was reported in seven government Otherwise Illegal Activity [OIA] Authorization Reports that were used for the Bid Rig III sting from February 21, 2007 thru August 8, 2008.

The notations by the FBI agents read, "OXLEY also tips off SD (Solomon Dwek) to upcoming foreclosure sales. OXLEY provides SD with the list of upcoming foreclosure properties to be auctioned off by the county. The list is normally given to SD two weeks before it becomes public. This gives SD the opportunity to negotiate a deal with the property owner before the auction and avoid competition and potentially higher prices. SD stated that he purchased property as a result of tips from OXLEY approximately three to five times. SD stated that he raises money for OXLEY every year." The pair hit it off so well that "SD stated that OXLEY gave him an honorary Sheriff's badge and identification with SD's photo. SD further advised that he meets with OXLEY every month," the 302 documents further reported.

According to *The Jersey Sting,* August of 2008 is the same approximate period when Todd Christie and Bill Palatucci were making their political rounds and lining up support for Christie from county chairpersons, after which there was no further mention of Oxley in any government OIA Authorization Reports. Miraculously, statements about Oxley's corrupt activities suddenly disappeared from the OIA reports as well. Copies of two reports, dated the same day, have Oxley's alleged criminal conduct mentioned in one and missing from the other. *How does that happen?* The United States Attorney's Office under Paul Fishman called this a "typographical error." (When you stop laughing, please continue reading.)

Within months of the purging of Oxley's alleged corrupt activities from the OIA reports, he became one of the first Republican Party county chairpersons to endorse Christie's candidacy in the Republican primary election. In June of 2012, not forgetting Oxley's loyal support and contribution to his election, fully aware of the crimes alleged against him by Solomon Dwek, Governor Christie nominated Oxley for a judgeship to the New Jersey Superior Courts. The Dwek and Oxley FBI 302 reports – filed as part of my Hyde Amendment petition to recoup my legal fees after my false arrest – were now public domain. Oxley was outed, and his nomination to the court did not sit well with the New Jersey Senate committee that would be hearing his nomination.

Senator Raymond Lesniak, a senior member of the Senate Judiciary Committee, demanded that Dwek appear before the committee to testify. "Based on Dwek's information, the U.S. Attorney's Office raided (former Department of Community Affairs Commissioner) Joe Doria's house shortly before Christie's election. So obviously they thought that he had credibility in what he was stating," the veteran Senator observed. The government raided Doria's house, despite already knowing he was innocent of any charges. It was a nice play though; Doria was in the cabinet of Governor Jon Corzine, Christie's gubernatorial opponent. Stories about the Doria raid appeared in Christie political ads and paid dividends according to polling results. It took well over a year for the feds to get around to clearing Doria after intentionally smearing his name. This again is our federal tax dollars at work.

Senator Nicholas Scutari, the New Jersey Senate Judiciary Committee Chairman, supported Lesniak's contention and went one step further. "Obviously it raises questions and concerns for myself and members of the committee. There's no way around it," he said. "And it smacks of political, selective prosecution," Scutari stated. The charge of "selective, political prosecution" hinted at a charge of prosecutorial misconduct.

Assemblyman John Wisniewski, also Democratic Party State Chairman, made public an analogy that everyone was thinking, "If you deny this and suggest Dwek is lying, does that raise the possibility with you that Dwek's testimony that convicted others should be questioned?" If Dwek's allegations were valid for targeting Democrats in Hudson County, did Christie's office, and his subsequent successor, Paul Fishman, apply a double standard for which prosecutions were to be pursued and which were not?

Following Oxley's nomination and the revelation of Dwek's allegations, the *Star-Ledger, Asbury Park Press,* and *The Jersey Journal* all editorialized in support of Lesniak's demand for Dwek to testify before Oxley's nomination proceeded any further. The *Jersey Journal* put it rather bluntly, even echoing the former editorial of a rival newspaper, "When Christie came to the U.S. Attorney's Office in Newark, he was considered a partisan figure. In a 2001 editorial against Christie's nomination to the post, the *Star-Ledger* used this sentence: 'His motives will inevitably be questioned if he indicts Democratic office holders or fails to indict important Republican donors who are under investigation.' It's late, but is it time to question those motives?"

Over the summer of 2012, the Oxley nomination sat simmering on the back burners of the Senate Judiciary Committee. Obviously, Oxley was not pleased. In October, Christie tried his favorite tactic: deflection. Never mind the serious nature of Dwek's allegations concerning the nomination of a candidate for a judgeship – Christie was attributing the Oxley nomination hold-up to partisan politics. "The Governor said the request is 'just another excuse by Lesniak and Democrats on the Senate Judiciary Committee not to deal with judicial nominations from the Supreme Court right on down. All they're looking for is excuses to not hold hearings on judicial nominations,'" the *Star-Ledger* reported.

It seemed as though the sitting United States Attorney at the time, Paul Fishman, would be used to help the Oxley nomination-succeed. His office's response to the Dwek allegations filed in the filed courtroom documents was: "the FBI looked into the accusations and turned up no evidence of wrongdoing." This is the same office that had previously attempted to minimize 28 obvious instances of government forgery and evidence tampering by labeling them "typographical errors." Christie and Fishman were in essence saying that Dwek was to be relied upon when he made allegations against Democrats, but not Republicans.

Christie picked up where Fishman's court filings left off. "I think that should end it," the Governor concluded. "Let me tell you as someone who has read over the course of my career a lot of raw FBI data from cooperating witnesses. Sometimes it can be reliable and sometimes it can be absolute fiction. And I think it's unfair to put that type of fiction out into the public stream." Christie seemed to think that everyone should just accept his word about Oxley's qualifications and integrity. When pressed for more candidness, Christie declined to comment further, claiming that he was still "bound by certain grand jury secrecy rules." He made it sound like a Freemason initiation.

However, Senator Lesniak was not backing down. He "insisted there was enough information to raise questions about Oxley's fitness for the bench." He went right back at Christie, "Put up or shut up, Governor. I'm not going to take his word for it and I have no reason to."

"We did a full vetting of Sheriff Oxley in the Governor's office prior to putting his nomination forward and I felt confident reading everything that I read in that vetting in moving forward with his nomination," Christie countered.

Lesniak, however, did his homework, and in June he filed a Freedom of Information Act request regarding Oxley, seeking "all records of investigations, interviews and reports" including "any and all information relating to allegations and evidence provided by Solomon Dwek about Mr. Oxley and information about any investigations of Mr. Oxley in the Solomon Dwek matter."

The government posture was that there was nothing to hide, but they were relentless and determined that no one should see the "nothing" they claimed they were not hiding. *Star-Ledger* correspondent Matt Friedman, who originally broke the Dwek-Oxley story, reported, "David M. Hardy, the FBI's section chief for record and information dissemination, denied Lesniak's request in July, citing Oxley's right to privacy. He said if the bureau had information about Oxley, it would release it only if he consented or if Lesniak demonstrated the public interest in the disclosure outweighed privacy concerns."

Lesniak then wrote to Oxley asking him to sign a form authorizing the FBI to release the information. He had a better chance of getting Oxley to donate a kidney. With no response from Oxley, Friedman reported that Lesniak then "appealed to the Justice Department in July, saying his request was 'in the public interest' and 'should be accorded greater weight than the privacy interest of a person who has accepted the nomination for judicial office.'"

The Department of Justice denied Lesniak's request and refused to overturn the FBI's denial for information – no sense releasing the nothing that was still not being hidden! "The letter, written by Janice Galli McLeod, associate director of the department's Office of Information Policy, made no mention of Lesniak's public interest argument. 'That's what's so bizarre about the decision,' he said. 'They didn't address the standards to which they're supposed to apply in all cases,'" Friedman reported.

However, the third time would prove to be the real charm for Oxley, as Christie once again pushed the nomination of the man responsible for delivering Monmouth County votes for his elections. Christie might have employed some political horse-trading to secure the confirmation, perhaps by sweetening the slate of nominees for Superior Court judgeships with a number of Democrats; effectively, peddling judgeships the way he had once peddled monitoring contracts for deferred prosecution agreements when he was United States Attorney. Oxley's lawyer friends, many of whom were also substantial contributors to Political Action Committees, lobbied the Judiciary Committee on behalf of Oxley as well; as a number of the panel members acknowledged.

"Oxley was expected to be grilled by Democratic lawmakers over his connections with federal informant Solomon Dwek. Instead, Democratic lawmakers surprised onlookers by not asking the former Monmouth County Sheriff and chairman of the Monmouth County GOP a single question about his connection to Dwek. Democratic Sens. Ray Lesniak and Paul Sarlo told Oxley they had planned to present Oxley intense questions or even oppose his nomination if not for all of the phone calls they received from people who spoke positively of Oxley. 'Quite frankly, you have a great resume,' said Sarlo, adding he planned to vote against Oxley being appointed to the Superior Court. 'Your colleagues called me right up to this morning on behalf of you,' he said," reported PolitickerNJ.

The committee made the United States Attorney's Office the heavy for their corrupted Bid Rig III investigations and prosecutions. Senator Raymond Lesniak labeled the prosecutor's actions "a miscarriage of justice," and determined that Oxley should not have to pay the piper. The irony of the situation was pointed out by correspondent Matt Friedman of the *Star-Ledger*, who reported, "Democrats used the opportunity not to grill Oxley, but to allege that the FBI and U.S. Attorney's Office – which at the time Dwek made the Oxley allegations was run by Gov. Chris Christie – went aggressively after some officials Dwek named, but not others." Nonetheless, Christie's office's misconduct was not going to be held against Oxley. "Quite frankly that has nothing to do with you, nor does it have anything to do with your qualifications to be a Superior Court judge," Senator Lesniak said, trying to make some sense of it all.

The Candidate

If you could nominate someone under a cloud for a judgeship, what would be wrong with running someone for United States Senator who was under a similar cloud? That must have been his thinking when Christie cleared the Republican field and announced his support for his dear friend and New Jersey State Senator, Joseph Kyrillos, when the latter decided to challenge United States Senator Bob Menendez in 2012.

Kyrillos and Christie first bonded in 1992 when they worked in New Jersey for the campaign of George H.W. Bush. Christie prompted Kyrillos to ask out a campaign staffer, Susan Doctorian. A few years later, they were married. When Christie was elected Morris County Freeholder in 1994, Kyrillos was asked to swear him in at the inauguration. Kyrillos also supported Christie in his rise to U.S. Attorney in Newark, while serving as chairman of the state Republican Party between 2001 and 2004 – the time of Christie's appointment. Christie campaigned for Kyrillos and helped raise close to a million dollars for his friend. Apparently, Christie did as good a job in vetting Kyrillos for a United States Senate seat as he did in vetting Oxley for the Superior Court judgeship.

Kyrillos would never truly know the value of Christie's friendship until the notorious Solomon Dwek coughed up the goods on the State Senator to the FBI. Dwek's troubling allegations concerning Kyrillos are documented in an FBI report that was never made public until my Hyde Amendment petition filing. These were allegations Dwek would allude to in testimony that the United States Attorney's Office vouched for as truthful. In the courtroom, the government was careful to ensure that Dwek would not mention names in his direct examination, because the FBI 302 reports were chock full of the names that the United States Attorney's office did not want to make public.

In an FBI 302 report dated August 22, 2006, Dwek told the FBI that he met with Kyrillos concerning campaign contributions, and then again at a later meeting, to implore the State Senator to help out in a matter concerning a Rabbi Baruch Lanner of Monmouth County. In a true testament to his character, Dwek was pressuring ing for Kyrillos to use his influence with the Monmouth County Prosecutor's Office to assist Lanner, who had been convicted of sexually abusing two teenage girls at a religious school where he was the principal. A New Jersey Appellate Court had ordered a retrial and Dwek interceded on Lanner's behalf to have the charges dropped. Just the everyday, run-of the-mill, constituent services that one seeks from their state representative.

Dwek also told the FBI that Kyrillos exerted his influence with West Long Branch New Jersey Republicans to help smooth over Dwek's building plans for the expansion of the Deal Yeshiva, the same religious school that Dwek had turned into a "crime scene."

Dwek further squealed to the feds that Kyrillos, at Dwek's suggestion, pushed for a judgeship for a Long Branch municipal prosecutor, Steven C. Ruben. Dwek alleged that, in exchange for free rent, the prosecutor was using his official influence to fix traffic tickets for Dwek and his friends. In response to a brutal cross-examination by Defense Attorney Michael Critchley, during the Suarez trial, Dwek stunned the courtroom with his revelations. "Do you recall saying that he [Ruben] used to fix tickets and other miscellaneous matters at your request in the court?" Critchley asked.

"I just said that he would fix tickets. He would reduce the fines, reduce the points, or just give them a fine instead of points." Dwek clarified.

Critchley pressed on. "So basically you corrupted that court, correct?"

Dwek clarified his answer again. "I had a corrupt agreement with Steven Ruben. That is correct."

Now it was Critchley's turn to clarify things. "And as a result of corrupting the prosecutor, he received free rent?"

"Correct," Dwek admitted. The government said nothing to contradict their witness; instead they vouched to the jury for what they considered honest testimony.

According to Dwek, Kyrillos pushed for Ruben's nomination for a judgeship, but another Monmouth County State Senator, Joseph Palaia, used his senatorial courtesy to knock down the nomination. None of this seemed to bother Christie, either as the United States Attorney deciding whether to target Kyrillos, or as the Governor who supported Kyrillos for a seat in the United States Senate. For Kyrillos it was just a case of a prosecution Passover.

In the very first rollover authorization for Dwek's initial Otherwise Illegal Activity (OIA) report, FBI and United States Attorney's Office representatives reported the following to the Criminal Undercover Operations Review Committee (CUORC): "The CW (Confidential Witness) has paid bribe/kickbacks and made substantial political donations to several State, Local, and County officials in exchange for official action and/or for future access should he need their assistance."

During the trial of Assemblyman Daniel Van Pelt, Monmouth County residents learned that "Dwek has said under oath and in his answer to questions from the prosecution this week that he has bribed a number of politicians over the years, including some who are still in office in Monmouth County," as correspondent Erik Larsen reported in the May 6, 2010 edition of the *Asbury Park Press*. Again, the tactic was for the prosecutors to never solicit, in questions put to Dwek, the actual names of the public officials who accepted bribes. After all, corrupt politicians deserve their privacy too.

Dwek's *modus operandi* was typically a campaign donation in exchange for official favors. Therefore, if one were to speculate on whom Dwek was bribing, a good bet would have been to follow the money; in this case, the campaign contributions. A review of the New Jersey Election Law Enforcement Commission (ELEC) data bank indicates that, since 1997, Dwek donated to a combination of forty-three candidates and political action committees (PACs) for a total of $95,675 ($66,275 for Republican affiliations and $29,400 for Democrat affiliations). Forty of those donations went to candidates and PACs in Monmouth or other PACS for potential use in Monmouth County (such as partisan State legislative committee PACs), for a total of $91,575.

Of Dwek's donations that were affiliated with Monmouth County candidates and PACs, thirty-two were for Republicans, totaling $65,275 and eight were for Democrats, totaling $26,300. Many of these contributions went to public officials who are still in office today and ran on Christie's ballot line in New Jersey's November 2009 general election. This may include the public officials who Dwek claimed he bribed during his testimony in the trial of Assemblyman Van Pelt – numerous Monmouth County elected officials who are still in office.

There is no indication that Christie pressed to investigate any of Dwek's claims. If he had, it might have proved suicidal in his run for Governor. Many of the officials listed on the New Jersey ELEC reports would have stood for re-election on the ballot that Christie headed in November 2009's general election. Those names were extremely familiar to voters and an invaluable asset to the top of the ticket.

All of the other Democratic powerbrokers that Christie had prosecuted, the likes of Senator John Lynch, Senator Wayne Bryant, Senator and Newark Mayor Sharpe James, and Bergen County Democratic Chairman Joseph Ferriero, were never cut the same slack as the Gilmores, Oxleys, Kyrillos, and other unnamed Monmouth County officials who were allegedly bribed, never prosecuted, and allowed to remain in office. Because they practiced a different political faith from Christie, one that did not entitle them to a prosecution Passover, the unfortunate Democratic politicians who were indicted and prosecuted became election carnage that benefitted Christie's gubernatorial prospects.

Judgment Day: A Fine Madness

Solomon Dwek's day of reckoning, his sentencing for bank fraud charges, kept getting pushed further back as the Bid Rig III trials dragged on and on. Dwek did not mind at all; he was out of jail and still earning his monthly stipend from the bankruptcy trustee. However, during the spring of 2012, as the United States Attorney's Office prepared for the prosecution of the next Bid Rig III defendant, Secaucus, New Jersey Mayor Dennis Elwell, the flimflamming confidential informant was about to flim his last flam.

While in Baltimore, Maryland, Dwek filed a false affidavit with the Hertz rental company while trying to lease a car. Somehow, as the legend is told, an acquaintance of Dwek had the vehicle and failed to return it. To complicate matters further, Dwek used his father's credit card to rent the vehicle: *apparently, the more than ten grand a month from the bankruptcy court just wasn't enough to make ends meet.* Hertz reported the car as stolen and the Maryland police issued a warrant for Dwek's arrest, which turned up shortly afterwards on the desk of one of Dwek's FBI handlers. When the FBI questioned Dwek, the confidential informant whom prosecutors had praised to juries as having turned over a new leaf and vouched for as the salt of the earth, did what he always did best – he lied! That put Dwek in the hot seat.

What could the prosecutors do? Dwek could open his mouth at any time about the corruption he had exposed in South Jersey and which Christie's office had taken a pass on or covered up. Dwek was back in the driver's seat. Christie's friends in the United States Attorney's Office, now under the direction of Paul Fishman, asked Judge José Linares to go easy on Dwek, suggesting a modified bail and house arrest. The Judge, who sat through the majority of the Bid Rig III proceedings, Dwek's arraignment, and trials, was fed up with Solomon Dwek and his defenders. "Linares, however, rejected any semblance of freedom. While acknowledging Dwek's 'substantial cooperation' with the government, he nevertheless called him an 'extremely accomplished liar' who tried to obscure what he was doing and 'showed a total disrespect' for the law," the *Star-Ledger* reported.

"He knew what he was doing was illegal and improper.... He has proven to be a consummate defrauder and an extremely cunning liar.... I do not accept house arrest. He's not above lying to the FBI, Hertz, and thumbing his nose at this court," Linares barked. The Judge ruled that Dwek had violated his cooperation agreement with the government, revoked Dwek's $10 million bail, and ordered him directly into jail. You could tell Linares was not a former United States Attorney.

A few months later, Dwek arrived back in court before Linares for his sentencing. His defense dropped a bombshell on the court: *Solomon Dwek was mentally ill*, and had been so throughout his targeting of defendants in Bid Rig III, and while testifying at trials. This threw a monkey wrench into everything. The Judge had already accepted guilty pleas and sentenced convicted defendants based upon the credibility of a confidential informant now alleged to be a legally non-credible witness. Surely, U.S. Attorney Fishman's office would object. They certainly would not let Dwek cast aspersions on the earlier trials in which he had testified. Assistant United States Attorney Mark McCarren made not a whimper, let alone an objection. In fact, he chimed right in, describing Dwek's history as "almost schizophrenic."

Dwek's attorney had supplied the court with a report containing a forensic evaluation of Dwek, documented by Dr. Jerome Rubin, Ph.D. and stating that Dwek had a "history of serious mental disorder," characterized by, among other symptoms, "illusory thinking." The evaluation further concluded that Dwek's disorder was affecting him during the same time that he was committing his crimes, was recruited by the government as a confidential informant, used as a witness at trials, and gave evidence that was dominated by his interactions and statements presented to grand juries for acquiring indictments.

The revelation created a serious problem for the government that harkened back to the trial of Mayor Anthony Suarez. During that trial, defense attorney Michael Critchley had requested Dwek's psychological report. The United States Attorney's Office pulled another of their famous fast ones. The government sought an ex-parte order regarding its obligation in disclosing the medical and psychological records of the examining doctor, Dr. Howard Silverman, for his treatment of Solomon Dwek. Judge Linares told Critchley that he reviewed Dwek's psychological records *in-camera*, in response to and anticipation of defense counsel's request for the Court to "review Mr. Dwek's psychological profile."

The Court then ordered the material turned over to the defense counselor. "This is the psychological report?" Critchley asked.

"Treatment records," Linares clarified. "It is not a report. It is actual treatment records."

In the same colloquy, the prosecutor for the government, the same Assistant United States Attorney Mark McCarren, then corrects the Court's description of the document and clarifies that the document consisted of "notes from Dr. (Howard) Silverman." In response to a question from defense counsel, McCarren further indicates, "June 14, 2006 was the first treatment." This was after Dwek's arrest, when he was under the control of the government. They *absolutely knew* about Dwek's condition if Dr. Rubin's subsequent diagnosis was correct. More troubling, while knowing that they had a defendant who was mentally incompetent, the government, nonetheless, recruited Dwek as a confidential informant and gave him the plea deal of the century.

Conspicuous by its absence was the diagnosis report and any forensic evaluation of Mr. Dwek conducted by Dr. Silverman, which would have served as the basis for the treatments being administered to Dwek. Despite defense counsel and the Court's request for "Dwek's psychological records", they were merely given "notes" related to Dr. Silverman's treatment of Dwek. The government may have potentially shielded itself from disclosure and discovery obligations by purposefully hiding behind the ex-parte order they had sought.

Clearly, the "notes" disclosed to the Suarez defense and others did not indicate that Dwek exhibited "illusory thinking" nor referenced his "serious mental disorder" as the subsequent forensic evaluation by Dr. Jerome Rubin did, or there would have been a defense challenge to Dwek's competency. Absent such description, diagnosis or forensic evaluation, apparently purposefully withheld from defense counsel and the court, the District Court determined the evidence to be "potentially impeachment stuff, not Brady (material)," and proceeded to move the case of Suarez and other Bid Rig III defendants to trial, without knowing the true competence of Dwek's mental state. The government, potentially shielded by the ex-parte order, may have purposefully situated itself in the position of not disclosing the diagnosis and forensic evaluation of Dwek, so that the very ex-parte order they sought would serve as their alibi, in case they were ever caught.

The diagnosis of Dwek's "serious mental disorder" and "illusory thinking" could have been used to impeach Dwek's testimony and challenge indictments. Moreover, the withholding of such evidence would further qualify as a violation of Brady disclosure laws. Subsequent to the Suarez trial – without explanation – Dwek was suddenly scrapped as a government witness for all future Bid Rig III cases, never to return to the witness stand.

He was mysteriously scratched from the trial of Assemblyman L. Harvey Smith, scheduled right after Mayor Suarez's trial. Something was up ... perhaps Critchley had come too close to exposing the psyche scam. It is ironic that the prosecutor in the Suarez trial did a turn of 180 degrees when he supported Dwek's sentencing report, as prepared by Dwek's attorneys. By so doing, the prosecutor was contradicting whatever had been deduced about Dwek's mental state from the "notes" that were previously provided to the same District Court during the Suarez trial.

All of the Bid Rig III defendants indicted by grand juries had presentments of evidence that were dominated by interactions and statements made by Dwek. Some defendants (Tabbachino, Beldini, and Van Pelt) would largely be convicted because of the testimony provided by the "illusory" thinker at trial, which was then supported by the opening and closing arguments of prosecutors. Those trials, primarily Jersey City Deputy Mayor Leona Beldini's, were peppered with objections by defense counsels concerning Dwek's testimony – principally dealing with his continuous over-exaggeration of facts and evidence in his direct examination – the "almost schizophrenic" behavior perhaps alluded to by Attorney McCarren.

This may be the reason the Department of Justice refused to honor State Senator Raymond Lesniak's Freedom of Information Act request relative to Dwek's interactions with Monmouth County Sheriff Joseph Oxley, when Christie nominated the latter to the New Jersey Superior Court. It might have shown that the government failed to charge Oxley because Dwek's mental condition was an impediment to any prosecution. Yet, the same prosecutors then decided to use Dwek to prosecute Democratic candidates in Hudson County, boosting Christie's gubernatorial campaign and burying the psych report that undermined their cases. The files requested by Senator Lesniak will never see the light of day.

In pleading for leniency for Dwek, McCarren gave the pride and joy of the United States Attorney's Office Babe-Ruthian stature, declaring Dwek, "the most significant cooperator," his office had turned in ten years. Thank God for those ten years. In pleading for leniency, Dwek referred to himself as a "piece of dirt," and choked up repeatedly as he expressed his remorse and asked forgiveness. Referring to his father, whom had since disowned and shunned him, Dwek said, "It is my hope that one day I can make it up with him and the rest of the family." One could almost still hear the echo of Uncle Joey telling Dwek to "go fuck yourself," when he realized that his nephew had beat him for some $60 million. Solomon Dwek had a lot of making up to do.

Judge Linares would have the last word in the courtroom. The prosecutors were seeking a substantial downward departure of the sentencing guidelines for Dwek, but the Judge was not buying in. Linares hammered Dwek with a six-year sentence and ordered him to pay approximately $23 million dollars back to the government in restitution – about one visit's worth at the drive-in teller's window of the Eatontown, New Jersey PNC Bank.

Afterwards, United States Attorney Paul Fishman expressed sympathy on behalf of the felon who had robbed and destroyed religious schools in order to fund casino boats and prostitution, who turned profits by purchasing life insurance policies on the terminally ill, who had sought pardons for child molesters and judgeships for prosecutors who fixed his parking tickets, and bribed key politicians essential to Chris Christie's gubernatorial campaign. Commenting on the sentence handed down by Linares, said Fishman, "Obviously, we're a little disappointed."

Obviously, however, not as disappointed as the defendants sitting in jail cells who were convicted by a mentally incompetent witness for whom United States Attorney Paul Fishman's office had apparently covered up.

Chapter Six

Two Trails Converge in Bid Rig III

As the 2008 presidential election campaign evolved, and with the 2009 New Jersey gubernatorial election on the horizon, time was pressing United States Attorney Chris Christie to make his move. He had been exploring his burning ambition for the governorship ever since the chance blew by in 2005, when United States Senator Jon Corzine squashed any notion Christie had of running.

The Too Long Goodbye

It is not known just how much planning Christie did for his 2009 candidacy while serving as United States Attorney (the Hatch Act clearly prohibits such activity). However, during testimony given to Congress on July 7, 2009, concerning the national scandal of the Bush Administration's firings of United States Attorneys throughout the country, former Bush Presidential Advisor Karl Rove shed some light on how early Christie was contemplating his 2009 run for Governor: apparently as early as 2007. "I talked to him twice in the last couple of years, perhaps one time while I was at the White House and once or twice since I left the White House, but not regarding his duties as U.S. Attorney, but regarding his interest in running for Governor, and he asked me questions about who – who were good people that knew about running for Governor that he could talk to," Rove said in his testimony.

The context of Rove's statement was a bombshell in itself, coming at the beginning of the 2009 campaign. Rove's testimony indicated that Christie had breached DOJ guidelines and regulations while serving as United States Attorney by discussing plans to seek partisan political office in the state where his office was overseeing investigations and prosecutions of his political opposition. "It's now clear that Christie was laying the groundwork for his gubernatorial campaign while he was serving in the U.S. Attorney's office,"

Corzine's running mate (for Lieutenant Governor) State Senator Loretta Weinberg (D-Bergen), complained to the *Star-Ledger*. "His phone calls with Karl Rove and meetings with high profile Republicans to plot his run for governor appear to directly violate the Hatch Act." Corzine's campaign also alleged that during another more recent meeting, in 2008, Christie spoke with State Senator Jennifer Beck about possibly becoming his Lieutenant Governor candidate, as well as Atlantic County Executive Dennis Levinson, who went onto serve as Christie's campaign co-chair.

In choosing Rove as a mentor, Christie was seeking advice from one of the most notorious figures at the center of the scandal involving the firings of selected Unites States Attorneys. As the *New York Times* inferred at the time, "It is now clear that United States attorneys were pressured to act in the interests of the Republican Party, and lost their job if they failed to do so. The firing offenses of the nine prosecutors who were purged last year were that they would not indict Democrats, they investigated important Republicans, or they would not try to suppress the votes of Democratic-leaning groups with baseless election fraud cases."

The *New York Times* further surmised, "It is hard not to see the fingerprints of Karl Rove. A disproportionate number of the prosecutors pushed out, or considered for dismissal, were in swing states. The main reason for the purge – apart from hobbling a California investigation that has already put one Republican congressman in jail – appears to have been an attempt to tip states like Missouri and Washington to Republican candidates for House, Senate, governor and president."

These coincidences give one pause. While Rove was mentoring Christie, was he contemplating the tipping of the New Jersey gubernatorial election by a similar methodology? This is not to suggest that Rove laid out the plan for Bid Rig III and targeted the eventual defendants, but merely to point out a disturbing fact that has been documented in federal and congressional investigation reports. Rove was alleged to have a propensity for encouraging the use of federal prosecutions to thwart Democratic Party efforts and advance his own political agendas.

The findings of one such Congressional Committee held that, "The Justice Department had been derelict in failing to address the issue of political prosecutions and reassuring the American people, that federal law enforcement is impartial and fair." The committee cited "evidence that indicated the prosecution of political figures was directed or promoted by Washington officials, inclusive of Advisor to the President Karl Rove." At the same time, in an historic gathering of forty-four former state Attorney's General of both parties, former federal prosecutors and former U.S. Attorney General Richard Thornburgh all expressed concern to Congress about what they termed were "apparent political prosecutions" being implemented by the Department of Justice.

Christie finally took the formal leap and announced his candidacy in December 2008. Pursuant to federal law, namely the Vacancy Reform Act, he would be able to select a temporary successor until a permanent appointment could be made. Christie ran an extremely tight ship at the Unites States Attorney's Office, and he would set in place a close-knit band of prosecutors that had always backed him up.

During the course of several cases, investigations, and other matters; McGreevey, Menendez, Dwek, deferred prosecution agreements, and the launch of Bid Rig III, a core advisory hierarchy had evolved in the United States Attorney's Office, consisting of such Christie confidents as Ralph Marra, Michele Brown, Charles McKenna, and James Nobile. They were colleagues whom, according to Christie, were his "front office," with whom he remained in contact. "We talk all the time," Christie claimed, even after leaving office in December of 2008. These were colleagues whom Christie now had in place in the United States Attorney's Office, facilitated through his choice of successor, Ralph Marra. These same Christie handpicked architects would soon guide the course of the Bid Rig III sting. As the case proceeded from targeting and investigation through the prosecution phase, a secondary, but just as essential team of Assistant United States Attorneys evolved: Brian Howe, Mark McCarren, Christopher Gramiccioni, Thomas Calcagni and others, who were assigned the roles for prosecuting the cases.

Two Trails

Now a full-fledged candidate for the New Jersey Governor's seat, Christie quickly hit the campaign trail and begin to put into place an ever-evolving campaign team. Of course, two essential operatives, his brother Todd, and close confidant Bill Palatucci, had already been maneuvering on Christie's behalf before he ever left the U.S. Attorney's Office. Another savvy strategist, Christie enrolled, was a bright up-and-coming political advisor, Mike Du-Haime, who was allegedly suggested by Karl Rove during his discussion with Christie's about a gubernatorial run. The strategy was easily understood: win the Republican primary while expending minimal resources, then plot an effective strategy for taking down the Democratic incumbent Governor of a Blue State, Jon Corzine, who had bottomless pockets of cash to fund his own campaign. It was a tough task that lay ahead, but, given Corzine's aloofness and his not so hot favorability rating, it was doable.

The sure way to secure the GOP nomination would be to line up as many Republican Party county chairpersons as possible behind Christie's candidacy. Perhaps because of Christie's decision to look the other way when Solomon Dwek implicated George Gilmore and Joe Oxley in criminal activity, Oxley and Gilmore threw their support behind Christie early on. They represented two of the largest Republican Party organizations in the State. The clout of these endorsements automatically made Christie the favorite to win the primary, but running against former Bogota Mayor Steve Lonegan and Assemblyman Rick Merkt would deplete financial resources that could be better used to battle Governor Corzine in the general election.

Quid Pro Quo

Leading up to the June primary election for the Republican Party gubernatorial nomination, candidate Chris Christie addressed remarks to a gathering at a morning campaign stop in West Windsor, New Jersey on February 28, 2009. "You know, we're going to ferret out waste and fraud and abuse in government. I think you know I'll do that better than anybody. I've got a group of U.S. Attorneys sitting down in Newark still doing their jobs. But let me tell you, they are watching the newspapers. And after we win this election, I'm going to take a whole group of them to Trenton and put them in every one of the departments because they saw a lot of waste and abuse being investigated while we were in the U.S. Attorney's office that didn't rise to the level of a crime. So I told them, the good news is, when we get to Trenton we don't have to worry about beyond a reasonable doubt anymore," stated the former United States Attorney in his videotaped remarks.

Christie eventually publically acknowledged that he had remained in contact with his former colleagues in the United States Attorney's Office throughout the course of the gubernatorial primary and general elections – this was also the same time frame for the Bid Rig III investigation and prosecutions. According to New Jersey Election Law Enforcement Commission records, within days of announcing his intentions to appoint Assistant United States Attorneys to Trenton jobs, the first of several donations by prosecutors, their family members and their staff began pouring into Christie's campaign coffers.

Marvin S. Goldklang, the father of Deborah Gramiccioni, the former Chief of the Commercial Crimes Unit of the United States Attorney's Office in 2004, and then State of New Jersey Criminal Justice Director, gave the first contribution on March 2, 2009. Goldklang's son-in-law and Deborah's husband was Christopher Gramiccioni – the Assistant United States Attorney prosecuting my case. Deborah Gramiccioni was given a raise and promoted to the New Jersey Attorney General's Office as Director of the Authorities Unit. She became a favorite confidant of Christie, and when Bill Baroni resigned at the Port Authority during the Bridgegate scandal, Deborah Gramiccioni was appointed by Christie to replace him as the Deputy Executive Director of the agency.

Chris Gramiccioni had to wait a while longer. He was hired as First Assistant Monmouth County Prosecutor by Christie's appointee, Monmouth County Prosecutor, Peter E. Warshaw, Jr. The job was negotiated while Gramiccioni was still working the ongoing Bid Rig III investigation and prosecution. First Assistant Monmouth County Prosecutor was a more prestigious job than Assistant United States Attorney and, as such, it put Gramiccioni first in line for Monmouth County Prosecutor if Christie got the urge to nominate Warshaw to a State judgeship, which did happen in due time. Gramiccioni was made the Acting Prosecutor succeeding Warshaw.

Chris and Deborah Gramiccioni also personally contributed to Christie's campaign on July 13th and September 29th of 2009 – two weeks before the July 23rd arrests and a week and a half after my indictment, for which Chris Gramiccioni made the presentment before the grand jury. Christopher Gramiccioni's brother Gregory, who lived in Cheektowaga, New York, also donated to Christie, on July 13, 2009. Christopher Gramiccioni's parents, John and Kathleen, both donated to Christie from individual bank accounts on the same day – September 6, 2009. The United States Attorneys' Manual places restrictions on Department of Justice employees, prohibiting solicitation of political contributions. If Christopher Gramiccioni did not break the law by soliciting or collecting the donations for Christie from his family and in-laws, his family relations have exceptional telepathic skills, as was demonstrated by their contributions to Christie occurring on the same days.

On March 3, 2009, a contribution from former Assistant United States Attorney Robert Hanna was recorded. Hanna would make a subsequent donation on September 1 of that year. Hanna was appointed by Governor Christie as Director of Law in the New Jersey United States Attorney's Office. In December of 2011, Christie manipulated Hanna's appointment as President of the state Board of Public Utilities.

In December 2012, Christie nominated Hanna to a seat on the prestigious Supreme Court of New Jersey. Hanna certainly got his money's worth from the only traceable campaign contributions that he had ever made to anyone's campaign. Questioned about Hanna's donations and his knack for landing prominent appointed positions, Christie quipped, "There comes a point in time where if you make two $300 contributions to your old boss when he's running for governor, some people might not say that's partisan. Some people might just say that's smart." *Smart*? Hanna should go to the head of the class.

On April 26, 2009, Charles McKenna, the former Executive Assistant to the United States Attorney (handpicked by Christie) and then Assistant United States Attorney in-charge-of the Criminal Division, had his contribution to Christie's campaign documented. When Christie left office, McKenna was switched over to the United States Attorney's Office Criminal Division. The Criminal Division oversaw the Special Investigations Unit, which was responsible for the Bid Rig III investigations and prosecutions. During the ongoing proceedings, McKenna negotiated a job in Governor Christie's administration as the New Jersey Homeland Security Director. Eventually, McKenna was appointed Chief Counsel to the

Governor, and was serving in that position during the time of the Bridgegate scandal.

Lee Vartan from the United States Attorney's Office Criminal Division donated to Christie's campaign on May 28, 2009. Richard E. Constable III, who had worked in the Criminal Divisions' Special Investigation Unit and made a donation on June 17, 2009. He wound up being appointed by Christie as New Jersey Labor Commissioner, and later DCA Commissioner, where he was accused by Hoboken Mayor Dawn Zimmer of pressuring her to approve a development project in exchange for Superstorm Sandy relief funds.

John Romano from the United States Attorney's Office Appeals Division donated to Christie on June 23, 2009. Peter Gaeta of the Criminal Division did likewise the following day. They didn't get jobs, but United States Attorney's Office public relations guru Michael Drewniak and Chief Administrator Rosemary Iannacone – both donated to Christie on June 26, 2009, and both wound up being hired by Christie. Drewniak, who choreographed the media coverage for Bid Rig III, was hired as Governor Christie's Press Spokesperson. Christie appointed Iannacone to the position of the New Jersey Governor's Office Director of Operations.

On July 8, 2009, Lisa Rose from the United States Attorney's Office Criminal Division's Government Fraud Unit donated to Christie. On August 3, 2009 and September 12, 2009, James B. Clark III did likewise. Michael Kramer brought up the rear with a donation on October 25, 2009.

Three other prominent figures in the United State Attorney's Office, who had oversight of the Bid Rig III investigation and prosecution, also negotiated jobs in Governor Christie's administration: Acting United States Attorney Ralph Marra, who signed every Bid Rig III initial indictment, First Assistant United States Attorney Michele Brown, and Assistant United States Attorney Thomas Calcagni.

Marra was once the subject of a Department of Justice ethics probe for comments he made at a Bid Rig III press conference in alleged support of Christie, and the subject of calls by two Congressmen to be investigated for his alleged inappropriate conduct during the 2009 New Jersey Gubernatorial election. Under Christie, he was appointed in February 2010 to the position of Senior Vice President for Legal and Governmental Affairs at the New Jersey Sports and Exposition Authorities. The position was a boost in pay of $35,000 from his federal salary to a new yearly compensation of $190,000.

Michele Brown, whose conduct in the United States Attorney's Office during the course of the election would eventually cause her to resign, eventually landed a job on Christie's transition team and later on Christie's senior staff as the Governor's Appointment Counsel. Brown was in charge of job placements as well as recruiting and guiding nominees for cabinet-level and judicial posts – including some of the very same prosecutors she was in charge of when they oversaw Bid Rig III.

Brown was eventually appointed CEO of New Jersey's Economic Development Authority with a substantial raise in salary. Brown was a pit-bull for Christie, perhaps his most loyal employee while he served as United States Attorney. She even went so far as to attend what appears to have been senior campaign meetings in Christie's home as early as January of 2009, while still serving in her capacity at the United States Attorney's Office.

Thomas Calcagni negotiated for the position of New Jersey Acting Director of Consumer Affairs while the Bid Rig III cases proceeded. He prosecuted the first case to come to trial – against Leona Beldini. His new state position also increased his yearly income compared to his federal salary. He was soon promoted to the position of First Assistant Attorney General. Calcagni had assisted in the grand jury presentment for my first superseding indictment and was one of the prosecutors that became the focus of my misconduct motions.

Last, but not least, on April 19, 2012, the *Star-Ledger* reported that Governor Christie tapped Eric Kanefsky as the new Chief of the State's Consumer Affairs Division, replacing Thomas Calcagni. Kanefsky had co-prosecuted the trial of Secaucus Mayor Dennis Elwell. He also handled the misconduct arguments, including the conflicts and recusal issues, that were raised in my case. Assuming that no one just walks into a prominent state position like that at the drop of a hat, if Kanefsky had discussions with anyone from the Governor's Administration regarding his new-found job, while he was handling the misconduct motions pertaining to members of the Governor's Administration, he had a serious conflict of interest. And had an obligation to recuse himself.

It should be noted for the record that Kanefsky replaced former United State's Attorney Thomas Calcagni as the Consumer Affairs Chief, who moved to the State Attorney General's Office.

The Merkt Matter

In attempting to preserve resources during the course of the primary election, the Christie camp perhaps got a bit over-rambunctious. On May 7, 2009, the *Star-Ledger* reported that, speaking at a New Jersey Statehouse news conference, Republican Gubernatorial Primary Candidate, Assemblyman Rick Merkt, said a close associate of Christie's campaign, John Inglesino, a lawyer with Stern & Kilcullen, told him in 2008 that Merkt "could have a role in Christie's campaign or administration if he decided not to run."

On May 8, 2009, in a letter to acting U.S. Attorney Ralph Marra and State Attorney General Anne Milgram, State Assembly members Reed Gusciora and Valerie Vaineiri-Huttle said such an offer would be "completely unacceptable." They cited a 2007 case where former Carney's Point Mayor John Lake attempted to convince an opponent not to run for a position on the township committee in exchange for a municipal job. Lake was convicted of bribery and sentenced to three years in prison for his conduct.

Inglesino's law firm benefitted from a multi-million dollar no-bid contract conferred by the United States Attorney's Office for a monitoring agreement involving the University of Medicine and Dentistry of New Jersey. According to NJ ELEC (New Jersey Election Law Enforcement Commission) reports, Christie's campaign was the benefactor of tens of thousands of dollars in campaign contributions from principals and associates of Inglesino's law firm.

At the same time that the United States Attorney's Office received the allegations of the Christie campaign representative's promise of future political influence in exchange for a patronage benefit, they were also constructing a prosecution against me alleging that I was intending to use my future political influence to bestow a *patronage benefit*.

There is no indication that the U.S. Attorney's Office ever investigated the allegations by the New Jersey lawmakers concerning Inglesino, or transferred the matter elsewhere because of the apparent conflicts. Apparently, Christie had placed the right people in charge before departing office, and the promise of jobs in Christie's

West Windsor speech was perhaps already paying selective dividends.

War Plans

Christie won the primary election in June 2009 comfortably, and the campaign's full-time focus turned to Governor Corzine. The New Jersey electorate was volatile in 2009. Property taxes in the State continued to rise uncontrollably as they had done for years, and the masses were angry with publically elected officials at all levels of New Jersey government: state, county and local. Living decently in New Jersey was fast becoming unaffordable for most New Jerseyans. Any evidence of the waste of taxpayers' dollars or public corruption drew the extreme ire of the already overtaxed populace.

Jon Corzine, just four years prior, had been elected on a platform of reform and a commitment to do something about unbearable property taxes. He did not deliver. The issue-oriented electorate would focus their judgment on Corzine's term in office and cast their ballots accordingly. As challenger, Christie was the new reformer. His record as a United States Attorney who prosecuted allegedly corrupt public office holders (most of whom happened to be Democrats) served to give him an advantage with an electorate who rightly vilified such politicians.

Although Democrats out-register Republicans in New Jersey, as the results of previous statewide elections indicate, nothing is a given. With New Jersey's seemingly vast number of registered voters who remain independent, not all statewide elections can be won merely on the strength of partisan party affiliation. While the competition for independent voters is what drives the campaigns of the candidates, there are certain basic things that Republican and Democratic candidates for statewide office must do to ensure their base vote. There is a select core of counties that each respective party must roll up pluralities in to ensure victory.

Democratic statewide office seekers need to dominate the vote in counties such as Hudson, Camden, Essex and Union. Republican statewide candidates need to dominate counties such as Morris, Ocean and Monmouth. In addition, with rare exceptions, candidates for statewide office of either party cannot win an election without carrying Bergen County.

As the campaign evolved, Corzine tapped into the popularity of newly-elected President Barack Obama, who stumped for him on occasion during the course of the election. Vice President Joe Biden also campaigned for the incumbent Governor at Corzine's behest. The Nation's top two Democrats accentuated a Corzine campaign theme: an aggressive attack linking Christie to unpopular former President George W. Bush and his policies.

Christie campaigned on the issues of ethics, reducing corruption, and ending government fiscal waste. However, Christie's campaign could not match the high-profile endorsements that Corzine as an incumbent Democrat with a sitting Democratic President could muster. When President Obama came to the PNC Bank Arts Center in Holmdel, New Jersey for a Corzine campaign rally, there was angst and concern among Christie supporters that the popular President could help tilt the electorate back towards Corzine. Christie needed a game changer to stifle any possible momentum created by the President's visit.

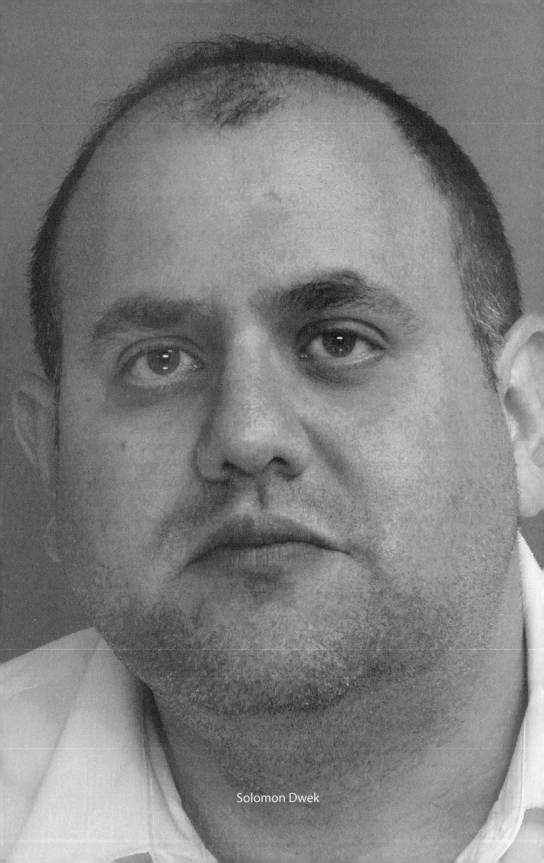
Solomon Dwek

Chapter Seven

Anatomy of a
DOJ Sting

T he game changer for Chris Christie's 2009 campaign was about to develop in the form of the Bid Rig III investigation that now rested in the hands of prosecutors with a stake in his election. They were about to okay Christie's confidential informant Solomon Dwek to target candidates for office in the springtime's nonpartisan Hudson County municipal elections. The Democratic field could typically be counted on to unite and work for the Democratic gubernatorial candidate in the fall general election, once their intra-party squabble was over.

"Legal Alchemy"
D ue to the obvious implications that Bid Rig III could have for the gubernatorial election, some of the prosecutors in the United States Attorney's Office had a legal obligation to recuse themselves from the Bid Rig III investigation. With visions of sugarplums dancing in their heads, the prosecutors ignored the law. The United States Code of Federal Regulations requires that "the Attorney General shall promulgate rules and regulations which require the disqualification of any officer or employee of the Department of Justice, including a United States attorney or a member of such attorney's staff, from participation in a particular investigation or prosecution if such participation may result in a personal, financial, or political conflict of interest, or the appearance thereof."

The threshold for recusal cited in the United States Attorneys' Manual (USAM) is "where a conflict of interest exists or there is the appearance of a conflict of interest or loss of impartiality." In determining whether to commence or recommend prosecution or take any action against a person, the standard imposed by the USAM is that "the attorney for the government should not be influenced by political association ... or the possible affect of the decision on the attorney's own professional or personal circumstances."

The United States Code of Federal Regulations states that an employee of the federal government "may not use his official authority or influence for the purpose of interfering with or affecting the result of an election." The Code further states that "an attorney for the Government shall be subject to State laws and rules, and local Federal court rules, governing attorneys in each State where such attorney engages in that attorney's duties, to the same extent and in the same manner as other attorneys in that State." The New Jersey Court Rules of Professional Conduct prohibits attorneys from engaging "in conduct that is prejudicial to the administration of justice."

Evidenced by the voluminous and clear language of laws guarding against conflicts of interest and mandating recusal it was clear that such matters were to be taken seriously. The prosecutors in charge of Bid Rig III obviously felt otherwise.

The Public Officials

When Chris Christie curtailed Solomon Dwek's activities in South Jersey after Republican Party financer Lawrence Bathgate turned up in Dwek's crosshairs, Dwek began rolling his confidential informant's candid camera elsewhere. Using the cover of the fictitious prominent developer named David Esenbach, Dwek had wormed his way into Hudson County in March of 2007. Dwek settled in on connections he had established in his real estate ventures over the years, and initially began ensnaring business executives in his money laundering scam. Two of those prominent businessmen were Moshe Altman and Shimon Haber, who opened the doors for Dwek to launder money. Josh Margolin and Ted Sherman wrote in *The Jersey Sting* that Chris Christie was becoming frustrated. He had thought Dwek was going to snare him some of Hudson County's overwhelmingly Democratic officeholders.

Eventually, in July of 2007, because Altman knew of Dwek's intentions to develop in Jersey City, he hooked him up with defendant John Guarini, whom Altman incorrectly thought was a Jersey City Building Inspector. It was then, through Guarini, that the dominoes for the eventual targeting of Hudson County political figures began to fall. In March of 2008, John Guarini introduced Dwek to defendant Maher Khalil, then a Jersey City Zoning Board member and a Deputy

Director of Jersey City's Health and Human Resources Department. In December of 2008, Khalil introduced Dwek to defendant Ed Cheatam, then Vice President of the Jersey City Board of Education and a Commissioner on the Jersey City Housing Authority; and later, in January of 2009, to defendant Dennis Jaslow, a Hudson County Board of Elections Investigator and political soldier of fortune. Cheatam, two months later, introduced Dwek to defendant Jack Shaw, a New Jersey business and political consultant based in Hudson County.

As the fictitious David Esenbach, Dwek's con was that he was about to finalize a deal on an enormous parcel of abandoned property on Grand Street in Jersey City. The site had once hosted chromium-contaminated structures that had long since been compromised and razed. As a former City Health Chief who dealt with the city's chromium contamination crisis, I knew the property well. Dwek was trying to dupe his public official targets into assisting him in acquiring or expediting permits in exchange for money. Primarily through Cheatam, Shaw, Khalil, and to a lesser extent Jaslow, Dwek was introduced to the officials who were alleged to be able to take care of his needs.

Before he ever targeted a candidate for office, Dwek appeared to know exactly how and from whom the official assistance he was buying would be provided. In some of Dwek's numerous taped meetings, Cheatam and Shaw outlined precisely how they would assist him. In meetings at the Casa Dante restaurant on February 16 and 17 of 2009, they identified the public officials who would be expediting Dwek's permits. The exclusive evidence indicates that Cheatam and Shaw were alleging that assistance for Dwek's Garfield Avenue development would be provided by building inspectors, contacts on the Zoning Board, the Jersey City Business Administrator Office, and contacts on the Planning Board. The government ignored the evidence.

In his weekly commentary for the *Hudson County Reporter*, journalist and columnist Al Sullivan offered this analysis: "Some of the defense attorneys in the case claim federal records show that there were numerous other officials who received money but were not charged, suggesting that these people either cooperated with the current crop of arrests or those that might be pending. The question is: who did the federal informants working with Dwek give up and who did they choose to protect from the feds?"

The public officials targeted by Dwek at this point were not of the caliber that would merit earth-shaking news if they were arrested. They had no ties to Jon Corzine, and if they were to support or endorse him, the impact of such actions would be negligible. However, the candidates running for the mayor and council seats that were up for election throughout Hudson County were prominent names with followings, most of whom would be rallying support for Corzine in the November election. *Someone took notice.*

Calling All Candidates

Investigative agencies must comply with guidelines that require an assessment and predication be conducted on those being targeted. It is, one might argue, what separates our American system of justice from that of third-world countries. Subsequent to 9/11, the Department of Justice decided to loosen predication guidelines but still held that the basis of the targeting "cannot be arbitrary or groundless speculation, nor can an assessment be based solely on the exercise of First Amendment protected activities or on the race, ethnicity, national origin or religion of the subject."

Up until the middle of February of 2009, only six of the Hudson County defendants had met with Dwek. The other sixteen, mostly candidates for office, had yet to be approached. The clock was ticking for the U.S. Attorney's Office. To make matters worse, according to Josh Margolin and Ted Sherman in *The Jersey Sting*, United States District Court Judge Kathryn Ferguson was bearing down on the prosecutors. Presiding over the Dwek bankruptcy case, the Judge was anxious to have Dwek deposed by his creditors – fearful that Dwek's assets would dwindle away. Solomon Dwek was being sued by his creditors in the bankruptcy proceeding that coexisted with his occupation as a confidential human source.

According to *The Jersey Sting,* on several occasions, the United States Attorney's Office – James Nobile, Brian Howe, and Ralph Marra – pleaded with Judge Ferguson to delay the deposition because of Dwek's role in Bid Rig III. Ferguson was growing impatient, but after personally being visited by the U.S. Attorney's Office on at least four occasions, from November 2008 through April 2009, she continuously put off the Dwek deposition.

The extensions were contemplated and requested by the United States Attorney's Office when there were only the six targeted Hudson County defendants. So why was there a need to ask for the extensions when the prosecutors had not even charged the public officials

(Building Department, Planning Board, Zoning Board, Redevelopment Agency and Business Administrator's Office) whom Cheatam and Shaw had already identified as the individuals who were going to expedite Dwek's fictitious development? The only thing missing from the sting was the prominence of candidates who were running for public office. As it stood, Bid Rig III was far short of the defendants necessary to constitute "New Jersey's largest public corruption bust" as U.S. Attorney's Office public relations guru, Michael Drewniak, would eventually spin it. But Dwek and the government had a plan.

Through primarily Khalil, Cheatam, and Shaw, and to a much lesser degree Dennis Jaslow, Dwek and the government initiated a bounty scheme. Dwek would pay a hefty monetary bounty to these defendants for introductions to anyone they thought could help him. Dwek then promised to match back to the intermediaries whatever money he paid to the targets they had introduced to him. As Dwek stated to Cheatam and Shaw during a taped February 17, 2009 meeting in Jersey City's Casa Dante Restaurant, "… Yeah, you know, I give you the money and you pay it, and whatever I pay him, I'll take care … I'll give you an equal amount." Then, "… So, Jack, setup this Doria meeting and whatever I do for him, I'll do for you. Just handle it." Just the day before, Dwek reiterated to Cheatam as he handed him a FedEx envelope stuffed with $10,000 cash. "… you know the guys, the building inspectors, this and that. Whatever I give them, I give you."

The *pay for prey* concept kicked off the parade of candidates running for office that Cheatam, Shaw, Khalil, and Jaslow began lining up and marching into meetings with Dwek. In order to lure in their unsuspecting prey, they billed Dwek as a legitimate developer who wanted to make a campaign donation. Dwek was a virtual ATM machine that would spit out cash for Cheatam, Shaw, Jaslow, and Khalil as they each took turns swiping their victims in and out of the government's teller. Had the investigation gone on any longer, there was a good chance that all of Hudson County would have been smiling for Dwek's candid camera.

The scheme also set off a mad competition between Dwek's handpicked accomplices, as each tried to outdo the other for bounty money. It was not long before Dwek's taped conversations began depicting Cheatam, Shaw, Khalil, and Jaslow backbiting, double dealing, and badmouthing each other while attempting to sow seeds of distrust in Dwek for their competition, hoping that they would be the one the government informant would rely on for setting up meetings. An FBI affidavit reported, "Cheatam and Shaw then lie to each other as to the stories they told Dwek in an effort to resolve Shaw's inconsistent statements." Another FBI report states, "Shaw stated that he made up the story about paying colleges on behalf of Doria. Ed Cheatam does not know Shaw did not pay Saint Peter's College on behalf of Doria;" and, "Cheatam thinks Shaw skimmed $5,000 of the $25,000 cash payment...." Once, when Dwek apparently shorted Jaslow of $2,500 in bounty money, the defendant's anger was caught on tape, "What happened? I thought you were hooking me up, man? You're cuttin' me down. You told me you were gonna give me the same as you were gonna give the guy."

Overall, each of the defendants' indictments had alleged that Dwek and/or Cheatam, Shaw, Khalil, or Jaslow had conspired to commit a number of offenses, with whatever particular defendant was named in the indictment, in order to reap the benefits of the conspiracy. What the Government did not specifically lay out in the authorization forms sent to Washington DC, nor detail in the indictments, nor say in the context of any other related prosecution is that, unbeknownst to any of the defendants, Dwek, Cheatam, Shaw and Jaslow had formed their own illicit agreement.

Essentially, the government, through Dwek, was paying Cheatam, Shaw, Khalil, and Jaslow with government money to set up the conspiracy and provide it with additional co-conspirators. Dwek's bounty had seemingly corrupted the assessment process and made suspect any statements made about any defendant by Cheatam, Shaw, Khalil, and Jaslow. They each had a cash motive to be less than truthful or simply lie. It is highly doubtful that this was the type of strategy that the Department of Justice anticipated when deciding to relax the FBI's assessment standards.

With an abundance of candidates campaigning for public office, the government was about to ratchet up the pace of the Bid Rig III sting. Dwek began meeting targets at breakneck speed. For a better understanding of how fast and furious the sting began to run, it is important to note that in the more than year-and-a-half since the sting targeted Hudson County, according to filed criminal complaints, Dwek had only conducted approximately thirty-two taped meetings with the eventual Hudson County political targets. That figure excludes meetings with defendants not charged, and the defendants in the money laundering cases and political corruption cases outside of Hudson County.

According to criminal complaints filed from February 1, 2009 until the conclusion of the sting on July, 23, Dwek conducted 63 taped meetings with the Hudson County political targets over a course of only 34 days. On March 24, 2009, Dwek conducted six taped meetings; and, on April 23, 2009, he conducted five taped meetings. When combined with the money laundering cases and non-related Hudson County political corruption cases, Dwek set a blistering pace of 107 taped meetings over the course of 51 days.

The target meetings also required consultation and instruction from Dwek's FBI handlers. When cross-examined by Defense Attorney Brian Neary in the trial of defendant Leona Beldini, Dwek stated in sworn testimony that the consultation and instruction sessions were held in sync, either before or after, with each target meeting and that there were "hundreds" of such sessions. Dwek stated that the briefing sessions ran anywhere from "between ten minutes and an hour." During an evidentiary hearing concerning the government's destruction of evidence in the trial of Ridgefield Mayor Anthony Suarez, FBI Special Agent William Waldie elaborated on the instruction sessions. "So, we prepped before a meeting, he went in for a meeting, and then we would talk after the meeting."

Again, all of the figures for the number of meetings exclude the mounting number of taped meetings with public officials never charged. Neither do these figures account for the thousands of phone conversations recorded between Dwek and the defendants as well as others not charged. Not to mention that between these rapid paced encounters with the governments' targets, Dwek was working another job for the U.S. Attorney's Office to assist the bankruptcy trustee unraveling the assets remaining in his real estate scams. It is doubtful that any confidential informant was ever utilized as frequently by the federal government as Dwek.

Ironically, there was a VIP candidate's campaign that was not targeted; the only time Dwek turned down an opportunity to snare someone; in spite of the fact that the 90-day rollover authorization forms sent to the DOJ were consistently asking for more time for Dwek to cultivate relationships with corrupt officials for the purpose of conferring bribes. An FBI 302 report depicting an interview with defendant Denis Jaslow on August 8, 2009, documents the defendant's interactions with Dwek, Hudson County Republican Chairman José Arrango, and Hudson County Republican Party operative Russell Maffei (spelled as McVeigh in the 302).

The 302 reports an attempt to lure Jaslow into soliciting Dwek for a contribution to Chris Christie's campaign for governor in exchange for political patronage – an appointment to an unnamed State board. Jaslow identifies the meeting date as the night that Peter Cammarano was elected Hoboken mayor. That would have been on the runoff election date of Tuesday June 9, 2009, or Friday June 12, 2009, when the election was certified.

Despite the government's objectives stated in the DOJ reports, Dwek declines to engage in targeting the Christie campaign, and tells Jaslow that it was because of Christie's law enforcement background; though Dwek had pursued other targets with law enforcement backgrounds. Dwek testified at trial that the government directed whom he could and could not target. In the jail cell holding the defendants after their arrests, Dennis Jaslow was second-guessing himself; regretting he had not gone along with his gut instinct that told him something was up when Dwek avoided making a payoff to Christie's campaign. He was the first defendant to associate the arrests with Christie.

The decision to target candidates who were not public officials, or public officials in their capacity as a candidate for office, would eventually present dire legal hurdles for the prosecutors running the sting. The prosecutors ignored DOJ laws and protocols prohibiting the targeting of local candidates without authorization. The prosecutors failed to document the targeting of candidates in the sting's rollover authorizations, and breeched the constitutional boundaries prohibiting federal encroachment into the matters of a State.

To carry out this purposeful breech of guidelines the prosecutors had to figure a way to get around the approval of the Criminal Undercover Operations Review Committee (CUORC), who were responsible, in part, for authorizing Dwek's conduct and ensuring the integrity of the sting. With the bankruptcy court judge running out of patience and pressuring the government's use of Dwek to wrap up, prosecutors ignored the Attorney General Guidelines mandating that a "specific description" of Dwek's activity be documented. They reported his conduct as involving only public officials, purposefully misleading the CUORC and not emitting a peep about targeting candidates for office. The agents filling out the forms describe the same conduct quite differently in the criminal complaints, indictments, and press releases after the fact. On those documents, the aforementioned conduct is depicted as *illicit campaign contributions to candidates* running for office.

In order to lure the targeted candidates into his lair, Dwek began to use the bait of campaign contributions and not out-and-out bribes. There is a legal distinction between a bribe and a quid pro quo, and a campaign donation and a campaign pledge. Dwek's reason for targeting the candidates was primarily election-related conduct, not pure public corruption. Prosecutors with the caliber of Assistant United States Attorneys should damn well know the difference. Apparently, the lure of Trenton jobs was clouding their thinking.

The Manzo Conundrum

Once the federal prosecutors decided to breach the guidelines and the law by targeting candidates for office who were not public officials, they had their work cut out in preventing overseers from the Department of Justice from shutting down the sting. As each of the ninety-day rollovers for the investigations authorization elapsed, they continued their game of hide-and-seek with Main Justice – camouflaging the facts and evidence produced from the investigation.

In my case, there were further complications. Before the government's concept for Bid Rig III ever began, before Solomon Dwek was arrested, my brother Ron Manzo, who dabbled in development himself, was desperately trying to get rid of a parcel of property that he owned on Garfield Avenue in Jersey City not too far away from the parcel of property that Dwek fictitiously claimed to own. My brother had engaged Ed Cheatam and Jack Shaw, who would both later fall prey to Solomon Dwek, to see if they could unload the property on any of the developers they dealt with. Cheatam and Shaw did business with Jersey City development projects and developers, mostly navigating government offices and potential pitfalls that occasionally got in the way of bringing a project to fruition.

When Dwek popped into Shaw and Cheatam's lives as David Esenbach, courtesy of Department of Justice targeting, they brought my brother's Garfield Avenue property to his attention. They didn't know it at the time, but Dwek's interest wasn't in Ron's property. Dwek, in the guise of Esenbach, feigned interest in Ron's Garfield Avenue property in order to target me, his brother, who was a mayoral candidate in the Jersey City election. The government had directed Dwek to target me, knowing full well that I was not a public official. At the infamous Dwek, Shaw, and Cheatam February rendezvous at the Casa Dante, the trio discussed the plot for roping me into a meeting with Dwek.

Dwek was insistent to Shaw and Cheatam that he wanted to be supportive to my campaign, while at the same time he was being supportive of the campaigns of my two opponents: incumbent Mayor Healy and Assemblyman Harvey Smith. It was arranged that Cheatam would be the conduit to set the meeting up with me. Cheatam first met with my brother to try and grease the skids. Cheatam told my brother that he had someone interested in buying his property. With a down real estate market in 2009, and the property's value declining every day, Ron told Cheatam that he was obviously anxious to meet with Dwek.

Cheatam then worked me into the picture, explaining to my brother that as a future developer in Jersey City, Dwek (as Esenbach) had an interest in the upcoming mayoral election. Cheatam told my brother that because of his relationship with the developer, he had worked out a contribution for my mayoral campaign. He asked Ron if he would arrange a meeting with me. Ron obliged Dwek's request and arranged my meeting with the pretend developer.

Insensitive Targeting

The FBI Domestic Investigations and Operations Guide defines one of the categories classifying a "sensitive investigative matter" as a situation "involving the activities of a domestic public official or political candidate (involving corruption or a threat to the national security)." A "sensitive investigative matter" initiated by the FBI's Newark field office would have required a review by the Chief District Council, approval by the Special Agent in Charge (Weyson Dun), written notification to the appropriate Unit Chief and Section Chief at FBI Headquarters in Washington DC, and notification to the United States Attorney and the Department Of Justice. No discovery was ever provided to our defense that would demonstrate the government had complied with the requirements of the guidelines relative to the "sensitive investigative matters" stipulations.

The FBI Domestic Investigations and Operations Guide establishes guidelines for the protection of First Amendment rights and civil liberties guarantees, such as election conduct, as provided by the United States Constitution. The Guide proclaims, "The FBI is responsible for protecting the American public, not only from crime and terrorism, but also from incursions into their constitutional rights. Accordingly, all Attorney General Guidelines for Domestic Investigative Activities must be carried out with full adherence to the Constitution, federal laws and the principles of civil liberty and privacy.... Furthermore, there are constitutional provisions that set limits what on that purpose may be. It may not be solely to monitor the exercise of rights that are protected by the Constitution."

The bait the government had used to build its conspiracy was campaign donations for candidates. Because this involved a First Amendment issue, special precautions were required. In my initial meeting with Dwek on February 23, 2009, the government seriously crossed the line. The vast majority of the meeting was innocuous talk, mostly Dwek in the role of David Esenbach establishing his fictitious background. At one point, his associate, Cheatam tried to get to the heart of the matter, explaining that he and Dwek wanted to meet, "so that you guys would be favorable to what we're trying to do in Jersey City." Neither Cheatam nor Dwek ever tied a *quid pro quo* to what they were trying to accomplish. On that note, Dwek began to spin his yarn of how he was all set to close on this property on Garfield Avenue in Jersey City.

I then began a lengthy interrogation about the location of the sight, and concluded that this was the massively chromium-contaminated parcel of property that I had uncovered when I served as Jersey City's Health Chief. Dwek acknowledged that the property had contamination problems, but then stated that he had a "No Further Action Letter" from the New Jersey Department of Environmental Protection.

What Dwek obviously did not know is that I am also a licensed New Jersey Registered Environmental Health Specialist; and that as a former New Jersey State Assemblyman, I had sat on the Assembly Environmental Committee. I knew that what he was saying was impossible. I thought calling him out would be embarrassing to Cheatam – who claimed that he was working for Dwek – so I let him ramble on, instead of confronting him on his bullshit. As a candidate, I had seen plenty of this before – a bullshit artist trying to make an impression. Eventually, I cut Dwek off and began to elaborate on my campaign platform.

The conversation that Dwek and I engaged in was covered by the FBI "Sensitive Investigative Matters" section of their guidelines: "The exercise of free speech includes far more than simply speaking on a controversial topic in the town square. It includes such activities as conveying a public message or an idea through words or deeds.... Law enforcement activity that diminishes a person's ability to communicate in any of these ways may interfere with his or her freedom of speech—and thus may not be undertaken by the FBI solely for that purpose."

Campaign platforms and advocating public policies are positions affecting all, in contrast to an explicit *quid pro quo* affecting one or a few. In one of the landmark case laws regarding the Hobbs Act and the issue of campaign donations alleged to be bribes, the Supreme Court, in its historic McCormick ruling, defended the colloquy that had occurred at my February 23, 2009 meeting. "... To hold that legislators commit the federal crime of extortion when they act for the benefit of constituents or support legislation furthering the interests of some of their constituents, shortly before or after campaign contributions are solicited and received from those beneficiaries, is an unrealistic assessment of what Congress could have meant by making it a crime ... to hold otherwise would open to prosecution not only conduct that has long been thought to be well within the law but also conduct that in a very real sense is unavoidable so long as election campaigns are financed by private contributions or expenditures, as they have been from the beginning of the Nation. It would require statutory language more explicit than the Hobbs Act contains to justify a contrary conclusion."

This did not matter to the prosecutors and the FBI agents overseeing the sting. Neither I, nor anyone else, stood a chance against the whims of compromised prosecutors. Margolin and Sherman explained it more bluntly in *The Jersey Sting*, "The FBI and U.S. Attorneys Office have an uncomplicated view of Hudson County politicians. To them, there were only two types: the crooked and the dead.... Essentially, the FBI was trying to run up the body count."

Mutiny and the Bounty

The bounty money that Dwek was paying out to his alleged co-conspirators wreaked havoc with the investigation, corrupting any legitimate assessment that could be relied upon for targeting defendants. Every diner and restaurant was a stage, and the emcees, Cheatam, Shaw, Khalil, and Jaslow, performed like the hosts of a television game show, embellishing the resumé of each target's act that they were introducing in front of Dwek's camera.

In the government's case against me, I was victimized by the fierce competition between Cheatam, Khalil and Jaslow. Over the course of one weekend, they fought with each other over who would introduce me to Dwek and collect the bounty. Cheatam won out only because he was working on unloading my brother Ron's Garfield Avenue property, and therefore had the inside track; he used his clout with Ron to set up the meeting.

The jealousy and backbiting between Cheatam, Khalil and Jaslow was over the top. They lied through their teeth to one another, destroying any semblance of credibility for the sting and the subsequent prosecutions. Dwek and the government played games with the lies – choosing what to believe and not to believe in order to satisfy the needs of their contemplated prosecutions.

Linking the Sting to Corzine

Although he was never charged, the FBI's relaxed "assessment" protocol and the bounty scheme proved devastating for New Jersey Department of Community Affairs Commissioner Joseph Doria. His reputation was sullied and he was forced to resign his job on the day the sting went down. He had been a longtime associate of Jack Shaw since the time when Doria was Speaker of the New Jersey Assembly and then Bayonne Mayor. Shaw had advised Doria and worked for him on many of his campaigns.

The government evidence shows that Doria never intimated that he would violate the law or take any money. I served with Doria in the legislature and had actually beaten him in the only election loss of his career: for State Assembly in 2003. When the late Jersey City Mayor and State Senator Glenn Cunningham suddenly passed away, Doria sought his seat and won. Despite our previous campaign against each other, Doria and I developed an amicable working relationship and a great friendship. He was a gentlemen, a devoutly faithful Roman Catholic, and as honest as the day is long. I supported him for his run for Senate.

Doria only agreed to meet with Dwek because he felt it would help Jack Shaw out. Anyone without a dog in this fight could review the tapes of the meetings between Doria, Dwek, Shaw, and Cheatam and see that he was blameless for any untoward behavior; anyone except, perhaps, the FBI and the U.S. Attorneys. When Shaw and Cheatam talked to Dwek outside of Doria's presence they intimated that they were funneling over the payoffs that Dwek thought he was making to Doria. Not only were they swindling Dwek out of the alleged payoff money, they were also doubling down. Dwek's bonus bounty would compensate them for the money they convinced their targets to take.

Early on, Cheatam began to suspect that Doria was not taking any of the money that Shaw was supposed to be handing over to him. Shaw knew his comrade was suspicious, so he invented a story claiming that Doria had asked him to donate the money to St. Peter's College in Jersey City. Doria had worked for the college in years past and was an ardent supporter of the institution. But Shaw was actually stashing the money away on the side, not wanting to split it with Cheatam.

Doria, a high-ranking State Commissioner, was perhaps the biggest fish being targeted. Moreover, Governor Jon Corzine had appointed him to his cabinet. Doria was the direct link from the sting to Governor Corzine – Christie's opponent. The federal prosecutors with stakes in Christie's campaign had to be salivating.

On the evening before the sting went down, the FBI scooped up Jack Shaw for interrogation. While awaiting arraignment on the day of my arrest, I was retained in a holding cell with Shaw and some other defendants in the Federal Courthouse at Newark, New Jersey. I was actually in the cell for nearly an hour before I noticed Jack, whom I knew very well. He was sitting hunched over on a bench, eyes closed, frighteningly ashen in color.

Shaw was not a well man and the Government knew it. The Viet Nam veteran was going for kidney dialysis twice a week, had a bad heart, hypertension, and battled diabetes. He took myriad medications. Whenever he dined with friends at local eateries, he would be popping pills before and after the meal. In his February 17, 2009 taped meeting with Dwek and Cheatam at Jersey City's Casa Dante Restaurant, Shaw served up a dissertation to Dwek on all of his life-threatening maladies. His grave appearance in the jail cell made me fear that he was lapsing into a diabetic coma. I moved myself to a seat next to him on the bench. Little did I know that in a matter of days he would be dead; either over-medicated or just plain killed by the stress.

"Jack. Jack," I repeated, rousing him from his slumber. "Are you okay? Can I do anything?"

He said nothing at first, just a slight smile, and then a nod of his head in recognition. I was prepared to call a U.S. Marshall and get him medical attention, but he steadfastly pleaded with me not to do that. Then he began to share with me his tale of woe, as if he had to get his overnight ordeal off his chest. He told me that the FBI had detained him since early the last evening. He had not eaten anything, nor taken any of his medications. They incessantly interrogated him, focusing mainly on Joe Doria, trying to get Jack to say that Doria took money. He said he told them that he still had the money they thought Doria took and that he would return it to them; but, he said, they were just intent on trying to make him say that Doria took the money. "Guantanamo has nothing on these guys," he joked, though he meant it seriously.

He mentioned that they were asking if he knew anything about me, and whether or not I had promised jobs to anyone. He said he told them "no" and that he knew that I had "never taken any money." Mostly though, the interrogation focused on Doria, and trying from every angle to get Shaw to incriminate him in a crime. He told me that he reiterated to them, "Joe Doria is honest – he wouldn't take a dime!" I asked Jack if he knew what was to become of Doria. He frowned, shook his head, and answered, "No. They just seemed hell bent on arresting him."

Because Shaw indicated to me that he told the FBI he knew nothing about me engaging in criminal activity, my attorney, John Lynch, asked during my first pretrial session that the tape or reports of Shaw's interrogation be turned over as part of discovery. One would think that, after the thousands of hours and dollars spent on secretly taping the targets, the government might have wanted to spare some resources in order to record one of the investigations most crucial interrogations, but they did not.

Only an FBI agent's notes of Shaw's debriefing preserved the event. The government rigidly resisted turning over the evidence. The Judge upheld their argument to keep their notes on the Shaw interrogation under seal. Sometime after my pretrial session, the FBI's 302 report of the Shaw interrogation popped up on my door-step in a folder with other sensitive and incriminating government documents. It was from an unidentified sender but, judging from the documents, I could only assume an honest, government law enforcement source. It was a bombshell.

Crucial excerpts from the 302 report depict what the FBI learned from Shaw on the evening before they executed the mass arrests: "Shaw never collected money on behalf of Doria and Doria never instructed Shaw where to give money. Shaw stated that he made up the story about paying colleges on behalf of Doria. Ed Cheatam does not know Shaw did not pay Saint Peter's College on behalf of Doria. Cheatam thinks Doria received cash through Shaw.... Shaw claimed he never made a donation to anyone on behalf of Doria. Doria just wants to see Shaw make money. Doria helped Shaw make money and wanted nothing in return."

The report then described the last encounter between Doria and Dwek, where Doria actually turned down a bribe. The report makes it clear that Doria never wanted nor got the money, and Shaw was going to give the money to the FBI the next day. "Shaw advised that the $25,000 cash he received from the CW on July 21, 2009 was never intended for Doria. Shaw stated that he planned to keep the cash and give a portion of the cash to Cheatam. Shaw stated that he deposited $2,500 of the cash into his bank account and gave $2,500 cash to Cheatam. Cheatam thinks Shaw skimmed $5,000 of the $25,000 cash payment and Doria got $20,000.... The remaining balance of $20,000 is in a secret hiding place not in his home.... Shaw claimed he will produce the cash tomorrow." Cheatam confirmed this very point to FBI agents interrogating him at his house on the morning of the takedown.

Despite this knowledge, the FBI and the United States Attorney's Office still decided to storm the home and office of Joe Doria on the morning of the takedown. Somebody made sure that the media had been tipped off about the raid and they turned out *en masse* in front of Doria's home. It was a perfect setup. According to *The Jersey Sting*, FBI agents then proceeded to carry out empty evidence boxes from Doria's house, against his objections that the press outside might be given the wrong impression. The news of the incident led to Doria's resignation. The news of FBI agents raiding Doria's home made it into Chris Christie's political spin, and by linking Bid Rig III to Corzine, they were helping to affect the outcome of the election.

The lethal fallout on Governor Corzine and his campaign was as inevitable as the future Trenton jobs and perks that were eventually bestowed upon Marra, Brown, McKenna and others in the United States Attorney's Office.

Having sat on this crucial evidence of Doria's innocence for more than two years, and under mounting pressure from the media for access to the FBI 302 exculpating Doria, the United State's Attorney's Office begrudgingly conceded to Doria's attorney, John Azzarello, and issued a letter finally clearing Doria of any wrongdoing. The *Star-Ledger* broke the news in an article written on October 7, 2011. "It is rare for prosecutors to clear potential targets left under a cloud of suspicion caused by their investigations," the *Ledger* reported.

Following up the *Ledger's* initial story, columnist Bob Braun was granted a rare interview with Doria: "'I was caught up in this even though I wasn't raising money for anyone,' said Doria. 'This was all about raising money for political campaigns.'... Doria won't criticize federal authorities or even mention the name of Gov. Chris Christie, under whose tenure as U.S. attorney the so-called 'Bid Rig III' investigation began."

The columnist also interviewed Alan Zegas, a prominent criminal defense attorney not involved in the Bid Rig III cases. "A 'terrible injustice occurs' when searches are publicized or investigations leaked. The innuendo is that the person has committed a crime that caused a judge to sign a warrant permitting the search," he said. Zegas also says defense attorneys won't criticize prosecutors– and don't want their clients to– because they don't want to 'reawaken' interest in their clients' activities," Braun reported.

No Quid Pro Quo

One of the more farcical assessments in the investigations pertained to Assemblyman and Mayoral candidate L. Harvey Smith. Despite declaring to Dwek at an April 24, 2009 meeting, "I don't do *quid pro quo!*" and, despite the fact that he returned a campaign donation to Dwek when he found out it was cash, it did not stop the prosecutors and the FBI from attempting to nab Smith at all costs.

"I don't do *quid pro quo*. What's that suppose[d] to mean," Dwek puzzled. "He's tough," Dwek confided to Cheatam and Shaw. Perplexed, Dwek was not giving up; he still had years to knock off his potential sentence. "Maybe you can talk to him and straighten him out.... The thing is he doesn't want no cash – How are we going to operate with this guy?" Dwek would not have long to wait for his answer.

Meeting again on July 17, 2009, the government got creative. This time, Cheatam shadowed Smith in his car as he pulled out of the restaurant parking lot, and then tossed a FedEx envelope containing cash onto the back seat of Smith's car. Smith attempted to return the money when he discovered it in his car, but the government needed to fulfill the sting's billing as the nation's largest public corruption bust ever. Innocent or not, Smith had to be charged and prosecuted. United States Attorney Paul Fishman had to uphold the reputation of his office.

The throwing of alleged bribe money through the open window of a car being driven by an unsuspecting defendant hardly epitomized what prosecutors promised Smith's jury in opening arguments: "The evidence will show that the defendant had no problem with David Esenbach paying him bribes, and that the defendant had no problems accepting those bribes." Smith's jury was not buying any of it and they acquitted him of all charges.

Likewise, other defendants just did not fit the mold of public officials on the take. Lori Serrano was a working mom raising two daughters and would not have been targeted had it not been for her candidacy for elective office. The hounding of Serrano represented the most brazen abuse of the bounty system implemented by the government. Not only did Cheatam set up her meeting with Dwek for his cash reward, he had also convinced her to run on my ticket for City Council. Still, the government wore her down into pleading to a misdemeanor.

Jimmy King was a retired senior citizen who ran a civic association. Jimmy made sure that on each Thanksgiving Day the city's elderly shut-ins all got a hot meal delivered to their doorstep. Seniors with nowhere to go were also treated to one of the thousands of meals the Jimmy King Association shipped out. The homeless were also served up a feast at the church hall where Jimmy and his volunteers prepared the meals. Christmas was just as busy a time for King, when he would deliver hundreds of toys to children in city hospitals. Even after his prosecution ordeal, King returned to Jersey City to provide the needy with Thanksgiving meals.

The targeting of King and Serrano was all in a days work for prosecutors and FBI agents who were intent on keeping America's streets clear of 'dangerous criminals'.

Corrupting Elections

One of the huge hurdles facing the prosecutors was the fact that Dwek was giving donations to candidates in an active election cycle; sometimes directing the money to the candidates through straw donors. The money was obviously being used for campaign purposes and, as such, was corrupting the results of the election. There are strict federal laws prohibiting federal prosecutors and the FBI from affecting the outcome of an election. During his testimony at every trial, Dwek reminded juries that his conduct was at the direction of the federal government. He followed their instructions.

As previously mentioned, because of the Tenth Amendment's constitutional restrictions and the prohibitions cited in the Public Integrity Section guidelines, any Otherwise Illegal Activity (OIA) regarding or involving the local elections and campaigns that were underway, were off limits and could never be authorized. Moreover, in order not to leave any lingering doubt, the OIA guidelines further declare, "... the Confidential Human Source is authorized only to engage in the specific conduct set forth in the written authorization and not in any other illegal activity.... Under no circumstances may the Confidential Human Source initiate or instigate a plan or strategy to commit a federal, state, or local offense."

A reading of the government's descriptions and recordings of the statement of facts, which are depicted in the investigation's criminal complaints and indictments, portrays election misconduct. Indeed, the approach to candidates who were not elected or public officials was the entrée for the ongoing election. Dwek was practically demanding that his targets take his campaign donations and not report him, as was required, on their election financial disclosure forms. Sometimes he gave his donations to straw donors, who then fraudulently cut checks to candidates' campaigns.

Councilman Mariano Vega's criminal complaint summarized it best: "CW further told defendant Vega that the check CW gave defendant Vega was 'only a small token,' and that the CW could be more generous as the election got closer, but had to figure out ways to contribute without the contributions coming back directly to the CW." Dwek's language was unmistakably clear and prolific. The crimes he advocated were New Jersey Election and Campaign Finance Law violations, which capture bribery during the course of an election as well. "I'll give you another 5 before the election as you need.... Then after you get in, when you're Mrs. Councilwoman, I'll give you more.... Just make sure my name doesn't show up on any of those lousy reports or anything."

Under the government's direction, Dwek was instigating and initiating the action at the taped target meetings, which were sandwiched between his instruction sessions with FBI agents, according to sworn testimony in court. Under cross-examination by defense attorney Michael Critchley, Dwek confirmed that he was "schooled somewhat" on what to say "by way of verbiage" and "what points" that he "should bring out" by the FBI agents. "I received talkings from the special agents of the FBI," he declared.

Both the authorization forms and the *Attorney General's Guidelines* require the FBI to implement "precautionary measures" and that they "must take all reasonable steps to monitor closely the activities of the Confidential Human Source." They further required that the FBI "must take all reasonable steps to minimize the adverse effect of the Otherwise Illegal Activity on innocent persons." Here, the government failed miserably.

Through Dwek, the government was cavalierly shoveling some $400,000 to candidates for use in their campaigns – knowing that most of this cash was going to be used in ongoing and active campaigns. In fact, it was actually suggested by Dwek. This was another slight detail left out of each and every one of the authorization forms the Newark FBI and United States Attorney's Office sent on to Washington, DC. There was no authorization (CUORC was never told), nor could there ever have been, for this conduct. Federal laws, Department of Justice guidelines, and the United States Constitution prohibit the federal government from affecting the outcome of an election. The money was spread over Hoboken's mayoral race and Jersey City's mayoral and city council races. The monies corrupted the election results and disenfranchised every voter and all of the nearly one million inhabitants of the two cities.

The government had another problem; they were required to document each and every instruction given to Dwek, which then had to be placed in his file. If the prosecutors and the FBI followed the guidelines they would be hanging themselves. When the instructions they texted to Dwek before, after, or during his target meetings became a center of controversy in the trial of another Bid Rig III defendant, Mayor Anthony Suarez, their cover-up was blown.

Chapter Eight

A Justice Department Cover-Up, Sanctioned by the FBI

"Oops" ... Destroying Evidence

An evidentiary hearing on missing text messages between Dwek and his FBI handlers in the trial of Bid Rig III defendant, Ridgefield Mayor Anthony Suarez, led to the unearthing of damaging revelations regarding other government misconduct. The disclosures in the courtroom indicated that missing text messages were not limited to the Suarez case, but widespread among the other cases against Bid Rig III defendants. During his meetings with targets, Dwek was incessantly texting back and forth to the FBI agents with his Blackberry phone. The action is caught in much of the tape-recorded evidence. The main FBI agents who were texting back and forth with Dwek were Special Agents William Waldie (nicknamed by colleagues "The Magnificent Waldie"), Sean McCarthy, and Donald Russ.

Text messages between the agents and Dwek were not the only information that was found to be missing – government witnesses testified that text messaging units of other attorneys and agents working the investigation were missing as well. Once Suarez's defense attorney, Michael Critchley, a former federal prosecutor, assisted by co-counsel John Vazquez, opened an attack on the FBI's careless disregard for what they termed "evidence" in the case, it turned out that the messaging was not just missing, but had actually been deleted and destroyed by the government.

At first, the government denied the existence of any text messages, despite the requests made by defense attorneys for the material, dating back to ten months (December 2009) prior to the start of trial. Then, in October of 2010, just as the trial kicked off, the prosecutors acknowledged that they were wrong and that records of text messages did exist. There was a caveat: while they had the records of the texts, some of the contents had been deleted, *accidently*, they claimed, by a communications computer server. There was another caveat: it seemed that some of the content of the internal texts between the agents had been preserved, but the content of the texts between the agents and Dwek had been deleted.

Straight faced, Assistant U.S. Attorney Maureen Nakly explained the dilemma to the court: "At the time, there was no policy to preserve the text messages, and I do not believe there is any evidence that any agent or government employee decided that these text messages were exculpatory or material to the defense and determined that they should be deleted or not preserved. It was a pure matter of happenstance that certain text messages were not preserved."

Critchley was livid over the government excuses after being put off for the discovery up until the trial date, waiting for evidence he had been told, at first, did not exist, then did, and finally, was selectively deleted. He revved up and delivered a scorching argument that led to the court granting the defense an evidentiary hearing. His argument and delivery were a classic presentation for lawyers.

"Your Honor, today I think we heard at least a third version of the Government's position regarding this rather not too complex of an issue, just basically a discovery obligation, ramifications of which could be dire, and trying to follow the Government is like trying to nail Jell-O to the wall because it keeps moving....

"I look at the letter that Mr. McCarren sent us August 31, 2010, and I will tell you my reaction when I first read this. 'The FBI retained text messages of its agents only for so long as limited storage space on its servers allowed.' When I first read that, it didn't even pass the giggle test. We have not heard anybody who has put first-person knowledge by way of an affidavit or oath that, in fact, this is the case....

"Last week, when I read this letter into the record that was given to us by Mr. McCarren, Ms. Nakly stood up and said, stop reading that letter, I told you, it is wrong, these are the facts, and she laid out on the record the facts as they existed last Wednesday. Now, we come before the Court on Monday, and she says, disregard not only the August 31 letter, the factual representations made, I'm going to disregard the factual representations we made last Wednesday. Now I am giving you another version, again based on the third person. Then she said things like, in terms of the Court asking the question, 'how do you determine what is preserved,' her response is, 'I don't believe they deliberately picked or choose what to save, it was just happenstance.'"

Critchley then offered his own critique. "I hope our Government, particularly the FBI, does not operate the way that it was described in the discovery letter, because I don't think it should be based on happenstance…. Judge, you could buy one of those thumb drives, one of these things, Judge. These cost about $25 or $30. You could save like 4.5 million pages of paper on this. You could buy a regular cheap laptop with 180 gigabytes that could save 25 million pieces of paper.

"You mean to tell me that the FBI has a retention policy that, oops, if it is gone, it is gone? I don't think the FBI works on oops, especially with the nature of the investigation they conduct. What do they do with terrorists when they have these text messages; they are just gone? There's no backup?"

In a damning accusation, Critchley suggested his own explanation for the deletions. "The Government, through the agents, I think cherry picked, cherry picked what conversations they were going to retain and what conversations they were going to remove. And the conversations that were going to be removed are those that were favorable to the defense or damaging to the Government or to the agents…. That is why I am saying, Judge, that did not pass the giggles test when I first heard it, and now it is no longer a laughing matter. Now, I am not smiling. Now, I'm saying, guess what, there is something wrong here. There's something very wrong here."

The agents handling Dwek were called to testify during the evidentiary hearing on the deleted evidence. The agents stated that they would sometimes send instructions to Dwek through text messages. Both the admonishment and authorization forms that Dwek and the agents signed off on state: "The CHS must abide by the instructions of the FBI." The agents also testified that Dwek would text to them, on occasion, his own interpretation of what was going on at the meetings. They felt these messages were irrelevant because what was being recorded on the tape was evidence, but Dwek's interpretations were not. Defense co-Counsel John

Vazquez pointed out a conflict: "Agent Russ testified. He testified under oath that Solomon Dwek's interpretations of what was happening during those meetings was irrelevant, because the information was on the tapes. Judge, the government has taken the exact opposite position during these cases. They have said his interpretation and his understandings are critical."

Initially, Agent Russ had told the court that he had hardly any reason to text Dwek with instructions, since Waldie was the lead agent on the case. However, evidence was produced that showed that Russ had in fact texted Dwek more than a thousand times. Russ told the court that despite not being able to recall if he had texted Dwek with any instructions, he was certain that there was nothing of evidential value in his thousand text messages to and from Dwek. Vazquez then pointed out that Solomon Dwek's testimony made the agent's claim highly unlikely. Vazquez then quoted to the court, Dwek's testimony: "The only time that I was texting with the agents when I was in a meeting where I was wearing a wire is if it was important. We weren't just, you know, talking."

The agents also claimed that they had deleted the text messages because, as they testified, they knew of no FBI policy requiring them to save them, and that they were further told that the messages were filling up the storage capacity of their Blackberries. They then testified under cross-examination that they could not remember ever being told by anyone that the storage space of their phones would be affected by the texts, nor that they had ever experienced a problem with their Blackberries' storage capacity.

Critchley and Vazquez emphasized that Dwek had been consistently testifying about his interpretation of the taped meetings for the juries in the various Bid Rig III trials. They pointed out that, if any of Dwek's texted interpretations of the target meetings were found to be in conflict with his interpretation of that same meeting in trial testimony, it would be exculpatory or impeachment evidence. They argued, for this very reason, that the government was required to save the messages between the agents and Dwek. The agents held their ground – claiming that, in the thousands of text messages between them and Dwek, there were not any, not a one, which would have evidentiary value.

This point of the trial provided the court with one of the proceeding's high drama marks. Judge Linares had sequestered the FBI agents. During the testimony of The Magnificent Waldie, solicited over a phone call from Afghanistan, Assistant U.S. Attorney McCarren slipped out of the courtroom and tipped off the other agents as to a key portion of Waldie's testimony. Unbeknownst to McCarren, Critchley stealthily followed him outside the courtroom and caught him dead to rights. He called him out, pranced back into the courtroom and reported the unethical behavior to Judge Linares. The Judge was angry and scolded the prosecutor, threatening to take sanctions. This was a truly disgraceful and embarrassing courtroom performance by the District of New Jersey United States Attorney's Office.

Critchley was unaware that the agents had been playing cute with their answers. There might not be an FBI rule specific to saving text messages, but as Critchley pointed out, evidence – in whatever form – has to be preserved. If the FBI Domestic Investigations and Operations Guide did not say so, the Attorney General's Guidelines Regarding the Use of FBI Confidential Human Sources did, especially when those text messages contained *instructions* from the FBI agents, as the agents and Solomon Dwek had already testified they did. Those guidelines make it clear under a section dedicated to "Record Keeping Practices" that "The FBI shall maintain a file for each Confidential Human Source containing all written authorizations, findings and instructions regarding Tier I Otherwise Illegal Activity." The Attorney General's Guidelines are explicit: "shall maintain ... all instructions" and "as required." It did not matter if the instructions were verbal, texted, or chiseled on stone tablets; the guidelines required that they were to be preserved.

The FBI Domestic Investigations and Operations Guide also addressed the agents' requirements for following the directives relative to handling Dwek. It offers little wiggle room for the lame excuses given in their testimony. In fact, it is airtight! "All FBI personnel must fully comply with all laws, rules, and regulations governing FBI investigations, operations, programs and activities, including those set forth in the AGG-Dom. Under no circumstances will expediency justify disregard for the law."

During the same evidentiary hearing, the technicians servicing the FBI Blackberries, computers, and servers were called as witnesses. They explained the intricacies of the messaging retention capabilities of the servers and then detailed the steps they had taken to retrieve the missing messages. They could offer no explanation as to why only certain Department of Justice employees' messaging units were selectively deleted and remained irretrievable. However, this contradicted a representation that had been made by Assistant U.S. Attorney Mark McCarren to defense counsel. In his letter to Suarez's lawyers, McCarren had claimed that the reason the messaging was deleted was the need to conserve space on servers. The technicians stated under cross-examination that they never told anyone in Newark that was the specific cause for the deletion of the messages. Pressed to explain, McCarren stated that the letter he drafted to Suarez's defense was based upon a letter sent by another Assistant United States Attorney to the Beldini defense during that trial.

Ironically, McCarren was one of the prosecutors who had signed off on the authorization forms for the Tier I Otherwise Illegal Activity and Dwek's admonishments; which, it so happened, had camouflaged the election-related conduct of the sting to Department of Justice overseers in Washington DC. McCarren, for sure, had an obligation to know the intricacies of the Attorney General's Guidelines Regarding the Use of FBI Confidential Human Sources; particularly, the guidelines requiring that evidence (which had already been deleted by the agents) be retained and kept in Dwek's file. McCarren's role in attesting to the authorization forms calls into question whether or not he had an obligation to recuse himself from arguing the matter before the court; or at least let the court know of his involvement in the matter.

The FBI technicians then explained to the court that had someone from the FBI or United States Attorney's Office requested a litigation hold, the messaging units would have been preserved. It was learned that subsequent to the discovery of the crucial missing messaging, a litigation hold was finally put in place for New Jersey's largest public corruption bust ever, in January of 2010, six months after the arrests and indictments of the defendants. By January of 2010, the litigation hold was useless. At that point, there were no pertinent messages to be preserved; they had already been deleted. No one could explain why the litigation hold did not commence with the initiation of the investigation, or sometime shortly thereafter, when the government knew they were attempting to prosecute the cases.

Assessing the evidence presented at the hearings, Judge Linares made his finding of fact. "There was an actual deletion of the text messages by the FBI agents who did have it in their handheld devices, so they willfully deleted those, and there was obviously the failure to preserve the text messages in conjunction with the investigation. This is not some independent investigation by the FBI of which the U.S. Attorney's Office was not involved, and there was no litigation hold in connection with this matter. There is still to this day no clear explanation as to why some of the text messages were preserved and some were deleted, and there is also no clear explanation to this Court as to why the litigation hold, which was put in place in January of 2010, why that was not put in place before that," Linares opined.

The Judge told the lawyers that he was going to give the jury an adverse inference instruction allowing them to weigh the government destruction of evidence against the prosecution's case if they wanted to do so. Without the evidence of the numerous conflicts involving the government personnel who were overseeing the Bid Rig III prosecution still not put before the court, Linares decided on a milder sanction against the government. The Judge had earlier cautioned that had he found the government acted in bad faith, the evidence might have been ordered inadmissible or the case might have been dismissed.

The matter was resolved for the time being, but the question and the mystery lingered. As Suarez defense attorney, John Vazquez, pondered aloud before the court, "Why did the FBI in Newark make a false representation as to what happened to those text messages by saying it was limited server space?"

Why would Dan McKenna of the Newark FBI office originally request FBI technicians to search cell phone and computer servers for the messaging information units of select agents and lawyers, and Solomon Dwek? It did not make sense for McKenna to call technicians to search for documents not required to be preserved, as the FBI agents had testified to in the Suarez trial. However, if the request was *to make sure* that the already deleted incriminating messages had not been stored on the servers that handled the Blackberries and the computers used by government employees, then the baffling questions raised by co-Counsel John Vazquez were answered. The government was making sure the deleted text messages did not exist elsewhere and that evidence of the government telling Dwek to break the law was completely destroyed.

The evidence, the testimony and the agency guidelines that the government was obligated to follow boils down to one of two distinct possibilities.

1) If Dwek's instructions did not come from the agents, Dwek broke the law by committing a criminal act for which he had no authorization. The agents further breeched their guidelines by not admonishing Dwek and reporting his crime in their reports.

2) If those instructions came from the agents, then both Dwek *and* the agents broke the law (under federal law there could be no authorization to use money for impacting an election, not even as an Otherwise Illegal Activity). It was constitutionally impermissible. In addition, there was no authorization to break New Jersey election laws under the guise of an Otherwise Illegal Activity.

Subsequent to the District Court ruling in the Suarez evidentiary hearing, my defense uncovered information that proved the government might have willfully misled the Suarez defense and the court during the hearing. It seems that while the government expert witnesses went to great lengths in explaining why the text messages were unrecoverable on the FBI servers used to transmit the messages, they played dumb as to how the messages were likely still retrievable from another source.

Consulting with forensic experts in the field of telecommunications, my defense learned that the government could have possibly retrieved the text messages had they subpoenaed the commercial carriers that their expert witnesses testified the FBI uses. Messages are stored on servers in the commercial carriers' systems, before being transmitted to the FBI server, and then from the FBI server to the server of the recipient of the message (such as Dwek's Blackberry), where it would be stored again. Commercial servers have practically unlimited capacity and some store information forever according to the experts we consulted. Apparently, the FBI technology witnesses were never asked about retrieving the messages from the commercial carriers and they never volunteered the information to the court. The cell phone server, located in Canada, is the most likely place for the government to retrieve the deleted text messages ... *if they really want to retrieve the contents.*

The text message issue in the Suarez case led to another troubling discovery regarding other government misconduct. In lieu of the deleted instructions given to Dwek through the texted cell phone messages, what about all of the instructions that were being given to Dwek on the fly, during the hundreds of prep sessions before target meetings and which lasted up to an hour, based upon the FBI's and Dwek's courtroom testimony? According to the Attorney General Guidelines, when instructions are given to a confidential informant regarding his contemplated criminal conduct (Otherwise Illegal Activity), and which were given outside of the investigation's mandatory 90-day reporting sessions, and which also might differ or expand the OIA that the informant has already been authorized to engage in, then the instructions must be commemorated in the informant's file within 72 hours. According to the testimony at trial, those instructions were never preserved and placed in Dwek's file.

The unpreserved evidence would have been classified as Jencks material, which by law *must* be preserved and turned over to the defense in discovery. The Jencks Act covers documents related to testimony, or relied upon by government witnesses at trial. Typically, it may consist of police notes, memoranda, reports, summaries, letters or verbatim transcripts used by government agents or employees to testify at trial. The law holds that after the government's witness testifies, the court shall upon motion of the defendant order the government to produce any statement of the witness in their possession relating to the subject matter upon which the witness testified. Apparently, in order to potentially cover up the government's participation in directing Dwek to commit unauthorized crimes and illegally entrap his targets, the instructions were never commemorated in writing or inserted into Dwek's file as the Attorney General Guidelines mandate.

All of the defendants in the case were denied the Jencks material.

There was still other startling evidence uncovered pertaining to the ninety-day rollover reports and authorizations: tampering and forgery. The instructions given to the FBI agents for filing the Otherwise Illegal Activity (OIA) authorizations are contained in the body of each report and direct that "both the OIA approval process, as well as the execution of admonishments, must be completed *prior to actual engagement* in OIA," and that "OIA admonishments must be *administered for each period of approved* OIA by the CHS (Confidential Human Source)."

There is evidence that the OIA reports used in the investigation had the signature acknowledgements by Dwek for the admonishments that he was given, along with the witnessed affirmations by the FBI agents, signed in advance of the approval process and the admonishments actually being conferred to Dwek. On many of the OIA reports' acknowledgement and affirmation pages, the dates at the top of the document differ from the date of the report and bear the date of a previous report, indicating that the document may be a duplicate. While the handwriting for the signatures of Dwek and the two FBI agents are different, the handwriting for the date confirming the signing of the affirmation appears identical for all three.

In order to complete the execution of the admonishments, the instructions explain to the agent handling the document to "physically separate, execute, and reattach the OIA admonishments." The directions do not state copy, clip and paste; which is what the agents handling the OIA reports in this investigation apparently did. Numerous OIA reports indicate that the many of the "SUMMARY OF THE INVESTIGATION" and the "SPECIFIC DESCRIPTION OF TIER I/II OIA" sections were copied from other reports, with the dates of the copied OIA report still intact at the top of the pages, and then simply attached to the form that was claimed to have been executed.

In court briefs, the government argued in its defense that, "Dwek's illegal activities with all defendants were subject to high levels of DOJ review and scrutiny, including by FBI Headquarters, the U.S. Attorney and the FBI SAC for this region, as well as the CUORC throughout the investigation, regardless of whether it was classified as Tier 1 or Tier 2.... The CUORC is composed of FBI employees, designated by the FBI Director, and DOJ attorneys designated by the Assistant Attorney General in charge of the Criminal Division. The CUORC meets bi-monthly. Its charge is to review, approve and provide continuing oversight of Group I Undercover Operations such as Bid Rig III." The government's argument points out that if the process for adhering to protocols were corrupted at the initial stage of execution – prior to the scrutiny of the DOJ overseers – then the oversight and approvals authorized by those who were reviewing the reports was based on a faulty premise. How could the Criminal Undercover Operations Review Committee have authorized conduct (Dwek targeting and arranging for straw donors to put money into active elections) that was never reported to them?

Past is Prologue

The Newark FBI was not alone in the gross breaking of the Attorney General Guidelines. In fact, since their inception, the breaching of guidelines seems to be a time-honored tradition for the FBI. In 2005, the Office of United States Inspector General, then headed by the well respected Glenn A. Fine, conducted an investigation and analysis of the FBI's compliance with the Confidential Human Sources guidelines, among other investigative guidelines that were examined. Fine's inquiry was prompted by a spate of high-profile scandals, the most notorious of which was when former FBI agent John J. Connolly Jr., allowed a Boston mobster and FBI informant James J. "Whitey" Bulger to flee by tipping him off to an imminent federal racketeering indictment. Relative to the guidelines for the use of these confidential informants, the findings were shocking.

Breaking the news of The Office of Inspector General's report, *Washington Post* Staff Writer Dan Eggen reported, "Many FBI agents have ignored Justice Department rules for handling confidential informants.... In an analysis of 120 informant files from around the country, the Justice Department's inspector general, Glenn A. Fine, found that FBI agents violated procedures in 87 percent of the cases, including some in which informants allegedly engaged in illegal activity without proper oversight or permission.... The report, parts of which are redacted because they involve classified material, also faults FBI agents for in some cases failing to notify officials in Washington about the initiation of criminal intelligence probes and for consistently failing to obtain advance approval to listen in on informants' conversations."

Among the findings cited in the executive summary of the Inspector General's report, it was disclosed that there were "significant problems in the FBI's compliance with Guidelines' provisions. Those violations occurred mainly in suitability reviews; the cautioning of informants about the limits of their activities; the authorization of otherwise illegal activity; documentation and notice of unauthorized illegal activity by informants; and the deactivation of informants.... These compliance errors are troubling in light of the history of the Confidential Informant Guidelines."

The Newark FBI and U.S. Attorney's Office were filling out the 90-day authorization forms utilized for Dwek's Otherwise Illegal Activity in a fashion strikingly similar to what the Inspector general's report was criticizing. The Inspector General's findings revealed that "the files for 7 of the 25 CI files (28 percent) that contained OIA authorizations did not include sufficiently specific descriptions of the authorized OIA in that they failed to specify the time period or 'specific conduct' authorized."

If the FBI was having problems with informants in cases without the record number of target interactions that were documented in Bid Rig III, what could then be expected when the staggering 107 taped target meetings over the course of 51 days occurred? Notwithstanding the fact that the meetings were sandwiched between the ten minute–to-one-hour instruction and debriefing sessions accompanying them.

Solomon Dwek was to Confidential Human Sources what Alex Rodriguez is to baseball. Dwek's record will always bear an asterisk. That asterisk will serve notice that the bounty system he employed, and the careless breaking of guidelines and the law by government agents and prosecutors, served as steroids that illegally enhanced Dwek's corrupt performance.

Chapter Nine

Bid Rig III's 'Backroom Boss with a Badge'

Election Strategy

After their respective 2009 primary election victories, the campaigns of Governor Jon Corzine and Former United States Attorney Chris Christie slugged it out. When June and July polling indicated Christie had a five-to-ten point advantage, Corzine's campaign needed to strike. The Corzine opposition research team began sniffing out Christie's dirty laundry – namely, the no-bid contracts for deferred prosecution agreements that had resulted in Christie being hauled before a congressional investigative committee, and Christie's abuse of travel allowances for him and his staff while he served as United States Attorney. Besides the intention to go on the offensive against Christie, the campaign strategists also planned to take advantage of President Obama's popularity in New Jersey by convincing him to come in and personally stump for Corzine.

Christie's confidants at the United State's Attorney's Office, Michele Brown and Ralph Marra, were aware of the Freedom of Information Act requests looking for travel records that had been served on their office by the Corzine campaign. Brown, a Christie pit-bull, took the information requests out of the hands of staff and personally took charge of the matter, despite the fact that some of the documents being asked for pertained to her. Inserting herself into the process was a clear conflict of interest. The Corzine campaign was stonewalled as Michele Brown shoved their information requests into the deep-freeze. Another development had the potential of putting Christie's United States Attorney's Office appointments also in the deep-freeze: the nomination of a new United States Attorney.

On May 15, 2009, as the Bid Rig III investigation reached its zenith, President Obama's intention to nominate Paul Fishman to succeed Ralph Marra as United States Attorney was announced. It was a nomination certain to be confirmed. According to *The Jersey Sting* authors, Ted Sherman and Josh Margolin, who had inside access and were privy to the commentary of the staff at the United States Attorney's Office, the announcement was a cause for concern. "Marra and his prosecutors knew Fishman and thought he was a solid lawyer who would do well in the job. But they also knew if he walked in before the roundup of politicians and rabbis in the Dwek case, he would stop everything in his tracks," the book reported.

Fishman was subsequently asked what he might have done had he been confirmed and installed prior to the eventual actual takedown day for the sting. "I don't know if I would have pressed the 'pause' button, but I certainly would have wanted to wait." According to *The Jersey Sting*, "Marra and Michele Brown and Jimmy Nobile and Brian Howe and the rest of the crew did not want to wait for Fishman.... The U.S. Attorney has extraordinary authority, and just because hundreds of thousands – if not millions – had been spent, Fishman as the new boss would have been well within his right to review the case and simply exercise 'prosecutorial discretion' to turn it off. They just didn't want to chance it." Certainly not with the stakes that they had riding on Christie's election – capturing the governorship and the Trenton patronage that came with it.

It was time for the United States Attorney's Office to lay out the charges and plot the arrests of the targets in the Bid Rig III investigation. According to Department of Justice sources, Michele Brown inserted herself into the process as well; insisting that arrests went down before a new United States Attorney took office, in order for Christie to be credited with the sting.

The Shoehorn

Confronted with a sting chock-full of election conduct captured on tapes as evidence, the prosecutors had their work cut out. Rather than waste the millions of dollars already invested in the investigation, the government tried to be creative and shoehorn campaign conduct and state violations into federal extortion, bribery, and mail fraud charges. They did so by alleging that conspiracy and attempt were the "legal alchemy" that could provide the coercive element of a crime that legally only a public official could commit. They wanted to prosecute candidates for office as public officials when their guidelines and the law said they could not.

The government could not change the evidence that was already caught on tape and which would have to be presented to grand juries, so they would have to change the status of the targets. The prosecutors labeled candidates for office as *future public officials* and charged them with conspiracy. There had never been a prosecution in the history of United States jurisprudence to implement the tactic, but the prosecutors had little choice. The crime *du jour* for charging all of the defendants would be the federal extortion statute, otherwise known as the Hobbs Act.

The decision to distort the Hobbs Act by applying it to non-public officials was cited as an ill-advised strategy in the United States Attorneys' Manual, which quoted case law language to underscore the point: "We believe that, as a general matter and with caveats as suggested here, proceeding against private citizens on an 'official rights' theory is inappropriate under the literal and historical meanings of the Hobbs Act, irrespective of the actual 'control' that citizen purports to maintain over governmental activity."

The government had also charged me with the Travel Act. The Travel Act was enacted to provide a means for prosecuting individuals who conducted criminal activity in one state but resided in another: primarily criminal racketeering enterprises. The gist of the government's theory was that, since the significant meetings with Dwek, in my case, occurred in Staten Island, New York, I was then eligible for prosecution under the statute. Besides not conforming to the elements of the statute required for charging me under the Travel Act, the government had actually coerced what they claimed were those elements, and totally misconstrued the legislative intent of the law.

The government alleged that I was trying to avoid prosecution for bribery under New Jersey statutes by traveling to New York to execute the crime. There were several problems with this theory. First, despite Dwek referencing money he was giving to candidates as campaign donations, the New Jersey Statute curiously selected by the government for the implementation of the Travel Act was a criminal statute intended for use against public officials for crimes such as extortion and bribery, as opposed to the New Jersey Statute that regulated campaign donations and election conduct.

The Tenth Amendment prohibits federal intervention in the prosecution of state laws that regulate election conduct; a prohibition clearly reinforced in the *United States Attorney Manual* and the Public Integrity Section's guidelines. The government had blatantly pierced the constitutionally shielded separation between federal and state jurisdiction. To cover their tracks they were using the Travel Act and the New Jersey statute for bribery of public officials. The government's actions were tantamount to enforcing State campaign finance laws for local elections through an unjustified and contrived federal investigation, which was clearly prohibited by the United States Constitution.

Second, the legislative intent of the New Jersey legislature came into play. By constructing bribery statutes enforceable in the laws governing New Jersey's election conduct, it was clear that the legislature did not intend for the public official bribery statute to be used for the policing of elections by the very fact that they had enacted laws to capture such conduct and, specifically, the conduct of candidates for office.

Third, the provision of the statute the government cited was limited to the prosecution of a bribe giver and not a bribe recipient – as they were charging me. This was borne out by the fact that the New Jersey sample jury charges for the crime have two charges – one for a bribe giver and one for a bribe recipient. It also so happened that all of the case laws that were later cited in government briefs dealt with the prosecution of a bribe giver and not a bribe recipient. The prosecutors were trying me as an alleged bribe recipient using the theory derived from the prosecutions of bribe givers. This was a strong indication that the prosecutors had intentionally misled the grand jury on the application of the law.

Finally, the government, through Dwek, had established the key out-of-State element that was necessary to trigger the Travel Act. On no less than seven occasions, Solomon Dwek stated his preference for meetings to occur in New York. Dwek's conduct was caught on his own recording devices – it was clearly entrapment.

On subsequent superseding indictments, the prosecutors took liberties with the federal Mail Fraud statutes, again converting election conduct into federal crimes. The government represented Dwek's money as bribes to satisfy the elements of bribery and extortion, and then represented the same money as legal campaign donations to satisfy the elements of mail fraud to the same grand juries. In some instances, they represented the same evidence (money) as a bribe and as a legitimate campaign donation in the same indictment.

The government theory for charging Mail Fraud was that since the money being given by Dwek to the defendants who were candidates for office was characterized as campaign donations, then by allegedly pocketing the money, they were defrauding other running mates on their slate of candidates or themselves. Since the money was not claimed on campaign finance reports as a donation, then the mailing of a fraudulent campaign finance report provided the elements necessary to sustain the Mail Fraud charge – or so the government felt. The theory seemed to conflict with the theory of prosecution stated in the indictments for sustaining the extortion charges.

It is clear from reading indictments alleging mail fraud that, in order to sustain the charge, the government had to represent the evidence in question to be legal "contributions" as defined by New Jersey campaign finance and election laws. Since by law, a candidate cannot deposit a bribe into a campaign account, the identical monies deposited into the accounts could not then be represented as a bribe to the same grand jury in order to satisfy a bribery charge in the same indictment.

If the candidate did not deposit the money into the account then the candidate had defeated the object of the conspiracy as cited by the government in the indictments: "to fund the election campaign and otherwise support the election" of the targeted defendant. This also eliminated the element of fraud in the mail fraud charges, because the running mates of a candidate for public office were not entitled to bribes, and, therefore, even if the candidate had pocketed a donation intended as a bribe, the candidate could not defraud any running mates of something to which they were not entitled.

While the government may represent that it has the prerogative to present alternate theories of prosecution, the same evidence cannot be represented to sustain opposing theories of prosecution when it would only serve to confuse a grand jury, as well as the charges to the trial jury. Such actions would thus infringe on due process by not showing the defendants, with any degree of accuracy, to what extent they may plead to or contest charges in the event of a subsequent prosecution. The indictments could not likewise accurately reflect the elements of the offenses that were charged.

Incredibly, the government exclusively charged me with Misprision of a Felony, an almost antique law. The indictment alleged that I failed to report a crime that they alleged my brother and Ed Cheatam had committed: bribery. If I had observed any illegal activity, *which I did not,* I would have been part of the overall conspiracy. Compelling someone to implicate themselves in a crime is contrary to their right of due process.

The government had so stretched the legislative intent of the criminal statutes that they should have used a contortionist to write the indictments. They gambled that the poor Hudson County politicians would never be able to mount the resources necessary to fight a federal criminal prosecution, and just plead out. They took the chance that New Jersey's press corps was not perceptive enough and too lazy to pick up on their legal gambit. Then, with all the bold arrogance afforded them by their unchecked legal authority, they rolled the dice and attempted to run up a record-breaking body count for their sting.

The Second Longest Day: Election Day Comes Early

"Some began calling it the 'Normandy invasion.'" That is how Acting United States Attorney Ralph Marra described the execution of the FBI sting dubbed Bid Rig III to *Star-Ledger* reporter Josh Margolin. Margolin and *Ledger* reporter Ted Sherman would later write their own synopsis of D-Day II in their book entitled *The Jersey Sting.* The book depicts an unprecedented detailed description of the massive arrests executed from the FBI Headquarters command center in Newark, at 4:30 in the morning that July 23, 2009– a rare and unheard of privilege extended to the reporters by the government.

"Hundreds of federal agents gathered in the early morning darkness ... from Jersey City to Deal in a coordinated operation of military-style precision that shattered New Jersey's political landscape.... He [Marra] said it was like the Normandy invasion for two reasons: the large numbers involved and also the fact that once launched you just had to wait, hoping that nothing would go wrong. 'The ships are out there; they're on their way. You're not calling them back,'" Margolin wrote in his August 2009 follow-up newspaper story on the mass arrests. Snap, crackle, pop! "The morning of the arrests, Marra hurried through a bowl of corn flakes and blueberries at his home in Cranford and was in the office in Newark by 7:30 a.m. as the FBI teams and other federal agents swept across the state."

The Bid Rig III takedown had massive press exposure on virtually every major news media outlet throughout the country and across New Jersey. Unlike the actual D-Day, there was no press blackout leading up to the execution of Bid Rig III. There was a great deal of detailed planning given to maximizing media exposure. Press leaks and well-choreographed press conferences were framed around the arrestee's arraignments, and timed perfectly so the media could cover each event. Despite post-9/11, 2001 precautions for security surrounding government buildings, easy access to the garage entrance at the back of Newark's FBI Headquarters was made available for the media to drive up and position cameras.

The media had enough time to literally sketch pictures of the defendants during the slow parade of perp walks. Likewise, the government made sure that the only way to exit the Federal Courthouse in Newark was through the front doors, where a galaxy of reporters greeted each defendant exiting the building at the conclusion of the long day's events. The trek from the front steps of the building to nearby parking lots was like running a gauntlet.

In the official press release issued by the United States Attorney's Office and written by Public Affairs Officer, and soon to be Governor Christie's spokesperson, Michael Drewniak, Bid Rig III was described as "a two-track federal investigation of public corruption and high-volume, international money laundering conspiracy," charging 44 individuals. In actuality, only 43 arrest warrants were issued for individuals – my brother Ronald Manzo was counted twice. Two more defendants who would be arrested subsequent to the July raid, Acting Jersey City Councilman Phil Kenny and Ocean County Democratic Chairman Al Santoro, and were not mentioned in the press release.

Drewniak's news clip did its best to portray an abbreviated synopsis for what had otherwise been a very broad investigation. "Law enforcement personnel, with the assistance of a cooperating witness, first infiltrated a pre-existing money laundering network that operated internationally between Brooklyn, Deal, N.J. and Israel and laundered at least tens of millions of dollars through charitable, non-profit entities controlled by rabbis in New York and New Jersey.

"The investigation veered onto its public corruption track in July 2007 in Hudson County, where the cooperating witness represented himself to be a developer and owner of a tile business who wanted to build high rises and other projects and get public contracts in Hudson County schools. Through an intermediary, the cooperating witness was introduced to a Jersey City building inspector who, in return for $40,000 in bribes, promised to smooth the way for approvals of the cooperating witness's building projects."

The press release went to great lengths to tie together the recently concluded elections in Hudson County, along with the candidates running for public office and their associates, as a key component of the government investigation. "From there, introductions and referrals spread amongst a web of public officials, council and mayoral candidates, their operatives and associates – mostly in Hudson County, and primarily in Jersey City – who took bribes…. In part, the bribe-taking was connected to fund raising efforts in heavily contested mayoral and city council campaigns in Jersey City and Hoboken, and the bribes were often parceled out to straw donors, who then wrote checks in their names or businesses to the campaigns in amounts that complied with legal limits on individual donations – so-called conduit or conversion donations"

Acting United States Attorney Ralph Marra was quoted prominently in the press release. "In both parts of this investigation," Marra said, 'respected figures in positions of public and private trust engaged in conduct behind closed doors that belied the faces of honesty, integrity and rectitude they displayed daily to their respective constituencies.'" Practically all of Dwek's engagements with the candidates for public office were conducted in the middle of crowded public diners, restaurants and luncheonettes in broad daylight. Despite this fact, Marra's quote could not avoid the typical stereotyping of alleged corrupt officials, thus his use of the term "behind closed doors."

Marra's quotes were a bit bolder during his press briefings throughout the execution of the arrests and arraignments. "The politicians willingly put themselves up for sale," Marra told the press. "For these defendants, corruption was a way of life. They existed in an ethics-free zone."

A subplot to the morning's drama was the announcement that FBI agents were executing search warrants at the home and office of New Jersey's Department of Community Affairs Commissioner Joseph Doria, an appointee of Governor Corzine. As aforementioned, the FBI knew that nothing incriminating would be found during the searches. In *The Jersey Sting,* Margolin and Sherman captured a poignant portion of Doria's ordeal: "The agents finally left carrying empty evidence boxes as if they were full of documents, exiting through the front door in full view of the press. 'You walk out of my house with those two boxes, people are going to think you took two boxes of material,' Doria complained. It wasn't fair.

"'We can't help that,' the lead agent replied.'"

Against these news story backdrops, candidate for Governor and Former United States Attorney, Chris Christie, *just happened* to be conveniently and coincidentally campaigning at ground zero for the sting that day, Hudson County. There were media crews waiting. In another coincidental stroke of luck, Christie's campaign just happened to begin running anti-public corruption ads shot prior to the mass arrests. Soon those commercials were replaced with actual Bid Rig III-themed ads and references, which attempted to link Corzine with the Democratic figures who had just been arrested.

In the interim, despite the fact that Ralph Marra, Michele Brown and the other Christie appointees were driving the Bid Rig III investigations, *Harper's* Magazine contributing editor Scott Horton astutely observed, "The media proceeded to credit the man who launched and oversaw the probe for most of its course, former U.S. Attorney Chris Christie. As it happens, Christie is the Republican candidate to replace Jon Corzine as governor of New Jersey. He's running on an anti-corruption platform, and this news – which stole headlines for a solid week – helped to propel him to a solid lead over the incumbent in the polls."

No one could miss connecting the dots: the story of the sting was being driven by the public corruption angle, despite the fact that 18 of the 44 defendants were linked to the money-laundering takedown, and one for trafficking human body parts – a kidney. Several from this entourage were rabbis. Somehow, the money-laundering and organ-trafficking suspects just melded into the political corruption grouping in the reporting of the stories. The rabbis were used like Hamburger Helper – beefing up the numbers for the sting portrayed as a public corruption takedown. There was confusion aplenty, with much of the public left with the perception that all 44 suspects were involved in pure political corruption.

A few weeks after the dust settled, *Harper's* Scott Horton gave his take on what seemed to be purposefully created confusion. "Watching this unfold, it was hard not to notice how convenient it all was for the Christie campaign. The announcement reflected a substantial number of largely unrelated cases, but they had been aggregated and held for arrests all on the same day as a sort of batch-release. Whatever law-enforcement considerations justified this step, it clearly helped gain newspaper headlines. Moreover, the announcement came at the end of July, which is the last possible moment for indictments with political impact in an election year cycle. Department of Justice guidelines preclude a U.S. attorney from announcing politically-charged indictments in a campaign season, which, by general reckoning, would begin the following month."

Unbeknownst to the Department of Justice, the guidelines referred to in Scott Horton's column were meaningless, as gubernatorial candidates Corzine and Christie had charged right out of the gates after their primary election wins and were already in full campaign mode – engaging in a relentless, hotly-contested election battle. Just one short week prior to the execution of the arrests, President Obama had already visited New Jersey to stump on behalf of incumbent Governor Jon Corzine's campaign.

Because of the carefully staged notoriety for the Bid Rig III arrests, public corruption ascended to a front-page issue in the minds of New Jersey voters. Although Governor Corzine was not a target of the probe, the raid on his Department of Community Affairs Commissioner's office and home was something he would have to address. There would be no due process for Doria: Corzine asked for and received Doria's resignation that very day.

With the ramifications of the sting on the gubernatorial election glaringly evident, a large cross-section of print media and talking heads reflected on what it all meant. In his PolitickerNJ column on the day of the arrests, former EPA Regional Administrator Alan J. Steinberg predicted that "the corruption scandal would doom Corzine's re-election bid, as ethics would become a major issue again, thus helping Christie." Bid Rig III had turned the focus of the electorate onto ethics, and as State Senator Ray Lesniak, a prominent Democrat, acknowledged, "If it's about ethics, Corzine loses. Not because Jon Corzine's weak on ethics, but because it's Chris Christie's strength, and now it's national news."

Attempting to seize the stage from the former United States Attorney, Corzine's campaign attempted to portray Christie's ethics-themed campaign as hypocrisy, exposing and criticizing serious ethical lapses during Christie's tenure as United States Attorney. Corzine's campaign continued to bombard the United States Attorneys Office with more Freedom of Information Act (FOIA) requests, attempting to get a grip on incriminating and damaging documents regarding Christie.

Unfortunately for the Corzine campaign, Senator Ray Lesniak's words rang true.

So just how effective were the Bid Rig III arrests in altering the dynamics of the Governor's election? Other New Jersey political correspondents and those from academia seemed to be unanimous in the verdict: it was the game changer.

Ingrid Reed, Director of New Jersey Project at Rutgers University, commented, "It's something that he (Corzine) hadn't expected to deal with in the campaign."

Peter McDonough, Professor at the Eagleton Institute of Politics at Rutgers University commented, "The arrests will refocus attention on Christie's leading attribute as a corruption fighter. Despite what Corzine's campaign is saying about how much progress he's made, New Jersey set a new standard (yesterday) for perp walks. And that has to be good for Christie."

"It is huge," said Steve Adubato, a Jersey political analyst and co-host of a popular public affairs show, *Inside Trenton*. "It now frames the governor's race very clearly around the issue of political corruption."

Brigid Harrison, Professor of Political Science and Law at New Jersey's Montclair University commented, "The problem of corruption has been one that Republicans have tried for years to make hay with. This is, in my mind, one more sweep they will use."

A look at a track of the polling data taken during the course of the election bears these astute observers out. In the four consecutive weeks of polling coinciding with the Bid Rig III arrests, Christie posted his highest numbers (50 – 53%) and his widest margin over Jon Corzine (13 – 15%) – a lead that would eventually tighten, but one that Christie would never relinquish.

Writing in the *Bergen Record* on the day after the Bid Rig III arrests, columnist Charles Stiles focused on ground zero for the sting, Hudson County. "It disabled a sizeable chunk of the Hudson County Democratic machinery. The 19 Hudson politicians, operatives and activists who were expected to steer the get-out-the-vote machinery in November now have their wrists in handcuffs.... 'These are people who know how to get people to the polls,' said one North Jersey political strategist who has worked campaigns in Hudson County.

"When you get them off the chessboard, that's it. In one way or the other, they are the pawns on the chessboard but you can't win the game without your pawns.... No one is predicting that Corzine will lose Hudson County. But he needs to rack up 60,000-plus margins over Republican challenger Chris Christie. Failing to do so (as Democrat Jim Florio learned in his 1981 loss to Thomas Kean and his reelection loss to Christine Todd Whitman in 1993), he could lose the election, party analysts say. The hobbling of Hudson also comes as polls show startlingly soft support for Corzine among core Democratic voters."

In the end, Chris Christie became the first Republican to win a statewide election in New Jersey in more than a decade. The election's final vote tally saw Christie winning over Corzine by approximately four and one-half percentage points. Christie blew out Ocean and Monmouth counties – courtesy of Republican Party County Chairmen George Gilmore and Joe Oxley. Corzine failed to roll up the votes he needed in Hudson and Union counties. Middlesex County, which Corzine had expected to win, went to Christie. Christie's prior arrest of the former Middlesex County powerbroker, Senator John Lynch, helped to tilt the county Christie's way.

Commenting on the Hudson County vote tallies at the Bid Rig III epicenter, Political Columnist and Opinion Editor for Hudson

County's *Jersey Journal* newspaper, Agustin Torres, in his "Political Insider" column wrote, "The HCDO (Hudson County Democratic Organization) mustered 11,000 fewer votes this time (a 22,000-vote swing between the candidates). Massive FBI corruption arrests of political figures this summer was a turbo-boost for the eventual winner, Republican Chris Christie." Torres' observation corroborated *Bergen Record* columnist Charles Stiles' analysis on the impact of Bid Rig III.

Despite having a prominent Bergen County State Senator (Loretta Weinberg) as his running mate for Lieutenant Governor, Corzine just sneaked by in that County. The Democratic Party there was still in shock from Christie's indictment and prosecution of the Party's chairperson, Joseph Ferriero, which concluded in early 2009. A Federal Appellate Court has since reversed Ferriero's conviction, finding that the statute Christie's office had charged him under was too vague.

For Christie, Bid Rig III trumped Corzine's presidential endorsement from Obama.

"It was political. Marra was over-the-top. The timing of the thing was not about luck. Christie used his office as a political stronghold along the way. God bless him, but it doesn't excuse the behavior," then New Jersey State Democratic Party Chairman, Assemblyman Joe Cryan, would state.

"The Dwek case to Cryan marks the final act in a career at the U.S. Attorney's office in which Christie played the role of backroom boss with a badge," surmised the authors of *The Jersey Sting*.

Ralph Marra

Chapter Ten

Painting Conflicts of Interest as 'An Honest Mistake'

T he buried truth of how Christie's prosecutors corrupted the Bid Rig III investigation to help tilt the gubernatorial election in his favor did not take long to surface. Department of Justice staff, seemingly in the New Jersey District United States Attorney's Office, would play the role of a "Deep Throat" and *out* the corruption.

Comeuppance

I t started to unravel for prosecutors a few short weeks after the arrests went down. The Associated Press, quoting law enforcement officials, reported that Ralph Marra was "facing an internal ethics investigation over public comments that may have helped his ex-boss' campaign for governor."

During one of the nonstop press conferences on the day of the sting, when asked about corruption in New Jersey, the man who was in line to be tapped by Christie as the Senior Vice President of the New Jersey Sports and Exposition Authorities, said: "There are easily reforms that could be made within this state that would make our job easier, or even take some of the load off our job. There are too many people that profit off the system the way it is, and so they have no incentive to change it. The few people that want to change it seem to get shouted down. So how long that cycle's going to continue I just don't know." The Department of Justice has strict guidelines cautioning that prosecutors "shall refrain from making extrajudicial comments that pose a serious and imminent threat of heightening public condemnation of the accused."

The *Star-Ledger* questioned Patrick M. Collins, a former federal corruption prosecutor in Illinois who speculated, "It could be construed as an implicit endorsement of his former boss." Collins further inferred to the newspaper that "Marra's comments were particularly notable given his professional history with Christie, and the fact that Christie has centered his campaign on a vow to clean up the state and root out political corruption." Not to mention Christie's promise to hire prosecutors when he got to Trenton.

Marra's extrajudicial comments were the least of the misconduct issues for Christie to worry about, as *New Jersey Network* news reporter Zach Fink broke a news story that would send shockwaves through the Department of Justice and Christie's campaign. It turned out that Michele Brown, who had stonewalled the Corzine campaign's Freedom of Information Act requests to the point that Corzine's campaign staff filed complaints with the Department of Justice, had some skeletons locked away in her closet. By the good old-fashioned news-hound practice of document searching, Fink dug up evidence showing that a financial arrangement, obligation, and relationship existed between Christie and Brown, the First Assistant United States attorney who was kiboshing the efforts of Christie's campaign opponents to access public documents from the United States Attorney's Office.

It turned out that Brown had borrowed some $46,000 from Christie when, according to the *New York Times,* "Ms. Brown's husband lost his job and ran up credit card debt." The *Times* further reported that, "Mr. Christie said he and his wife offered Ms. Brown their help, and she accepted. The loan, which was recorded Oct. 22, 2007, with the Morris County clerk, carried a 5.5 percent yearly interest rate, with monthly payments of $499.22 over 10 years; Mr. Christie said he received a $500 check every month. He said that he charged interest because he thought it was 'important to have an arms-length transaction,' and that he and Ms. Brown agreed upon a rate that seemed fair." In 'fessing up to the hush-hush loan, the *Times* reported that, "Mr. Christie said others in the 'front office' including Ralph J. Marra Jr., now the acting United States attorney, knew of the loan; a spokesman for Mr. Marra confirmed that. But Mr. Christie did not disclose the loan to his superiors at the Justice Department, a campaign aide said Tuesday,"

Christie had also failed to *report* his loan to Brown, as required by law, three times: on ethics disclosure forms, on his income tax statement, and on New Jersey Election Law Enforcement Commission forms. If Christie had mailed those mandated forms to the appropriate agencies, he would have technically committed Mail Fraud, according to the standards for charging the crime by the United States Attorney's Office. These same standards would be used to charge some of the Democratic candidates in the Bid Rig III sting with fraud by mailing in an election contribution report that failed to account for donations. There was apparently no decision to charge Christie by the prosecutors, who had donated to his campaign, and to whom he had publically promised jobs in Trenton if he was to win the gubernatorial election. Washington DC turned a blind eye – the Department of Justice protects their own.

Christie put on a puppy-dog face and called it all an "honest mistake." The New Jersey media, still to this day, have swallowed his alibi.

In a letter to the Department of Justice, New Jersey Congressman Bill Pascrell called for them to investigate the matter. "Add this to the growing list of Christie capers. Is it mere coincidence that Mr. Christie's personal life is again in conflict with his public obligations? A prosecutor at his level should know that once he gave that loan, no matter how well intended it was, it changed the relationship between Mr. Christie and Ms. Brown. We have a right to know to what extent it changed. At the very least, this is a conflict of interest," wrote the Congressman.

An obviously embarrassed Department of Justice was forced to take action. David Halbfinger of the *New York Times* reported, "Justice Department officials told Mr. Christie's interim replacement, Ralph Marra, to remove Ms. Brown from acting as coordinator of the Freedom of Information Act requests about Mr. Christie's tenure because of the obvious conflict of interest, according to a federal law enforcement official briefed on the communications. Ms. Brown resigned from the prosecutor's office the same day, the official said." Brown's resignation saved her neck. Once out, the Office of Professional Responsibility had no jurisdiction to question her regarding her conduct.

In a not so discreet e-mail sent to his staff and leaked to the press, Acting United States Attorney Ralph Marra, promptly but indirectly blamed the Corzine campaign for the controversy. "I know how distracting these transitions can be, and this one has been made more difficult as the Office has been unfairly drawn into a political campaign through the barrage of FOIA requests; the purported controversy over Michele's personal loan, and a wholly trumped up (and then apparently leaked) complaint, reportedly about my generic and general comments at the Bid Rig press conference and the timing of the Bid Rig takedown.... We owe it to the public and ourselves to keep the work of the Office going at our usual pace and at our usual standard of excellence."

Marra's comments, which the media made public, so outraged United States Representative Frank Pallone that, within hours, he too was asking for a federal investigation into the circumstances and the principals. "Last nights comment from the Acting United States Attorney, whose neutrality in the face of the law is of paramount importance, makes it clear that he has completely compromised any sense of neutrality. I regard this as a serious breach of ethics. These statements and actions – or lack of actions – by Mr. Marra are even more disturbing in light of recent revelations about political and non-political activities undertaken by his predecessor, Chris Christie. Recently, through Congressional testimony, we have learned that Mr. Christie, while he was U.S. Attorney, sought and took political advice from Karl Rove. This appears to be a direct violation of the Hatch Act. Further, when it came to light that the second Assistant United States Attorney, Michele Brown, had received an unreported loan from Mr. Christie that she was in the process of paying back, Mr. Marra's office allowed her to continue overseeing the freedom of information act requests. This is despite the fact that they affected Mr. Christie to whom she was personally indebted," wrote the Congressman.

The October Surprise

Unfortunately for Former First Assistant United States Attorney Michele Brown, the truth had not yet finished marching on. On October 19, 2009, correspondent David Halbfinger of the *New York Times* disclosed that three Department of Justice whistleblowers had come forward to accuse the First Assistant United States Attorney of improperly using her position to leverage the Bid Rig III prosecutions in order to benefit Christie's campaign for governor. The revelation from Brown's colleagues became the subject of a *New York Times* front-page story in which David Halbfinger reported, "In mid-June, when F.B.I. agents and prosecutors gathered to set a date for the arrests of more than 40 targets of a corruption and money-laundering probe, Ms. Brown alone argued for the arrests to be made before July 1. She later told colleagues that she wanted to ensure that the arrests occurred before Mr. Christie's permanent successor took office, according to three federal law enforcement officials briefed on the conversation, presumably so that Mr. Christie would be given credit for the roundup."

Two United States Congressmen and a United States Senator excoriated what they described as unethical and illegal conduct on the part of the United States Attorney's Office, all demanding an investigation. "It is shocking to learn that a former deputy to Chris Christie was conducting a political campaign within the U.S. Attorney's Office. It was particularly distressing that this raw political agenda came into an office with a historic reputation for fair and unbiased dispensation of justice, and Ms. Brown went so far as trying to bring political campaign objectives into the planning of law enforcement actions.... Several incidents ... indicating a troubling set of facts that suggest at least one of his [Christie's] former colleagues coordinated with Mr. Christie's campaign to advance his electoral prospects," declared United States Senator Frank Lautenberg in his letter to the Department of Justice....

"On January 26, 2009, First Assistant Brown attended what appeared to be a senior campaign meeting at Mr. Christie's home. Also present at the meeting were Christie campaign consultant Michael DuHaime, fundraiser Jon Hanson and Republican political strategist and Christie advisor Bill Palatucci These undercover meetings continued for several months.... Also of concern ... should be testimony released by the House Judiciary Committee in which former White House Political Director Karl Rove acknowledged that, in late 2006, he discussed political strategy with Mr. Christie while he was U.S. Attorney regarding his intentions to run for governor of New Jersey. Mr. Rove went so far as to recommend a specific political consultant to the U.S. Attorney for his run. After Mr. Christie resigned and declared his candidacy, he hired Mr. DuHaime, the political consultant identified by Mr. Rove."

By this time, Michele Brown had found other gainful employment to fulfill her financial obligations, including the loan to Christie. Soon after her departure from the United States Attorney's Office, to fill her idle time, wrote Zachary Roth for the October 20, 2009 *Talking Points Memo*, "Brown takes a job at a law firm with close ties to Christie. The firm had represented one of the companies identified as targets in Christie's investigation of kickbacks among makers of medical devices. Brown had been the top prosecutor on the case, and she and Christie had negotiated a settlement in which the company paid a fine and avoided criminal charges." No, the United States Attorneys' Manual does not sanction such conduct but, by now, it should be evident that the Manual was to be ignored.

For that law firm, McElroy, Deutsch, Mulvaney & Carpenter, the payback was not forgotten: under Christie's administration, their state contract fees were boosted some $900,000. For Brown, the ostracism was short-lived, as she would soon be called to serve on Christie's campaign staff, later his transition team, and finally in his administration. She was recruiting and recommending for hire some of the very same staff from the United States Attorney's Office who had donated to Christie's campaign or were actively working the "ongoing" Bid Rig III investigation and prosecution – some of whom she had supervised before in such capacity. This included Acting United States Attorney Ralph Marra, Charles McKenna, and two Bid Rig III prosecutors – Christopher Gramiccioni and Thomas Calcagni.

Michele Brown's conduct made her by far the most egregious of all the members of the United States Attorney's Office. United States Senator Frank Lautenberg stated it bluntly, charging that Brown had "coordinated with Mr. Christie's campaign to advance his electoral prospects."

Christie and Brown, of course, staunchly denied any wrongdoing.

Slaying Goliath

After Christie's election and all of the campaign hoopla died down, the inevitable prosecutions of the Bid Rig III defendants progressed. My attorney, John D. Lynch of Union City, was about to make history and accomplish the unbelievable. At the time, the United States Attorney's Office was boasting of their approximately one hundred thirty cases and several years' unbeaten record in political corruption cases.

Immediately after my initial court appearance on the day of my arrest John told me, "I don't see a crime." Two of my brother Ronald's Attorneys, Samuel R. Deluca and George Tate of Jersey City, New Jersey, echoed the same sentiment. Some of the other defendants, strapped by their inability to finance a defense, were saddled with public defenders who worked out plea deals despite the fact that their clients were wrongfully charged. Private defense attorneys for others did likewise. Of the Jersey City candidates for election and their counterparts, only Assemblyman L. Harvey Smith, Lori Serrano, myself, and my brother held out with "not guilty" pleas. Mike Manzo, Jimmy King, Lavern Webb-Washington, Councilman Mariano Vega, Guy Catrillo and Phil Kenny pleaded guilty. Joe Castagna, charged as an accomplice, had still not been indicted.

John Lynch argued the case in court, with Sam DeLuca and George Tate collaborating on the strategy and the brief. As far as criminal defense attorneys go in New Jersey, Sam DeLuca was the Chairman of the Board. George Tate was a no-nonsense sharp legal mind that I had known since high school.

The trio made a great legal team. John Lynch put it right on the line, daring to charge in where other defense attorneys feared to tread. "My client was indicted for a headline," he prefaced in his remarks presenting our legal argument. Then he quickly addressed the issue of whether a private individual could be charged as a public official under the conspiracy or attempt provisions of the Hobbs Act, which became the great legal battle of my case's first set of pretrial motions and oral arguments. John Lynch, proffering a brilliant analysis, argued that the government's position would be akin to charging former *Smothers Brothers' Comedy Hour* comedian Pat Paulsen with extortion for making promises to supporters when he mockingly ran for President in 1968.

The gist of the government argument focused on their belief that the law was applicable for charging candidates even before they were sworn into office. They conceded the position that candidates for office were not public officials, but held firm that they could still be charged under the provisions of the Hobbs Act conspiracy and attempt provisions. Ironically, the government's courtroom position was in contradiction to the FBI agents who investigated the cases. Those agents considered that targets were future public officials for authorizing the investigations' continuance at various intervals. At the same time the government proffered their unique prosecution theory, they curiously moved for a superseding indictment; perhaps to harmonize any inconsistencies between the conflicting government theories that prosecutors might have presented to the initial grand jury.

There was not one single case law, in the approximately sixty years of jurisprudence since the enactment of the Hobbs Act, which had ever addressed the charges being lodged by the government. John Lynch hammered the point repeatedly that, without some existing color of public office, there was nothing to establish the element of inducement and, thus, no crime. The District Court Judge, Jose L. Linares, agreed. "The Government appears to believe that charging "conspiracy" or "attempt" is a legal alchemy with the power to transform any gap in the facts into a cohesive extortion charge.... The Court finds that they are not so magical as to altogether substitute for the coercion required by the statute," the Judge wrote in delivering his opinion.

The Hobbs Act charges were dismissed. "Essentially, the U.S. Attorney's Office in Newark suffered its biggest setback in about a decade," was how *Jersey Journal* columnist and editor Agustin Torres described the Court's decision. Within days of the decision, attorneys for defendants King, Webb-Washington, Serrano, M. Manzo, and Kenny were filing motions for dismissals and asking to retract previously entered guilty pleas. The government immediately announced they would be filing an interlocutory appeal with the Third Circuit Appellate Court in an attempt to have the District Court decision overturned. Effectively, all defendants were in a state of legal limbo until the Appellate Court ruled.

At the Third Circuit oral arguments in January of 2011, a prominent contingent of U.S. Attorneys, including the current United States Attorney, Paul Fishman, showed up in support of their argument. Among the assemblage were prominent members from the office, James Nobile and Christopher Gramiccioni, who had constructed and finessed the prosecution theory. It was embarrassing. From the get-go, the three-Judge Appellate panel besieged Assistant U.S. Attorney Glenn J. Moramarco's attempt to present the government argument. The distinguished jurists shredded and gutted, with their own legal acumen, the thesis being proffered by Moramarco. Fishman and entourage sat a few seats away from me, cringing with each judge's stinging criticism of his office's argument.

At one point, in a desperate attempt to rescue his case, Moramarco referenced Sarah Palin and John McCain, hypothetically suggesting that though they lost the 2008 Presidential election, had they committed extortion under color of official right, their election loss would not excuse their behavior. Embarrassingly, the panel of Judges reminded the U.S. Attorney that Palin and McCain were public officials and suggested that he revise his scenario by substituting someone who was not a public official; for example, Louis Manzo. Within in a month's time, the Third Circuit panel upheld Judge Linares' decision with a solid 3-0 Precedential Opinion decision.

"The ruling delivered yet another courtroom loss to federal prosecutors who are trying to vindicate the partisan methods that the Republican Christie used as New Jersey's U.S. Attorney from 2001 through 2008 on his way to his state's governor's mansion campaigning as a crime-fighter and reformer. But the loss by New Jersey's federal prosecutors of their last two jury trials in the case is unprecedented during the past decade," reported Andrew Kreig, Executive Director and lead writer for the Justice Integrity Project.

The next legal round involved the second superseding indictment's Travel Act charges that entwined the New Jersey criminal statute for bribery of public officials, and the obsolete Misprision of a Felony charge that was tacked onto my indictment. The government dropped my mail fraud charge, getting a whiff of John Lynch's planned argument in my defence. My brother by this time had pleaded out to his indictment in another of the Bid Rig III cases, and the charges against him in my matter had been dropped; the case was now solely against me.

John Lynch's brilliant legal brief and argument, along with his courtroom demeanour, was more than a match for the six prosecutors the government had stacked up against him. Lynch then dissected how the government had shoehorned circumstantial evidence into the elements of the federal crime they were charging. He dispatched every legal argument the government proffered with effective counter arguments and won the day. John also reamed the government out for basing their charges on speculation.

The government allegations were rooted in an assumption about what the government inferred from an approximately 30-second colloquy between Dwek and me, while he chased after me as I was exiting a restaurant. The colloquy from the secret recording was reproduced in the indictment, climaxed by the following exchange:

CW [Confidential Witness/Solomon Dwek]: "You got that thing I gave to (Cheatam) already, right?"

LM: "Yes. Yes, I did."

The government alleged that this signified the acceptance of a bribe. But it was all for show and an attempt to bluff me into pleading to something I did not do. *The government wanted me to lie.* They knew that their inference was false, having already deposed my brother about the circumstances, prior to and during trials, then accepting his answers as truthful. The government then vouched for the truth of his statements to trial juries and my brother's sentencing court in the other Bid Rig III case.

Moments before the aforementioned colloquy, the confidential informant had retreated to the restaurant's restroom, unable to record a crucial conversation of the other participants left at the table. The government knows what occurred during the tape's interlude by attestations from their own government's witness, my brother, that are documented in an FBI 302, which states, "Towards the end of the meeting, ESENBACH seems frustrated and goes to the men's room. LOU then asked CHEATAM if ESENBACH was going to give a campaign contribution or donation. CHEATAM assured LOU not to worry about it. CHEATAM then stated, 'if he (ESENBACH) says anything, tell him I have it.'"

The government assertions in my indictment are also contradicted by my brother's other statements, to juries and the District Court, that the government vouched for as true. It is documented in the same FBI report. "RON recalled LOU directing him to not set up any more meetings with ESENBACH. LOU specifically complained to RON that "no one's gonna tell me how to run my administration." LOU also instructed RON not to take any more campaign contributions from ESENBACH. RON did not want to get into a fight with his brother over the matter."

Finally, the government persisted with another false allegation that it termed "the promotion transaction." The government stated:

"Manzo acknowledged on audiotape that he was willing to promote Dwek's friend within Jersey City government ..."

The colloquy from the taped evidence the government relied on depicts that I acknowledged knowing that Dwek's friend [defendant Maher Khalil] wanted to become a department director and *not that I agreed* to the appointment. The FBI interrogation of my brother further documented, "... RON never had any conversations with LOU about promoting KHALIL in the Health Department. He recalled that LOU was angry about that coming up in the third meeting with ESENBACH."

Maher Khalil had been caught on a government tape telling Dwek and another defendant why he knows he *would not* receive a promotion from me if I were elected mayor. Another audio-tape in the government's possession indicates that Dwek told Khalil, subsequent to his meeting with me, that his promotion had already been secured through another candidate running for office. No charges were ever filed by the government pertaining to that matter.

The government was swimming in dangerous waters – they had vouched for my brother's truthfulness to the jury that convicted another defendant, Secaucus Mayor Dennis Elwell, and to the District Court that sentenced my brother. Now they were contradicting their own witness's attestations, and asking my trial Judge to accept their inconsistency. John Lynch argued that they could not have it have it both ways. This time, John had also filed motions of misconduct, accusing the prosecutors of breaking the law by failing to follow recusal guidelines and for charging crimes based upon political and personal motives. You could sense an uncomfortable uneasiness emanating from the Assistant United States Attorneys; no one had ever come at that them like this before. John Lynch had them off their game.

In a blistering 60-page opinion, dismissing all of the remaining charges against me, District Court Judge José Linares wrote what amounted to a law school primer, hammering the failures of indictment and the government's Travel Act argument into the ground. Judge Linares also tossed the Misprision of a Felony charge – he had ruled that my conduct as alleged in the indictment was not unlawful and, as such, exculpated my brother and Cheatam. "Since the Court does not find Defendant Manzo's conduct unlawful, principals Mr. Ronald Manzo and Mr. Cheatam cannot be found to facilitate it as a crime," stated Linares.

Linares' ruling was so sound and powerfully written that it dissuaded any thought on the part of the government to attempt an appeal. They were cooked. I was free!

The Greater Good

The *New York Times* reports that "prosecutors have the power to decide what criminal charges to bring, and since 97 percent of cases are resolved without a trial, those decisions are almost always the most important factor in the outcome. That is why it is so important for prosecutors to play fair, not just to win."

According to the National Registry of Exonerations, forty-three percent of wrongful convictions are the result of official misconduct on the part of the investigators or the prosecutors. In multiple studies conducted over the past fifty years, the Center for Prosecutor Integrity reports that courts punished prosecutorial misconduct in less than two percent of the cases in which it has been documented.

Had the Department of Justice initiated a serious investigation of the government misconduct in Bid Rig III, it would have put at risk some high-ranking officials within the Department. These were the overseers who simply covered for the sham investigation and prosecution of the Democratic candidates for office in Hudson County in order to benefit Chris Christie's campaign for governor. The fallout from such an investigation would have undermined, for certain, the nation's faith in its system of justice. So, for that "greater good", the government did nothing.

Whoever makes such calls might have reasoned that the only people hurt were the rabble that they consider comprises the political roster of Hudson County. The rabble they referenced to the authors of *The Jersey Sting* as either "corrupt or dead." What about the voters who were disenfranchised by the government's illegal placement of sting money into campaign coffers that corrupted election results? The same hierarchy could have come to the conclusion that the United States Attorneys did these voters a service by taking the "corrupt or dead" out of the picture.

The government's failure to preserve evidence and disclose Brady material served to help cover up their compromised sting. As Chief Judge Alex Kozinski of the United States District Court of Appeals for the Ninth Circuit remarked, in recently rebuking his peers for deciding not to sanction United States Attorneys who failed to turn over Brady material, "When a public official behaves with such casual disregard for his constitutional obligations and the rights of the accused, it erodes the public's trust in our justice system, and chips away at the foundational premises of the rule of law. When such transgressions are acknowledged yet forgiven by the courts, we endorse and invite their repetition."

So what happened to the Congressional complaints, documented in letters from Senator Lautenberg, Congressman Pallone, and Congressman Pascrell, that were lodged with the Department of Justice for the conduct of prosecutors running the sting? They were referred to an agency called the Office of Professional Responsibility (OPR), a self-policing office designed to police federal prosecutors– a redundant oxymoron!

Harper's magazine's contributing editor Scott Horton has written often about cases of misconduct reported to the OPR. "In theory, OPR exists to uphold the Department's ethical standards. In fact, OPR seems to have a double function. First, by engaging in infantile games of turf warfare, it effectively blocks the DOJ's Inspector General from doing his job. Second, when purporting to conduct investigations of wrongdoing, it proceeds at a glacial place, rarely succeeds in uncovering any facts, and, even when it does, usually issues a soft tut-tut, almost never administering any serious disciplinary measures. The DOJ consistently holds its own lawyers to a far lower standard than it holds others. In effect, OPR has become a whitewash organ for DOJ that specializes in whistleblower intimidation and shoring up U.S. attorneys engaged in highly abusive, and sometimes criminal, practices."

Commenting on the actions of the OPR for the *American Bar Association Journal*, Fordham University law professor Bruce A. Green, a former federal prosecutor and ethics committee co-chair for the ABA Criminal Justice Section, stated, "I used to call it (OPR) the Roach Motel of the Justice Department. Cases check in, but they don't check out." *Harper's* Scott Horton concurred: "OPR remains the organ of phantom investigations. The roaches go in, but nothing ever comes out."

Echoing that same sentiment in an interview with *USA Today*, Jim Lavine, the president of the National Association of Criminal Defense Lawyers, proclaimed, "OPR is a black hole. Stuff goes in – nothing comes out. The public, the defense attorneys and the judiciary have lost respect for the government's ability to police themselves."

USA Today, in its continuing exposé on misconduct in the offices of federal prosecutors throughout the country, revealed how extensive the problem remains. Writers Brad Heath and Kevin McCoy presented a series of blistering reports, which rocked the Department of Justice: "*USA Today* found a pattern of 'serious, glaring misconduct,' said Pace University law professor Bennett Gershman, an expert on misconduct by prosecutors. 'It's systemic now, and ... the system is not able to control this type of behavior. There is no accountability.' He and Alexander Bunin, the chief federal public defender in Albany, N.Y., called the newspaper's findings 'the tip of the iceberg' because many more cases are tainted by misconduct than are found. In many cases, misconduct is exposed only because of vigilant scrutiny by defense attorneys and judges."

Jack Wolfe, a former federal prosecutor in Texas and now a defense lawyer, commented, "Prosecutors think they're doing the Lord's work, and that they wear the white hat. When I was a prosecutor, I thought everything I did was right. So even if you got out of line, you could tell yourself that you didn't do it on purpose, or that it was for the greater good."

The prosecutors working for United States Attorney's Offices throughout the country believe they are untouchable. They are gifted public officials who are blessed to be able to walk between raindrops. Holding themselves to be above the laws they apply to everyone else is an inherent hypocrisy. They are the incarnation of the platitude *"absolute power corrupts absolutely."* To some, the law and the administration of justice was never a vocation – it was merely an instrument for advancing their careers and sometimes serving a political agenda at the same time. Is it any wonder that Chris Christie would think he could get away with finagling the Bid Rig III sting to help his election chances, or his administration could shut down the traffic lanes on the George Washington Bridge to get even with his political enemies, or that he could use federal disaster aid reserved for hurricane victims as a political slush fund to advance his agenda.

If you are outraged by what you are learning, do not hold your breath. Only the appointment of an independent prosecutor outside the Department of Justice, or a serious congressional investigation, could ever ensure that prosecutors are not using their powerful tools to advance their own personal and political agendas.

No one has the inclination or the guts to take such action. Therefore, federal prosecutors can break the law with impunity. They can arrest you on a whim. You just have to live with this frightening fact.

Chapter Eleven

Broken Promises and a Glimpse of a Christie Presidency

With the aid of the Bid Rig III sting, courtesy of his friends (and future employees) in the United States Attorney's Office, Chris Christie won the 2009 New Jersey gubernatorial election by a comfortable margin. Upsetting a Democrat incumbent for statewide office in New Jersey is considered a masterful political feat. His victory received national attention and thrust Christie into an even larger spotlight – now he was prime-time news. Christie became an overnight GOP rock star. The kudos rolled in and Christie went to work right away, translating his victory into a mandate from the people for his agenda. Acknowledging the victory, Christie continued to evoke his campaign pledge to "turn Trenton upside-down!"

Christie's in your face, what he coined, "Jersey style," made him a walking sound-bite for journalists and media outlets. Christie's oft' times candid and caustic remarks turned him into a *YouTube* sensation. The media could not get enough of him, and Christie pushed his advantage to the hilt. This former slick prosecutor would soon outmaneuver every one of New Jersey's entrenched Democratic *powerticians* – playing them off on each other to suit his own agenda. He beat them at their own game, many times embarrassing some of the sharpest New Jersey political heavyweights.

The Man Behind the Mirror

It did not take Christie long to begin manipulating his Trenton political adversaries. Within moments of his swearing in, he had the Senate President and Speaker of the General Assembly performing at his whim. During his acceptance speech, he uttered, "So today, right now, I ask Senator Sweeney and Speaker Oliver to come and stand with me and join in a handshake of resolve and

friendship. In a handshake of commitment to stand for our principles – but to never abandon our duty to serve the people." Both Oliver and Sweeney temporarily remained seated in a state of shock,
only seconds later to stand and shake Christie's outreached hand as
he thrust it towards them in front of rolling cameras and thousands
of eyes. "We've shaken hands as a symbol for our citizens of all that
is possible in a future that demands that who gets the credit finally takes a back seat to doing something worth getting credit for,"
Christie concluded afterwards. It was a showstopper.

Time would tell that the "credit" which Christie spoke about
would all be his to claim, while Sweeney, Oliver, and other Democratic lawmakers were left with open and empty palms. He would
write his own history of New Jersey and what he was accomplishing and crediting to himself; a version that differed greatly from
the actual reality. Christie would soon embark on a whirlwind tour
of endless town hall meetings throughout New Jersey, as well as
guest speaking opportunities throughout the country. At each venue, Christie proclaimed accomplishments that could only exist in
an alternate reality, but the naive New Jersey citizen or the out-of-
state uninformed had no idea or could care less ... *it sounded good
and they liked it.*

Christie would also add an extremely lethal weapon to his spin
arsenal. Prominent New Jersey radio station, New Jersey 101.5, became a huge supporter of his policies. Christie was given a prime-
time weekly show, *Ask the Governor,* in which the news director of
the station would host Christie on a live call-in show for New Jersey
residents. Christie came off affable and composed, nothing seemed
to ruffle him, so unlike the rather uptight Governor Corzine that
he replaced. Corzine could not handle a radio gig; Christie thrived
with it. Christie ruled – the program was a huge success for the station, and it became a valuable tool with which Christie could spin
his agenda and attack his critics.

Christie was The Man on the dial and on a mission.

Christie had promoted an aggressive agenda through his election
promises as he campaigned for Governor – a tonic for just about
every one of New Jersey's ills. Lowering New Jersey's crippling property taxes, improving education, preserving property tax rebates for
seniors, and improving the State's overall economy were all staples of
Christie's campaign platform. He even went so far as to promise nev-

er to cut union pensions and, in so doing, managed to garner support from some police, fire and other civil service unions. "The notion that I would eliminate, change or alter your pension is not only a lie, but cannot be further from the truth," he committed in writing to a firefighters' union.

Distinguished *Star-Ledger* columnist and editor, Tom Moran, who covers, opines, and reports about major New Jersey news events for the paper, assessed Christie's integrity. "After he won, he broke all those promises right away. The centerpiece of his first year in office was the following: cut pensions, cut education spending and cut property tax rebates. And for the Bible-thumpers in the South, here's a revealing coda on Christie's style: Bill Lavin, the firefighters' union chief, later attacked Christie over the flip-flop on pensions. He said Christie sent a personal emissary who stated he was instructed to relay these specific words to Lavin: 'Go f— yourself.' Neither the emissary nor the governor's office denies it," wrote Moran.

Christie had an ally in cutting government workers' pensions, none other than a private sector union leader himself, State Senate President Stephen Sweeney, a Democrat, who used the issue to enhance his own political resumé. Over time, the general public had become envious of the pensions negotiated by the government workers' unions. In fairness to the unions, the problem posed by the enormous amount of monies owed to workers' pension fund was caused by the failures of a succession of Democratic and Republican administrations to adequately fund it. They used money due the workers' pensions as an offset to fund other budget items and to offer the public property tax relief and rebates, which were always fantastic election year gimmicks.

Christie seized the opportunity of the bipartisan support provided by Senate President Sweeney to push through an agenda issue that would play well for the national Republican Party hierarchy as well – standing up to unions. A nice feather in the cap of a Republican elected official looking to enhance his status as a national party figure. He downplayed the fact that by not paying the State's fair share to the pension fund he too was building up future debt. The *Star-Ledger* called the Governor out. "The dirty secret behind Christie's pension reform is that it allowed the state to delay paying what is owed," the paper editorialized.

Over time, that enormous pension debt would rise to staggering figures, crushing the State's finances along with its financial standing, which had been downgraded under Christie's administration. However, in the end, Christie had his sound bite, while the pension crisis time-bomb kept ticking. The *Star-Ledger* editorialized on that portion of the "Jersey Comeback" – Christie's pet name for the mess he created and defiantly touted. "The guy who keeps telling the world that he's straightened up Jersey's budget, has made it worse. How has he done that? By following Jersey's bipartisan tradition of kicking costs into the future. Christie Whitman did it. Jim McGreevey and Jon Corzine did it. And Christie is doing it, too."

New Jersey's worst problem, the nation's highest property taxes, was exacerbated by Christie's policies. Unwilling to shift the funding for schools, the lion's share of the property tax bill, off of property taxes and onto more progressive taxes like the income taxes or sales taxes, the property tax burden on homeowners continued to bury New Jersey families.

Christie's draconian approach consisted of forcing hard caps on New Jersey city budget increases and then cutting aid to those towns in order to trim the state budget. This slowed the rate of the increases but not the depth. When Christie broke his promise and cut the funding for property tax relief that had been previously provided through the rebate program, the tax burden for the average family increased by 20 percent during his first two years.

Christie was only warming up. He wanted to reduce the state budget a second year in a row and the cuts to government programs would be steep. Some Democratic legislators railed against him, but Christie did not fret. Rather than kowtow and negotiate with individual assemblyman and senators, Christie dealt with the very group of people he chastised when running for Governor and at his forums around the nation – Democratic Party bosses. Why argue about costs with Trenton street politicians when you can make a deal with their pimps.

Writing for the *Star-Ledger*, Tom Moran spelled out the theory. "Christie's smartest strategic move was to make friends on Day One with Democratic bosses George Norcross in the south and Essex County Executive Joe DiVincenzo in the north. These two control Democratic votes in the Legislature, as do smaller bosses such as Sen. Brian Stack (D-Union City). What that means is Christie doesn't have to herd cats in the Legislature to round up the Democratic votes he needs. He just has to keep the bosses happy, then watch them round up the votes. That's happened over and over. Pension reform. Property tax cap. Tenure reform. Higher education reorganization."

Between them, Norcross and DiVincenzo could bottle up any legislator's bill they didn't want. Norcross was Senate President Sweeney's political godfather. Speaker of the General Assembly Sheila Oliver worked under DiVincenzo in Essex County. Not many legislators were willing to take on the leadership of their caucus if they wanted any of their bills to see the light of day. There were coup attempts, but the uprisings were quickly quashed and the upstarts punished by forfeiting their prime leadership and legislative committee assignments.

For delivering the votes to Christie, the party bosses were rewarded with political pork for programs and initiatives they desired to see in their respective regions of the state. The co-operation of Democrats with Christie's agenda drew criticism from United States Senator Frank Lautenberg, bemoaning how he was troubled by the state's legislative leaderships' deals with Republican Governor Christie.

With a mere lip service protest for their partisan minions, the Democratic majority in the state legislature approved Christie's budget while holding their noses, thinking they had a gentlemen's agreement, or backroom deal, with Christie. They would give him what he wanted and in return pet programs important to their constituents would not be cut. The ink had hardly dried on the budget legislation when Christie took out his red pen and used one of the New Jersey governor's unique tools – the line item veto. Christie was going to have his cake and eat it too. After all, he had struck his deal with the party bosses and not the legislators; the bosses apparently never put the legislative wish list on the negotiation table.

The Democratic legislators had tried to restore money to a few of their favorite programs such as college scholarships for poor students and legal aid for the needy. Not only did Christie veto the add-ons, he also added new cuts in funding to the programs as if to spite his adversaries. As for the Democratic wish-list they had inserted into the budget, Christie cut $45 million in tax credits for the working poor, $9 million in health care for the working poor,

$8 million for women's health care, another $8 million in AIDS funding and $9 million in mental-health services. Instead, for his fellow Republican legislators, Christie used the money to provide $150 million in school aid for the suburbs, which resulted in money doled out to some of the wealthiest towns in New Jersey.

Christie also used his veto pen to slash the Senate and assembly office budgets, an unprecedented action, and then seemingly got even with some of his other antagonists by cutting funds from the nonpartisan Office of Legislative Services, the outfit that sided with Democrats on the year's revenue estimates. He even cut a fellowship program run by Alan Rosenthal, the Rutgers University professor who served as referee in that year's legislative redistricting fight and sided with Democrats, to Christie's chagrin.

The big man in Trenton who drew the brunt of Christie's tirade was Senate President Sweeney, who attempted to preempt the budget massacre when leaks about Christie's intentions reached him. *Star-Ledger* columnist Tom Moran recapped the ugly Trenton scene. "Sweeney had just risked his political neck to support the governor's pension and health reform, and his reward was a slap across the face. The governor's budget was a brusque rejection of every Democratic move, and Sweeney couldn't even get an audience with the governor to discuss it. The details are even uglier. The governor, Sweeney said, personally told him they would talk. His staff called Sweeney and asked him to remain close all day Wednesday. At one point, the staff told him the governor planned to call in five minutes. No call. No negotiations. 'I sat in my office all day like a nitwit, figuring we were going to talk,' Sweeney says."

Sweeney personally knew how hard Christie's budget scalpel would fall on some other perhaps unintended victims. Christie had cut the Early Childhood Intervention Program by nearly $8 million. Sweeney's daughter had Down's syndrome and he knew the value of the program, as he told the press. "I was very angry, but (Christie) sat down at a desk and said: 'Hmm. Early Intervention Program, I'll cut that.' When my daughter came home after 75 days in a neonatal unit, the first person she saw was from Early Intervention. It is critically important for disabled children to have that program. Why do you do things like this?"

The frustrated and angry Senate President was just warming up. He unleashed a torrent of criticism about Christie's actions for a crammed gallery of reporters covering the Trenton statehouse. "This is all about him being a bully and a punk; I wanted to punch him in his head. You know who he reminds me of? Mr. Potter from 'It's a Wonderful Life,' the mean old bastard who screws everybody."

Sweeney continued, "Listen, you can punch me in the face and knock me down, do what you want, but don't be vindictive and punish innocent people. These people didn't do anything to him. It's like a bank robber taking hostages. And now he's starting to shoot people.... I'm just so angry that he hurt people like this to prove a point. He is a cruel man. He's mean-spirited. He's angry. If you don't do what he says, I liken it to being spoiled, I'm going to get my way, or else. He's a rotten prick!"

Christie could care less; he had finally *turned Trenton upside-down*– just not in the way he had promised.

In Christie's third budget year, the Democratic legislature was on guard; they did not intend to be duped again. Despite declining revenues, Christie called for an across-the-board tax cut of 10 percent, while at the same time increasing spending. A rosy budget forecast was used to support the planned tax cuts, but that forecast was contradicted by Christie's later decision to borrow $260 million for transportation projects. New Jersey's public radio reported, "A state-by-state analysis by the bi-partisan National Governor's Association shows Christie's proposal increases spending by 7.2 percent. But Christie's office said the actual increase is 3.7 percent. The national average is 2.2 percent." There was a serious discrepancy in Christie's budget numbers. "Christie's proposed budget was predicated on state revenues increasing by more than 7 percent. Current figures for this year are about $287 million below estimates, his administration said."

The month prior to Christie's budget announcement, the neutral Office of Legislative Services reported that the combined revenue shortfall for the current year and the next was over $1 billion. Christie excoriated that well-respected non-partisan office, resorting to personally attacking its fiscal analyst, Dr. David Rosen, calling him, "Dr. Kevorkian of the numbers," and characterizing Rosen as a "handmaiden" of legislative Democrats who don't want to cut taxes. "Why would anybody with a functioning brain believe this guy?" Christie asked. "How often do you have to be wrong to finally be dismissed?"

Fixated on a tax cut, Christie reneged on promises to rely less on one-time revenue sources, raiding various funds and money earmarked for transportation, even raising the state's debt load for road and bridge projects. Noting the budget's declining revenue picture, veteran State Senator Ray Lesniak said the state could not afford Christie's tax cuts. "Nothing's changed as far as I'm concerned except that it's gotten worse," he told the media. "To pay for this tax cut would involve borrowing money and that's a fiscal policy that is not only irresponsible but reckless."

In 2012, Christie was being considered as a potential vice-presidential candidate on the Republican Party national ticket or at least a prospect for the party convention's keynote speaker. Christie needed positive budget news – it would make a great story to tell at the convention.

Still pressing for the tax cuts, Christie proclaimed that New Jersey's economy had turned around, and then launched a new campaign theme to accompany his speaking engagements– The Jersey Comeback. Christie's imaginary comeback was short-lived. The New Jersey constitution gave the Democratic legislature the ability to force Christie's hand early on, rather then to await another budget ambush like the one they'd suffered the previous year. Assembly and Senate Democrats followed up with their own proposals. Senate President Stephen Sweeney offered a tax credit equal to 10 percent of a resident's property tax bill, capped at $1,000. The Assembly wanted to use a "millionaire's tax" to help boost the credit to 20 percent and cap it at $2,000.

Realizing that he was not going to get his way, Christie announced that he would support Sweeney's alternative property-tax-credit proposal, but still lambasted the Democrats for not supporting his plan. Then, Christie had the rug pulled out from under him. Troubled by the dismal revenue projections in the budget they had sent to Christie, the legislators placed a stipulation on the tax cuts – they would be tied to the revenue actually materializing.

For Assembly and Senate Democrats, the economic indicators were alarming enough to cool their dueling tax-cut plans. They decided to set aside $183 million for a new property tax credit, but they would only pull the trigger on the proposal at the year's end and only if finances improved and the revenue could be realized. In defending the strategy, chairman of the senate budget committee,

Senator Paul Sarlo, called Christie out. "The governor's insistence on tax cuts now, before we know if we can truly afford them and six months before they would even take effect, is a platform built on national campaign rhetoric rather than fiscal reality," he told the press.

Christie lashed out. "We agreed everybody was talking the same language," he told a crowd at one of his town hall meetings. "I got fooled. And it's hard to admit in front of 750 people you got fooled, but I got fooled." Christie then vowed a summer tour of town hall meetings to berate Democrats and continue to press for the tax relief. "I am going to kick their rear ends from one end of the state to the other to get you a tax cut."

Christie also got even with his veto pen. Though he left some additional funding in the budget that Democrats had provided for the elderly, child care, cancer research and legal services for the poor, Christie red-lined money out of other programs the legislature tried to fund. "The governor quashed Democrats' plans to restore money for social services and other programs. He nixed a bill to pump $7.5 million into clinics for women, refused to return $66 million in energy tax revenue to cities, and vetoed a proposal to bolster tax credits for the working poor after slashing them in 2010," the *Star-Ledger* reported.

Christie then embarked on his "kick their rear ends" summer tour. It would be interrupted by prep time for his scheduled keynote address at the Republican National Convention, campaigning for Mitt Romney's presidential bid, and some startling economic reality news: Christie's policies had worsened New Jersey, not helped it. In September of 2012, New Jersey's unemployment rate hit its highest mark in three decades – a staggering 9.9 percent. "The state's unemployment rate has been climbing since January, when Gov. Chris Christie began boasting of a 'Jersey Comeback,' and is at its highest level in three decades. Only California, Nevada and Rhode Island have rates above 10 percent," the *Star-Ledger* reported.

Christie's administration was in a state of denial. Charles Steindel, the chief economist for the Department of Treasury, questioned the unemployment figures and said they were at odds with signs of economic recovery seen around the state. Steindel argued that the household employment survey used by the Federal Bureau of Labor Statistics to determine unemployment was less reliable than a payroll survey of employers. The payroll survey showed a gain of 50,000 jobs in the past year, compared with the loss of 47,000 jobs depicted in the household survey.

The spin continued. "These are two totally divergent figures, the latter of which simply does not match other metrics of growth in the state," Kevin Roberts, a spokesperson for the governor, said in a news release. "In 2009, when former Gov. Jon Corzine made a similar argument, Christie – the Republican gubernatorial candidate at the time – dismissed the Democrat's explanation," the *Star-Ledger* remembered. "Look, unemployment is up again this month," Christie stated at the time, criticizing former Governor Jon Corzine's Steindel-like alibi.

Senate President Stephen Sweeney characterized Christie's alibis another way: "This feels like Groundhog Day. Every month we hear the same bad news, followed by the same inevitable spin."

Not to be forgotten was Christie's brutal budget cuts to aid for New Jersey towns and cities. The impact of those cuts forced New Jersey local governments to lay off workers and contribute to the rising unemployment numbers. A respected New Jersey think-tank, Policy Perspective, issued an October 2012 report, which stated that 61,200 public sector jobs were lost from the beginning of the recession through the end of 2011. They argued that had those jobs not been lost, New Jersey's jobless rate would have been more than a full percentage point lower, from 9.9 to 8 percent. The report concluded that those public sector job losses had a ripple effect in the private sector, discouraging businesses from locating in New Jersey, making communities less safe and contributing to the shrinking of the middle class; all problems confronting New Jersey under Christie.

On top of the bad unemployment news, Standard & Poors was next to lower the boom on New Jersey's credit outlook, downgrading the state's status from stable to negative. "While Standard & Poor's did not change the state's AA- rating – one of the worst among the states – it warned the more drastic step of a lower rating loomed if Christie's nearly 8 percent growth in revenue failed to materialize," the *Star-Ledger* reported. For the New Jersey taxpayer, a lower credit rating for New Jersey would significantly raise the cost for the state to borrow money. "We revised the outlook to reflect our view of the risk of revenue assumptions we view as optimistic, continued reliance on one-time measures to offset revenue shortfalls, and longer-term growing expenditure pressures," John Sugden, a credit analyst for Standard & Poor's, elaborated.

The Standard & Poors analysis of the overly optimistic revenue projections were in line with the assessments that the Office of Legislative Services had provided to the New Jersey State Legislature, which Christie had so publically castigated. Ironically, while Christie was arguing over the estimates of the future revenue forecasts with anyone who dared to challenge his Jersey Comeback delusion, out of the other side of his mouth, he was whispering to Wall Street investors that he agreed with his detractors' revenue estimates. Correspondent Jarrett Renshaw broke the news for the *Star-Ledger*. "Gov. Chris Christie didn't hesitate this week to blast the state's legislative budget officer, who said his revenue estimates were falling short, but his administration has told Wall Street something different. The administration advised potential investors in a preliminary bond offering statement filed Wednesday that lower-than-expected revenue collections may cause a 'significant' reduction in the state's projected surplus for the fiscal year that ended in June."

Christie's damage control spokespersons quickly stepped forward to downplay the hypocrisy. Michael Drewniak, the silver-tongued wordsmith who followed Christie to Trenton from the United State Attorney's Office, exhibited his doublespeak. "This is nothing more than the standard disclosure that indicates the fund balance is only an estimate at fiscal year-end and always subject to adjustment in the audit, and that there are always uncertainties in the budget that have to be managed," Drewniak told the media. Former State Treasurer David Rousseau, who worked under Governor Jon Corzine, disagreed. Rousseau said Christie could say what he wanted to in public, but the rules were not the same when dealing with Wall Street. "This confirms what we already know: that the administration did not collect as much revenue as they had hoped."

With a state left reeling in the wake of a fiscal policy predicated on sound bites, and a populous swallowing every excuse and alibi that their Governor spewed, Christie remained untouchable. His popularity in polling continued to rise as steadily as New Jersey's economy fell. The *Star-Ledger*, New Jersey's dean of newspapers, sounded a wakeup call on its September 30, 2012 editorial page.

The paper cast Christie's attacks and very public budget battles with the Democratic legislature as intentional. "The governor's intention was to create a media stir that casts him as the guy who wants to cut taxes. And because he's so damn entertaining and funny, it worked again. This guy belongs on national TV, and it's starting to look like that is more likely than a second term as governor. Because no sane person would want to clean up the mess Christie has created. That's right, this governor, the guy who keeps telling the world that he's straightened up Jersey's budget, has made it worse," the paper opined.

In reality, Christie had done very little to fulfill his campaign promises or address New Jersey's ills. No substance. No long-term policy. Just plenty of smoke and mirrors. Did he really intend to fulfill his empty promises or articulate policy, or was he merely using the Governorship as an intermittent gig on the way to the White House? Nonetheless, because of his extraordinary cunning, Christie was able to convince a majority of New Jersey voters otherwise. Despite a variety of conditions in New Jersey steadily worsening under his watch, Christie was the proverbial political placebo – convincing some 54% of New Jerseyans that he was curing the state's ills.

Out of Order in the Court

One would have thought that, coming from the background of a Department of Justice United States Attorney, Christie's judiciary appointments would be rock solid. Instead, his handling of appointments to the New Jersey Supreme Court proved to be another of his administration's biggest blunders. Perhaps it stemmed from his declarations to redo the judiciary in New Jersey according to his brand of politics. "I'm being much more discriminating about who I renominate. They have bills in to rubber stamp automatically. I'm not doing that. You're going to be seeing me do less of that in the coming weeks. I'm doing this because I'm at wit's end about how to change this bench in the state," he declared.

The *Star-Ledger* had reported, "A source with knowledge of Christie's plans said the governor is targeting several judges coming up for reappointment in the next couple of months." The Senate Judiciary Committee Chairman, Nicholas Scutari, was concerned that Christie was targeting Democratic judges; a tactic that he warned would "destroy the integrity and independence of the judiciary." The prominent legislator publically chastised Christie. "This governor has politicized our judiciary like no other," Scutari charged. Pensive Democratic legislators stood guard, awaiting Christie's next move.

A Supreme Court brouhaha erupted when Christie refused reappointment to the State Supreme Court's only black member, Justice John E. Wallace. Wallace became the first Justice seeking reappointment to be refused renomination by a governor since the State Constitution was adopted in 1947. Christie consistently criticized the court, once calling them "the kings and queens of legislation from the bench" at a visit to Harvard University. "Mr. Christie has called the court too liberal and activist, particularly in a long series of rulings mandating more money for poor, urban schools based on language in the state's Constitution," the *New York Times* reported. Christie aimed to teach the court a lesson.

The legislature bristled back at Christie. From that point on, he was only able to fill one vacancy on the court in three years. A series of blunders, unqualified nominees with questionable background issues, and distrust amongst legislators caused the Senate Judiciary Committee to shoot down one Christie pick after another.

Finally, at the end of Christie's first term, the courts of New Jersey found a hero who would hit back. In an unprecedented speech before the New Jersey State Bar Association, State Supreme Court Justice Barry Albin called upon lawyers and the public to defend the judicial system of New Jersey from political intrusion. "Albin called on hundreds of lawyers and retired judges to act as proxies for sitting members of the bench when their jobs are being threatened by the governor or state lawmakers for political reasons or as payback for unpopular rulings. Although he did not mention Gov. Chris Christie by name, Albin, a Democratic appointee who has drawn Christie's ire in recent years, appeared to be returning fire today – focusing his speech on some of the judicial controversies of Christie's term," reported Salvador Rizzo of the *Star-Ledger.*

Albin's remarks seemed to strike a chord with the audience – he received a standing ovation. "When one judge is punished for issuing an unpopular decision, other judges take notice and may be less inclined to invite controversy, perhaps at the expense of the fundamental rights of some disfavored group. A judge should not be concerned about whether doing justice is a bad career move.... Judges will not always make the correct decisions. If mistakes are to be made, and they will, it is better that they made for principled reasons and not for political ones. Judges should not be courting votes. Judges should not be looking in the rear-view mirror.... The debates concerning the judicial article of our state constitution clearly show that the drafters wanted an independent judiciary, not a timid one," Albin commented.

Then Justice Albin made it personal, not only to the bar, but to anyone who might need to rely on the justice system. "You have a very good reason to be concerned about the reappointment process. When you appear before a judge, you do not want that judge to have any extraneous considerations affecting his or her judgment. The application of the law to the facts is all that should matter."

The Justice's words would echo across New Jersey.

Chapter Twelve

The Art of Placing the Blame Elsewhere

The Christie Pulpit

Seventy-seven years young, New Jersey State Senator Loretta Weinberg is one of New Jersey's most progressive thinkers. She has championed practically every landmark Democratic initiative for nearly two decades. She is often affectionately referred to as the New Jersey legislature's feisty Jewish grandmother. Her compassion for the most needy of New Jersey's residents is unending. Weinberg has been recognized as "Legislator of the Year" by numerous organizations and associations – particularly those representing the voiceless and downtrodden amongst us. I know Loretta personally, having served on the General Assembly's Health and Human Services Committee, which she co-chaired. Loretta also chaired the Democratic assembly caucus meetings prior to voting sessions. She is a wonderful soul.

As such a prominent and outspoken Democratic leader, Loretta was not a favorite of Republican legislators. Seeking the Lieutenant Governor's office as Governor Jon Corzine's running mate in the 2009 election, Loretta was cast in the role of attack dog. Christie certainly did not appreciate Weinberg's function, as he was her number one target.

After the election, unfortunately for Loretta, her entire lifesavings were wiped out. She had been a victim of the infamous Bernie Madoff's investment swindle. Striving to keep her head above water, Loretta was forced to begin collecting her pension from her prior career as a public servant. Since she was already collecting a public salary for her position as Senator, Christie sought to capitalize on Loretta's pain, suggesting that Weinberg had a "double standard" since she had advocated pension reform that was critical of such conduct. He quickly added that she was "hiding behind Bernie Madoff." Christie made his allegations before a full array of media assembled before the podium at a press conference.

Ironically, Weinberg had actually outed herself, as she reminded the press in response to Christie's attack. "To clarify, I've never attempted to 'hide behind Bernie Madoff', as the governor suggested in yesterday's temper tantrum," she retorted. "I've never tried to obfuscate or hide the facts. In fact, I'm the one who first detailed all the facts. The governor may be trying to play 'gotcha' with this issue, but I'm the one who announced it to the world. I've never sought to hide from or distance myself from the facts – unlike the governor, who has routinely tried to use scapegoats and distractions to divert attention away from his administration's own failings to look out for the best interests of the people of New Jersey."

Weinberg called Christie's attack on her a diversion from media heat the Governor was taking for failing to chastise other state politicians for pension abuse who were Christie-friendly and had rounded up votes for his agenda items. "While the governor is in full-deflect mode, he's made me his latest target to help draw attention away from his own shortcomings as a supposed 'champion of good government'," Weinberg said. "This episode has proven that Governor Christie can apparently dish the criticism, but is hardly able to take it."

Christie also offered his advice to the press corps as to what they needed to do in dealing with the seventy-seven year old widow. "Can you guys, PLEASE, take the bat out on her just for once," he implored. He then nominated Weinberg for a "hypocrisy award," and described her criticism of the pension abuses of Christie-friendly pols as "gamesmanship." Christie had kept a straight face when calling for a "bat" to be taken to the widowed grandmother, while seemingly working Weinberg over with a Louisville Slugger of his own. Paradoxically, one of Christie's appointed cabinet secretaries, Lou Goetting, was receiving his state salary of $137,000 a year in addition to a public pension of $87,000. No one called for taking a bat to Goetting; Christie gave his own appointee a base on balls.

It seemed the "bat" remark incensed Weinberg and fellow Democrats more than Christie's flip accusations. "Most disturbingly, Governor Christie used the words 'take a bat out on her', in his admonishment of the press corps to make hay over my pension,"

Weinberg said. "Frankly, considering I've devoted my entire legislative career to fighting for the rights of women – including battered women – I think his words continue to show the level of insensitivity and poor judgment that the governor has demonstrated on women's issues since getting elected. I doubt that the governor will apologize to me personally regarding this latest attack.... However, I won't hold my breath."

Senate President Stephen M. Sweeney was more direct. "In the past, the governor's rhetoric has been silly, disrespectful and generally unhelpful," Sweeney stated. "But his comment that the press should 'take the bat out" on Senator Loretta Weinberg goes beyond any sort of decency or common sense.... Residents rightly expect more from people in public office than horribly inappropriate statements, embarrassing temper tantrums and over-the-top bullying. It's time the governor started acting like a grown-up."

Anyone who holds a sufficiently high position of authority is provided a platform known as the 'bully pulpit', which can be used to bring issues to the forefront, due to the the publicity that a prominent public office can lend in arousing attention to a cause – good or bad. When abused, a bully pulpit is a powerful weapon of mass-communication destruction that can be used to demonize and turn public opinion against a prominent official's opposition.

Most officials who abuse their office utilize the extreme powers of that office to enforce their own personal political agenda simply because they can. They use those powers to attack their critics or anyone who would dare stand in their way. Most elected officials usually have department heads or spokespersons respond to their critics. It is the demagogue who, using all the trappings of his office, delivers the response himself. There seems to be self-gratification in doing so. Loretta Weinberg was only one of many who were to become the victims of Christie's bullying.

Snow White

The bully pulpit also becomes a tool to deflect attention away from a public official's *faux pas*, and Christie made ample use of it for such purposes. At the end of his first year in office, Christie decided to take a Christmas holiday – he booked a Disney World vacation in Florida. It so happened that the week Christie's vacation jaunt was scheduled, New Jersey was hit with its worst blizzard ever; a storm that buried some parts of the state in well over two feet of snow.

To make matters worse, the newly elected Lieutenant Governor Kim Guadagno, serving in a position specifically created for the purpose of filling in for the Governor when he was out of state, had scheduled a trip to Mexico to see her ailing father, apparently so sick that he needed a cruise ship vacation. "The Great Blizzard of 2010 shut down much of official government business, but touched off a storm of criticism, with a handful of Democrats pointedly questioning why Gov. Chris Christie and Lt. Gov. Kim Guadagno, Republicans both, basked in warmer climes – he at Walt Disney World in Florida, she vacationing in Mexico – while the Garden State shivered under a blanket of paralyzing snow," *The Star -Ledger* reported.

The cleanup response to the snow was botched. Apparently, the state had failed to plow major roadways that were relied on by other snowplowers for getting to New Jersey towns and cities in order to plow them out. The criticism poured in, but Christie's minions downplayed the plight of New Jersey's stranded residents, burying them in an avalanche of excuses. Returning from his vacation, Christie took the state by a storm of his own, immediately calling a press conference and taking to his bully pulpit for the purpose of deflecting the mounting criticism.

Listening to him praise his administration's inadequate response to the blizzard, one would have to wonder if he was still vacationing in Fantasyland. "At his first public event since a blizzard slammed the state, Gov. Chris Christie praised state workers and his administration for their response to the storm and said he wouldn't have done anything differently. Christie signed a letter in Freehold officially requesting aid from the federal government and then took questions, blaming mayors for people being trapped in their homes and Democrats and the media for the attention being given to his decisions to remain in Disney World on a family vacation while the state was inundated with snow," *Star-Ledger* correspondent Ginger Gibson reported. "I know who these mayors are and they should buck up and take responsibility for the fact that they didn't do their job." Christie said, deflecting the blame, while sporting a Florida tan.

When pressed about why he did not cancel his vacation when he knew beforehand the forecasted severity of the storm, Christie stood his ground. "I wouldn't change the decision even if I could do it right now. I had a great five days with my children;" further stating that his wife warned him not to "even think about" cancelling the trip. "I would have been doing the same thing here as I was there. I would not have been out driving a plow. I would be in a room somewhere on a telephone. That's exactly the same thing I was doing in Florida." Christie claimed he was constantly on the phone working out the response with the competent officials he had put in place.

Christie then took a swipe at some of the local public officials, who, while out tending to the cleanups of their towns, managed to be captured in news stories covering the blizzard. "You can decide to be a showboat, hop on a plow and act like you're doing something or you can actually put leadership skills to work that put competent people with good character in important positions." Many of New Jersey's small-town mayors could not afford a vacation at Disney World over the Christmas holiday; they had no other choice but to fulfill their obligations to the people they represented.

"If you live in the northeast this is going to happen sometimes," Christie summed up at his press conference. "We just have to be the tough New Jerseyans that we are and grit our teeth and get through it."

Too Tall a Tale

Christie also took to the bully pulpit when the federal government rescinded a much-needed $400 million in Race to the Top funding for education in New Jersey, due to the failure of Christie's administration to provide State-funding figures to the federal government during the grant application meeting. Christie tore into the Obama administration, claiming that his Education Commissioner Brett Schundler had in fact given the feds the information they had requested in a subsequent meeting with the feds, and that it was a federal government bureaucrat who had, in fact, screwed up by not accepting the submission. "When the president comes back to New Jersey, he's going to have to explain to the people of the state of New Jersey why he's depriving them of $400 million," threatened Christie.

The United States Department of Education then released a videotape of the subsequent meeting, the evidence of which completely contradicted Christie's claims (*Woops!*). Proving that he was nonpartisan when deflecting blame, an embarrassed Christie took out his Weinberg bat and slugged his very own Education Commissioner, firing Schundler for allegedly lying to him and making him look bad. "As I have said before, I never promised the people of New Jersey that this would be a mistake-free administration. However, I did promise that the people serving in my administration would be held accountable for their actions. I was extremely disappointed to learn that the videotape of the Race to the Top presentation was not consistent with the information provided to me. As a result, I ordered an end to Bret Schundler's service as New Jersey's Education Commissioner and as a member of my administration," a holier-than-thou Christie declared.

Schundler was no slouch and he did not appreciate Christie calling him a liar. He responded a few days after his firing. He distributed a collection of e-mails between himself and the Governor's office that indicated he had told Christie and the Governor's Chief of Staff, Richard Bagger, that the missing information was never provided to the federal government and they should not say otherwise. "I will not accept being defamed by the governor for something he knows I did not do," Schundler told the press.

He said he informed the Governor's Office that "the only way to accurately sum up for the press what had happened was to admit my team made an error on the application and leave it at that. But that idea, that you simply admit making a mistake, obviously didn't sit well with the governor because the next morning while I was at my office, I received a phone call from him. The governor said he was angry about the missing information in our grant application, but that no one was going to lose their job over it. He said he was about to do a press conference about the matter, and that he believed it is always better to be on offense than defense, so he would accept responsibility for the error, and then go on offense against the Obama administration. He was going to try to make the story about their picayune rules. He (Christie) was going to say that I gave the reviewers the missing information, but the Obama administration refused to give us the points we deserved, and that this showed they put bureaucratic rules above meaningful education reform."

Schundler claimed that he interrupted the Governor, telling him *not* to state that he had given the federal government the information. "The governor ignored my correction of his mental script. Whether accidentally or on purpose, he went ahead and said what he had wanted to say from the beginning. He shouldn't have. Good prosecutors don't support their argument with claims they know are false. And they don't charge people that they know are innocent," Schundler stated, sounding a lot like a lawyer for a Bid Rig III defendant. The truth seemed to matter little to the former federal prosecutor. Christie counted on the bully pulpit to be the great equalizer.

Tunnel Vision

Sometimes a bully pulpit can provide cover to distract or get even. On the cusp of the Schundler fiasco, October 2010, Christie made an announcement that sent shockwaves through New Jersey and was felt in Washington, D.C. Christie pulled the plug on a proposed Hudson River commuter train tunnel intended to double rail capacity between New Jersey and New York, which at the time was the nation's largest public transit project. The project would have linked Secaucus Junction, North Bergen and the western Palisades of New Jersey to midtown Manhattan. The *Star-Ledger* reported, "Tunnel opponents maintained the project was rushed together so then-Gov. Jon Corzine could get a re-election campaign photo opportunity at a ceremonial ground breaking in summer 2009."

Of course, Christie wouldn't be so spiteful as to kill a transportation project of such magnitude for the sole purpose of deflecting attention or settling a score ... would he? Christie took to the podium and blamed the impact of the recession and his estimation that New Jersey would not be able to afford the project's escalating cost overruns. Christie had a tunnel vision of his own. "The only prudent move is to end this project. I can't put taxpayers on a never-ending hook," Christie stated, abandoning more than $3 billion in federal funding that had been earmarked for the plan. The project was estimated to create 6,000 construction-related jobs and another 45,000 permanent jobs upon completion – seemingly the perfect remedy for a recession.

However, Christie was claiming that his review of the project found that the Federal Transit Administration was estimating cost overruns that could climb to nearly $14 billion. "Simply put, the

$8.7 billion estimate was a fiction. And, I'm not going to ask the taxpayers of the state of New Jersey to take it on faith that a project tunneling under Manhattan Island and the Hudson River will run even close to these cost estimates," Christie argued, further disputing that the state would be leaving the $3 billion on the table.

The reaction to Christie's decision was brutal. United States Senator Frank Lautenberg called it "one of the biggest policy blunders in New Jersey's history." The Senator further stated, "Without increased transportation options into Manhattan, New Jersey's economy will eventually be crippled. The Governor has sentenced New Jersey to a future of insufficient access to New York City, fewer job opportunities, and lower home values." It initiated what was to be an ongoing nasty and very public feud between the Senator and the Governor. His counterpart, United States Senator Robert Menendez, also harshly criticized Christie, claiming that the governor was "intent on killing the tunnel no matter what the repercussions." Menendez added, "The governor's public statements portray surprise and uncertainty about cost estimates, but it's hard to understand how he has so little control of and information about a project that is directed by his own administration."

According to *Star-Ledger* news reports, many Democratic lawmakers in Trenton were expressing beliefs that Christie's ultimate goal all along was to redirect New Jersey's share of the tunnel project into the nearly bankrupt State Transportation Trust Fund, which pays for road and bridge repairs and transit services. That would enable Christie to avoid increasing the gas tax to pay for the fund, generally considered a politically unpopular move. Christie wanted to build up a national reputation as a tax cutter. Assembly Transportation Chairman John Wisniewski said, "It was hard to imagine a more irresponsible decision. In one massive careless swoop, Gov. Christie has destroyed economic development in the region, crushed job creation in New Jersey and put public safety at risk for decades to come."

It did not take long for Christie to show his hand. As predicted, he eventually maneuvered the money that had been reserved for the tunnel project into New Jersey's Transportation Trust Fund. The revenue helped him avoid raising the gasoline tax, and provided him with bragging rights, as the Governor who cut and would not raise taxes, for his frequent speaking engagements around the country. Two years later, in April of 2012, the Government Accounting Office issued a report after its thorough investigation of the matter. The report found that Christie had exaggerated the overrun costs for the purpose of scuttling the job-creation-rich project.

Writing for Thinkprogress, an economy blog, correspondent Pat Garofalo highlighted the GAO's findings. "The report by the Government Accountability Office, to be released this week, found that while Mr. Christie said that state transportation officials had revised cost estimates for the tunnel to at least $11 billion and potentially more than $14 billion, the range of estimates had in fact remained unchanged in the two years before he announced in 2010 that he was shutting down the project. Mr. Christie also misstated New Jersey's share of the costs: he said the state would pay 70 percent of the project; the report found that New Jersey was paying 14.4 percent. And while the governor said that an agreement with the federal government would require the state to pay all cost overruns, the report found that there was no final agreement, and that the federal government had made several offers to share those costs," wrote Garofalo.

The Christie flub was eventually dubbed by many as his "tunnel to nowhere." The GAO report provided Lautenberg with one last parting shot in the matter. The Senator did not mince words. "The tunnel was critical to the future of New Jersey's economy and it took years to plan, but Gov. Christie wiped it out with a campaign of public deception. The future of New Jersey's commuters was sacrificed for the short term political needs of the Governor."

Christie would not forget Lautenberg's critique. And, whenever he could, on whatever issue he could, Christie climbed into the bully pulpit and launched tirades against the octogenarian senator, blaming him for Washington's failed policies and constantly referring to Lautenberg as a "partisan political hack."

Whirlybird

In May of 2011, the Governor went from an underground tunnel blunder to one that would prove to be sky-high. Christie decided to hijack a state helicopter that had been purchased with homeland security dollars for a shortcut to his son Andrew's baseball game and then a later political meeting. The helicopters were designed for law enforcement, emergency medical transportation and homeland security duties. The choppers outfitted for medical transportation "can be used to ferry executives" also, according to the New Jersey State's Attorney General's Office.

The *Star-Ledger* described Christie's descent from the heavens: "As the game at St. Joseph Regional High School in Montvale was about to begin, a noise from above distracted the spectators who watched the 55-foot-long helicopter buzz over the trees in left field, circle the outfield and land in an adjacent football field. Christie left the helicopter and got into a black car with tinted windows that drove him about 100 yards to the baseball field."

Christie also had a late-afternoon meeting scheduled back at 'Drumthwacket', the Governor's mansion located in Princeton, with a group of Iowa business executives, who were trying to recruit Christie to run for President. Montvale is some seventy miles away from Trenton, and perhaps as much as a two-hour drive in afternoon traffic. Apparently, to save time, Christie evoked the privileges of his office in securing the helicopter. In the middle of the fifth inning, Christie and his wife departed the game and headed for the political meeting back at the Governor's mansion. The cost of the flight would later be estimated at $2,500.

By the time Christie and his wife came in for a landing, the criticism for the Governor's joyride was just taking off. While not objecting to Christie's attendance at his son's baseball game, Assemblyman John Wisniewski complained, "The people of the state of New Jersey should not be required to pick up the tab so he can meet with Iowa donors at Drumthwacket. It's not just contributors, it's people who want him to run for another office with a political agenda. That's where he's crossed the line," Wisniewski said. "He's a governor who as U.S. attorney would rail against elected officials blurring the line. But this governor has selective memory and selective outrage."

Assemblywoman Valerie Vanieri Huttle, who represented a portion of the county where the helicopter alit, offered a different perspective, characterizing Christie's antics as typical of a "do as I say, not as I do" attitude. "I can't remember how many times I had to skip political events because my children had games or school activities," Huttle said. "Leaving in the fifth inning to meet with wealthy Iowa political donors says something about the governor's priorities. Perhaps his presidential courters can help him foot the bill so our taxpayers aren't on the hook for such perks when he is calling for sacrifice."

Even conservative Fox News talk show host Greta Van Susteren weighed in. "In these very, very difficult times for most Americans, it looks really bad when a politician is spending (or appearing to be spending) taxpayer money in lavish ways," Van Susteren commented. More calls came in calling for Christie to reimburse the taxpayers for his flight of fancy – including from Christie's frequent nemesis, Senator Loretta Weinberg, who in an MSNBC television interview stepped up to the plate and took a swing at the Governor. She saw Christie's use of the helicopter as proof of "certain arrogance that he has displayed that needs much more self control. I'd like to see the governor, for once, stand up and say, 'You know what, I made a mistake,'" Weinberg stated. "And I'm assuming that he will reimburse the state of New Jersey," she added.

State Senator Barbara Buono called for the Attorney General and U.S. Attorney to investigate records of the Governor's travel "to ensure that he has not made a habit of using taxpayer dollars for personal or political travel." Apparently, she was unaware of the United States Attorney's Office's complicity with crime during the Bid Rig III investigation and prosecution. "If these reports are true, the governor has potentially violated the law by using public resources for private purposes," she declared. "This is a serious breach of public trust and necessitates a full accounting of his use of government resources, particularly, the state police helicopter."

Initially, Christie sheltered in his office, hiding behind the words of press spokespersons who tried to quell the turbulence. They reminded the press and public that many other New Jersey Governors have utilized the state's helicopters and Christie was no different. "It is a means of transportation that is occasionally used as the schedule demands. This has historically been the case in prior administrations as well, and we continue to be judicious in limiting its use. The governor does not reimburse for security and travel; the use of air travel has been extremely limited and appropriate," was the company line. An assortment of New Jersey Republican legislators lined up to support the Christie position as well. It was to no avail. The incident had "gone viral" according to the *Star-Ledger,* and Christie's national brand was rapidly being tarnished by the affair. Inevitably, two days later, Christie took to the bully pulpit, using it as a control tower for trying to ground the orbiting story.

Christie decided to reimburse the state, but still would not admit he did anything wrong. He stressed the fact that he was only coughing up the money because the issue was becoming a distraction while he was trying to solve the problems of the state, and not for any other reason. In vintage Christie, he blamed the lapse on the Governor's Office limitations on fatherhood, and then common courtesy. "And, so if you want to try and do all of the things that people want you to do as governor. And, also be a father, and try to make sure that you get to as many of the things for your kids that you want to be at, there are times when it is literally impossible to do that by car," he began. "But, I also understand that this is a really fun media story for all of you," he then surmised to the press corps in a sarcastic tone. "I get it. And, you like to write about these things."

Christie then unloaded his own air-to-ground missiles, particularly taking aim at Senator Buono and Assemblywoman Huttle for their comments – they seemed to have managed to get under Christie's thick skin. "And, I love these folks, you know all the people in the political hack world, you know who just do this stuff and just jump on and start saying 'Oh this might be illegal. This might be this.' You know these guys are a joke. And, this is why the people of New Jersey reject that kind of politics. They know full well, full well, that it was none of that stuff at all. I'm not going to allow the media and the hacks in the Democratic Party to turn this into something that allows them to do what they always like to do, which is get away from the serious issues where they have to make hard choices for things that matter, 'cause they want to have a circus."

Then it was time to go for the jugular. "I also saw an awful comment by Assemblywoman Huttle, who should be ashamed of herself," he said, quickly reciting the Assemblywoman's quote. "She should really be embarrassed at what a *jerk* she is for saying something like that. I mean really, you know, to score cheap political points. We stayed every minute we could to watch our son play. And, we had people who flew from Iowa to come and have dinner for us, and we didn't think that it was appropriate to be late for them. I mean I just call that common courtesy. So I guess we know that what Miss Huttle cares about more is scoring cheap political points for her hacks in her political party then thinking about what you really do as a parent, or maybe that's what she does as a parent … I don't know."

Sometimes the bully pulpit was a lonesome place to face the music when things went wrong. During such awkward moments, Christie employed a strategy of deflection, even after claiming that he would accept the responsibility as Governor.

The Art of Deflection

Having pretended to eat his humble pie after the whirlybird fiasco, Christie would soon be serving up a plate of blame for somebody else to swallow. One of the Christie regime's worst blunders was bungling some $300 million of federal aide provided through the Troubled Asset Relief Program (TARP), to supply relief to homeowners who, caught in the grips of the recession and rising unemployment, began defaulting on mortgage loans. The funds were designated to help the soon-to-be homeless refinance or transition into cheaper housing.

Christie's Department of Community Affairs (DCA) Commissioner, Richard Constable III, another of the federal prosecutors hired by the Governor, established the New Jersey Home-Keeper program. It was allegedly designed to help people facing foreclosure keep their homes, but Christie's initial Department of Community Affairs Commissioner, Lori Grifa, had created guidelines and an application process so stringent that practically nobody qualified. Some $250 million of funding went unspent as countless New Jerseyans in need of assistance went belly-up and lost their homes. Constable's program was too little, too late. Christie took to the pulpit and deflected. He accepted the blame on behalf of his administration and then blasted the bureaucracy as if he had nothing to do with it. "Sometimes, I know it's going to be shocking for everyone to hear, government doesn't always work the way it's supposed to," he declared. Then his new DCA Commissioner took to a podium of his own to take the rap for his boss.

The boondoggle was particularly embarrassing for Christie, who had already been outed for attempting to divert affordable housing funds for the purpose of plugging holes in his budget. Christie held aside some $140 million in funds for low-income housing by deliberately leaving towns in the dark about how they should spend the money so that Trenton could justify snatching it away. The foreclosure funding fiasco reopened an old wound.

Another issue that dogged Christie was the Democratic legislature's attempt to pass a gay marriage bill. Christie vetoed the proposal but the Democrats continued to resurrect it, as it seemed to resonate with their constituents. Christie held that the Constitution provided no formal right to gay marriage. Then he stated his compromise, "I have been just as adamant that same-sex couples in a civil union deserve the very same rights and benefits enjoyed by married couples – as well as the strict enforcement of those rights and benefits." Christie also renewed his push for a voter's referendum to resolve the issue – perhaps believing that the votes were not there for the measure to pass. He called for the appointment of an ombudsman to ensure the state's civil union laws were enforced. Democrats found Christie's suggestions insulting, roundly criticizing him.

Christie, being Christie, took to the bully pulpit and fueled the fire, making one of the most outlandish analogies that one could imagine. He compared the gay marriage initiative to the 1950s and 60s civil rights movement, declaring that the activists of those eras "would have been happy to have a referendum on civil rights rather than fighting and dying in the streets of the South." Christie was trying to compare his call for a referendum on gay marriage to the civil rights struggle. The remarks went over like a lead balloon. Assemblyman Reed Gusciora, an openly gay Democratic legislator, likened Christie to George Wallace and Lester Maddox.

Christie fired back, calling Gusciora a "numbnuts" – double entendre possibly not intended.

Then the Democrats brought out their big cannon in the form of honored civil rights activist, Congressman John Lewis of Georgia, who was so incensed by Christie's words that he traveled to Trenton to respond to the Governor. "People of color in the American South … could not register to vote simply because of the color of their skin," he said. "Could not take a seat at lunch counters in restaurants. Could not take a seat in the front of the bus. Could not visit state capitals. If it had been put to a referendum, we would have never ever won," Lewis countered.

Christie wiped the whipped-cream pie from his face and humbled himself. He could not afford a no-win argument with Lewis – it could cost him his national reputation. Now in damage-control mode, Christie called Lewis an "American hero," declaring that he would have cleared his schedule to meet with the Congressman had he known he was in New Jersey. "Any time he wants to come to New Jersey he will be welcomed with open arms because he led an extraordinary movement at great risk and sacrifice to himself," Christie offered, quickly convening a meeting with Black leaders across the state in an attempt to bury the issue.

As for Assemblyman Gusciora, he took Christie's name calling all in stride. "I'll take the numbnuts comment as a compliment. It's a term of endearment," he said. "My college roommates used to call me that."

Beat the Press

Two groups that Christie relished pouncing on from his podium were the press and the New Jersey Education Association (NJEA): the teacher's union. When given the chance, Christie would lampoon reporters who tried to ask tough questions, often belittling them. It was risky, but soon even veteran reporters in the Trenton press corps were so uptight about being singled out and ridiculed in front of their peers that they succumbed to Christie's tongue-lashings and eased off. Christie's had tamed the tiger. The NJEA, which had spent a small fortune opposing his election, was vilified by the Governor at every opportunity. He usually laid the blame for New Jersey's number one problem, high property taxes, on the organization's doorstep.

Christie went right to work breaking in the Trenton press corps shortly after his inauguration, singling out one of the most distinguished New Jersey media writers, the *Star-Ledger's* Tom Moran. Moran asked Christie what the chances were of one of his legislative initiatives getting through the New Jersey legislature, given Christie and the legislature's "confrontational tone." Christie took it as though Moran was holding him responsible for the "confrontational tone." In a crowded press briefing room, Christie lectured Moran like a parent scolding a toddler. "You know, Tom, you must be the thinnest skin guy in America. 'Cause, you think that's a confrontational tone ... then you should really see me when I'm pissed," Christie admonished.

Then Christie broadened his rebuke to include the entire press corps, letting them know what they were in store for with the new Governor. "Now I can say it really nicely. I can say it in a way that you all might be more comfortable with. You know maybe we can go back to [the] way of the last administration where I can say it in a way that you wouldn't even understand it. OK? But the fact of the matter is, this is who I am, and this is who the people elected.... Everybody plays to their part. This is who I am. Like it or not, you guys are stuck with me for four years."

When Christie held a press conference concerning a water main break at a Monmouth County reservoir, during the 2012 budget fight with Democratic lawmakers, he asked the media to stay "on topic." A not too sharp reporter asked about the budget fight, and Christie went ballistic. "Did I say on topic? Are you stupid?" Christie chastised. Seconds later, he called the Q&A to an abrupt halt. Before leaving, Christie took one last parting shot at the now befuddled reporter. "Thank you all very much, and I'm sorry for the idiot over there." Take care."

When WABC television reporter Jim Hoffer tried to pin the Governor down about his administration's botched foreclosure bailout program at an impromptu press conference, he got the Christie treatment. "And who are you by the way?" Christie sarcastically asked. Hoffer answered, but he was only opening the door a bit wider. "From where?" When Hoffer told him he was from Channel 7, it did not phase Christie one bit. "OK, yeah, no – don't watch you," Christie responded with more of his gleeful sarcasm. Hoffer persisted in challenging the Governor's excuses for the failed mortgage assistance program, but Christie shut him down. "Don't show up once in every blue moon and think you're going to dominate my press conference, OK?" Message delivered.

Careful What You Pray For

As for the NJEA, they seemed to be under Christie's skin all the time. He assumed a scorched-earth policy for dealing with the teacher's organization – never missing the opportunity to attack them. He referred to the NJEA as the "bullies of State Street," because of the powerful clout they carried when lobbying lawmakers. At one point, the relationship between him and the union leaders got so cantankerous that the head of the Bergen County affiliate, Joe Coppola, jokingly asked his membership in a newsletter to pray for Christie's death. "Dear Lord ... this year you have taken away my favorite actor, Patrick Swayze, my favorite actress, Farrah Fawcett, my favorite singer, Michael Jackson, and my favorite salesman, Billy Mays.... I just wanted to let you know that Chris Christie is my favorite governor."

Before the congregation of teachers could start lighting candles, the letter was leaked to the public and the NJEA President, Barbara Keshisian, had to offer a formal public mea culpa. "Language such as that has no place in civil discourse. It was intended as humor, but it is not funny," Keshisian stated. "We deeply regret that the 'prayer' reference was included in the letter, and we apologize to Gov. Christie for both the content of the 'prayer' and the lack of respect it demonstrated."

Christie was quick to seize on the issue, wanting to demonize the organization in the eyes of the public. He ridiculed Keshisian's apology. "I wonder. They said they didn't intend it (the prayer) to be public," he said. "So private prayer for my death would've been okay. Public prayer for my death somehow is not okay." A few weeks later, as the teacher's union campaigned for candidates they were supporting in local school board elections, namely office seekers opposed to Christie's education agenda, Christie had a caustic comment of his own. When a teacher in Monroe Township gave students a homework assignment that involved finding out if their parents were voting in the school board elections, Christie pounced.

"These are the typical kind of scare tactics that they involve themselves in," Christie elaborated. "Scaring students in the classroom, scaring parents with the notes home in the book bags, and the mandatory 'Project Democracy Homework' asking your parents about what they're going to do in the school board election, and reporting back to your teachers union representatives, using the students like drug mules to carry information back to the classroom, is reprehensible." The "drug mules" comment drew as much angst as the Christie death prayer gaffe, but unlike Keshisian, there would be no forthcoming mea culpa from Christie.

Sometimes, more than just words were used for making a point. When Christie suspected former Governor Dick Codey of sabotaging his judicial appointments in Essex County, Christie decided to shoot hostages. He accused Codey of being "combative and difficult," then suspended the former Governor's State Police driving detail. He then fired Codey's cousin and Codey's former chief of staff from the state payroll. The *Star-Ledger* editorialized, calling Christie's actions "vindictive bullying." Said the editorial board, "So if you are wondering why people consider the governor a bully, and why so many politicians in both parties are too intimidated to speak out against him, look no further. This is a classic case."

And, sometimes, the bully pulpit hit the television airwaves through the *Christie on the Line* television Q&A show. When an irate parent called the show in June 2011 to protest Christie's budget cuts for education, she got a bit personal: "You don't send your children to public schools. You send them to private schools, so I was wondering why you think it's fair to be cutting funding to public schools," the women challenged.

Christie let her have it. "You know what; first of all, it's none of your business. I don't ask you where you send your kids to school. Don't bother me where I send mine," Christie retorted.

No Mister Softy

The bully pulpit was also portable, traveling with Christie even while he enjoyed a Fourth of July break, vacationing with his family in Seaside Heights. While strolling the boardwalk on a sweltering hot summer night, a passerby offered a derogatory comment to Christie concerning the Governor's education policies. Licking a rapidly vanishing vanilla ice cream cone, Christie demonstrated his dexterity by challenging his critic without missing a single tongue stroke on the tasty treat. "You're a real big shot," Christie taunted back. *Lick. Lick.* "You're a real big shot shooting your mouth off." *Lick. Lick.*

"Just take care of the teachers," the man responded, walking away to diffuse the situation.

Christie proceeded after the retreating target. "Keep walkin' away … keep walkin'," he continued to taunt. *Lick. Lick.* One of Christie's security detail quickly placed a hand on the Governor's shoulder and guided him in the opposite direction. Unfortunately, for Christie, someone with a cell phone recorded the ugly incident. The video clip was quickly posted on the internet and went viral, depicting an unflattering other side to Christie that many of his fans had yet to see. Throughout the entire ordeal, Christie made sure that not a drip of ice cream hit the boardwalk or his shirt – true crisis management skills.

These spontaneous outbreaks, what Christie liked to call his Jersey toughness, would take their toll on the Governor. Despite his high favorability in polling, eventually hovering over 50 percent, his negatives also remained incredibly high. And, not surprisingly, the most common negative attribute shared by a large cross-section of New Jersey was that their Governor was a bully.

However, Christie was able to convince many of those already supporting his agenda that his abrasive style was not actual bullying but leadership. People sometimes have a morbid fascination with watching someone else getting the shit kicked out of them; especially when that person has been demonized as the source of their own miseries. This is classic history, the style of ruthless demagogues and dictators since time began, which may explain why Governor Christie, despite his bombastic style and tendency to berate the meekest of individuals, was able to keep his approval rating hovering above fifty percent.

As for polling high negatives, that was a problem he would have to deal with. Christie needed to reach out and touch in order to soften the bully image. He needed a shtick. After all, as an old-time Hudson County political muse once told me, "Politics is just show business for ugly people." Christie's solution was to employ a methodology unlike any other ever before implemented by a New Jersey governor. He went out to meet the people in an endless parade of so-called town hall meetings – more than a hundred to date. This was Christie developing a magical alibi for the bullying and his caustic style.

Chapter Thirteen

The Magical Mystery Tour

The ever-transforming town hall meetings became hallmarks of Governor Christie's administration. The road show always packed them in; usually a turn-away crowd averaging a little over 500 people per event, unless the venue would hold more. They started bare and bland, but with each successive event, Christie, his handlers and staff tweaked the format and content, somewhat like a director might tweak the performances of a play in previews, getting it ready for Broadway (i.e. the White House). Christie's production crew enhanced what worked, cut out what did not, and always added new ripples to keep the show fresh. Whether you loved Christie or hated him, one thing you would have to agree on is that his town hall meetings were sublime entertainment.

As the issues affecting the state changed, so did the signage and decorum adorning the assembly hall, gym, arena or indoor stadium hosting the gathering. From "The Reform Agenda" to "The Jersey Comeback", Christie had a theme and catchphrase to cover any issue. During the budget season or the end of the legislative calendar, a numbers dial would be prominently displayed for the audience, reflecting the amount of days that were left for action on whatever legislative agenda Christie was promoting at the time. Signs exhibiting phone numbers and beckoning the audience to call legislators to demand action were also commonplace at several of the functions. The walls were adorned with huge American and New Jersey State flags.

It was at these forums that Christie created and fed the myth that New Jersey was doing great under his governance. Throughout the course of the road tour, the comeback myth would soon be weaved into audiences' perception, which soon became a widespread false sense of reality. If they still did not feel good or couldn't feel the love that night, Christie exploited the audience's despair, blaming their anguished station in life on his enemies – Democrats and any other politicians who disagreed with him, including teachers, police, firemen, government workers and bureaucrats, newspapers that criticized his policies, and the more than occasional heckler.

At a Cedar Grove town hall event during his 2012 budget showdown with Democratic legislators, Christie cast his adversaries as vampires. "Two and a half years into my term you thought the Corzine Democrats were dead. Well they're back.... We thought we'd taken a wooden stake and put it through this type of Democrat's heart.... I thought I took care of them for you in 2009. I thought I got rid of them for you. But they're back. The same way Jon Corzine came back to Wall Street, and you see how that went," he concluded, referring to the stock scandal that almost resulted in Corzine facing criminal charges.

The people at the town hall meetings overwhelmingly bought into the Christie message, sometimes prompted by seeming shills nodding their approval for everything Christie mouthed. In an exposé of the town hall meetings Associated Press correspondent Beth DeFalco wrote, "Christie doesn't deny that invitations are sent early to Republican-friendly groups, but notes that the events are seated on a first-come basis and advertised in weekly newspapers. He said that audience plants have never been part of events, but he hopes that an entertainment factor is: 'Sure, I want to be entertaining.'" The events were a 21st century medicine show, complete with all the snake oil that Christie could sell combined with a revival meeting staged to spread the gospel of Christie's politics.

"Part stump speech, part quiz show, part comedy hour," as DeFalco described it. Sometimes, while demonizing his enemies (usually the state legislature) as the cause of the audience's troubles, Christie would whip the crowds into a frenzy. Soon Christie's enemies were the crowds' enemies as well.

Even in such Democratic bastions as Hudson County, the Democratic Senator and Mayor from Union City, mesmerized by the Christie persona, introduced him as "the greatest Governor ever." Despite facts and figures affirming that what Christie was spinning was not so, the town hall crowds were content to remain in a state of denial. They were a lot like a crowd attending a professional wrestling event: what they were seeing was staged and unreal ... *but, boy, was it fun!* Christie was their matinee idol, and they even hissed at the Governor's political enemies. Christie had the audiences eating out of his hands. He was P.T. Barnum, with his audiences sprouting newborn suckers every minute.

The typical setting was a squared-off area of a hall or arena cordoned off by belt stanchions, somewhat resembling a boxing ring, but with the audience on three sides. In the center, or off to one of the inner sides of the ring, stood a small podium or conductor's music stand to hold Christie's notes. No one else entered the squared-off space, strictly reserved for the main man. A host of prominent officials and VIPs from whatever town was hosting the event typically sat behind and formed the backdrop at Christie's rear. Once engaged, Christie rarely turned to face them, keeping his focus on the audience forward, left and right. The staffers thought everything out; when the meetings aired on *YouTube*, it looked good for Christie to have recognizable officials sitting behind him nodding with approval of everything that he was saying. "His team of 20-something new-media guys" typically posted the *YouTube* vignettes. And, yes, Christie has his own videographer.

The show usually begins, if the venue has the capability, with a video highlight reel of the best of Christie's sound bites edited over inspirational music. Sometimes a hosting town Mayor introduces him, and other times a staffer with a distinct voice, as if mimicking a ring announcer, caps the anticipation by announcing "the Governor of the State of New Jersey, Chris Christie!" The Governor trundles onto the stage, relishing the applause and thanking the crowd. He brandishes a wireless microphone and bottle of spring water.

Almost immediately, Christie begins stalking the confines of the ring marked off by the stanchions. In a press interview, Christie described the moment. "I need to take a deep breath and whatever I'm thinking, feeling at the moment, I gotta get rid of it. Because when I go out there, this will be the one time for many people that they will get to see me in person, and they are going to leave with an impression. I want people to walk away really knowing me."

Christie quickly dispenses with some minor formalities. This is the part he plays by ear, sometimes acknowledging dignitaries in the house, other times not. Then he quickly gets down to business, delivering his monologue while endlessly pacing back and forth. "I'm not under any illusion. You all did not elect me for my charm and good looks," he told a Lake Hopatcong audience. "I believe you elected me because you believed that this former federal prosecutor might just be tough enough to take these things on."

Associated Press correspondent Beth DeFalco, in her April 2012 close-up of the town hall, captured what happens next, "He greets the crowd, and explains that he's there because being governor is isolating. 'You travel in a bubble. I never walk through a front door to any place any more,' he says. 'I walk through more kitchens than you'll ever walk through in your life. And that's not good for me to be walking through that many kitchens,' he adds, as the crowd chuckles, acknowledging the fat joke at his own expense.

"Next comes the stump speech, or rant, depending on his mood. Sometimes it's about why the public should support whatever plan he has just unveiled. Sometimes he uses the speech to rebut criticism, or to single out Democrats and Republicans who refuse to fall in line. Sprinkled in between are stories of his childhood, stories from the road and people he's met, and stories about his home life: picking up dry cleaning, getting in trouble with the wife, whatever cute thing his four children said or did that week."

After the monologue, Christie is ready for the main event – questions and answers and interactions, and sometimes confrontations with the crowds. This is the part of the event that audiences really relish – the source of much of the show's controversy. The media loved reporting on the Q&A segment – especially the give and take. Like a prizefighter shedding his robe in the ring, Christie escapes from his suit jacket. The crowd usually responds with gleeful chorus of anticipation: "Uh-oh." Like a wrestler's routine, this part of the performance is staged for effect. "It happened because I was hot as hell one day," Christie explained to DeFalco, telling her that since the crowds reacted he keeps on doing it.

Christie now preps the audience and explains that there are rules. Rules? "While other politicians shy away from shouting matches with constituents, Christie has made it his trademark," DeFalco clarifies. "I'll call on hostile people intentionally," Christie said. "I don't want people to think I'm only calling on people with the big smiles and Christie lapel pins." At a Lake Hopatcong meeting, Christie told *Philadelphia Inquirer* correspondent Matt Katz, "Some of you may have seen some of these town halls on the Internet.... People love the confrontational part." To avoid chaos, "rules of engagement" were established, and Christie's presentment of them is part of the entertainment.

The scene is reminiscent of a grammar school teacher enforcing classroom discipline. Christie prompts the crowd that they have to raise a hand in order to be called on. "I want everyone to hear you." He directs them to state their name and hometown, before they begin. "I don't want to have to say, `Hey, you, in the red sweater,'" he explains. Christie warns them about using the moment to make a speech: "When you get this microphone, there will become an indescribable but undeniable desire to make a speech. Take my word for it." Christie even cautions the brown-nosers: "Don't come up here and blow sunshine at me," he warns. "If you've got something on your mind bothering you, ask me."

Forewarned is forearmed, and Christie stresses and reminds them about the give and take. "If you decide that today is the day that you want to show off for your friends, if today is the day you decide you want to take the governor of New Jersey for a walk, just understand the rules of engagement before you start: We are all from New Jersey. And I think you know what that means." The line usually draws laughter and applause. Christie then sometimes reminds them once more, "If you give it, you're gonna get it back." As *Philadelphia Inquirer* correspondent, Matt Katz, described this much-anticipated part of the show: "It is part Roman Coliseum, with the masses hoping for the gladiator guv to slay some unsuspecting opponent – senior citizen, high school senior, no matter."

But why even give your critics a chance to confront you in an unscripted question and answer period? Christie recalled for De-Falco a piece of advice he was given years ago: "It's hard to hate up close." He went on to explain how the events allowed him to not only "energize his base but also reach out to his critics and let them get to know him as a person, not just a politician whose policies they dislike." Ironically, it is the confrontational portions of the town halls, posted on *YouTube* by his public relations staff, that have helped to turn Christie into a national political celebrity. Snippets of the these portions of the town halls, played on television and radio talk shows, prompted invitations for Christie to appear on those very shows.

During a town hall meeting in Florence Township, 34-year-old law student William Brown, a veteran of three deployments in

Iraq, decided to take the Governor out for a walk. Brown calm-
ly explained that he was upset that Christie was allowing Rutgers
Camden to lose the "Rutgers" name when it merges with Rowan
University, and thus robbing students of the "Rutgers" brand. This
became a source of much consternation in southern New Jersey. "I
know that all my friends in the military no matter what state they're
from respect that fact that I go to Rutgers," Brown told Christie.
"It's also true that none of my friends in the military no matter what
state they're from have ever heard of Rowan."

Christie tried to explain that current students would still graduate with degrees from Rutgers. Brown ignored the answer and
shouted back at Christie. "What about my son? What about my
neighbors? What about my friends?"

It was time for Christie to lay down the law. "Listen we're not
going to get into a debate here, ok. I listened to you. You're unhappy
about it. You don't want Rutgers to merge with Rowan under any
circumstances. Well here's what going to happen. Rutgers is going
to merge with Rowan and here's why –"

"It's not a merger," Brown interrupted.

"I sat here and listened to your story and your position – excuse
me – without interrupting you," Christie volleyed back.

"It's not a story, it's the truth," Brown retorted.

"The exchange continued with Christie's amplified voice boom-
ing from the speakers and Brown yelling at him from his seat in the
back row of the fire hall," the *Star-Ledger* reported. "If you decide
that what you want to do is put on a show today, let me tell you
something, I can go back and forth with you as much as you want,"
Christie retorted. Nothing was getting resolved and not only was
Brown taking the Governor out for a walk, he was yanking Christie's chain as well.

"Do you want to hear the answer or no? Do you want to hear
me answer or don't you? Because I'm not going to – I've heard you,"
Christie fired back to no avail. Brown persisted in yelling back. By
now, Christie had lost his patience, and it was time to move on.
"OK, next question," he prompted the crowd.

Police then took Brown by the arms and walked him down the
aisle. "I'm a combat veteran Navy Seal, how's that?"

As the police continued to escort the Navy seal out of the hall,
Christie gave Brown a sendoff: "Let me tell you something, after

you graduate from law school, you conduct yourself like that in a courtroom, your rear end is going to be thrown in jail, IDIOT!"

With Brown out of the hall, Christie made an apology for the Navy Seal's disruption. "You know, I tried to be patient with the guy. Every time I tried to answer him, he started yelling over me again and everything. Well, DAMN MAN, I'm Governor! Could you just shut up for a second?"

Outside, Brown shared his opinion with the media. "I thought he lost his cool," he said. "He was trying to shut me down ... I thought he's a bully sometimes and I don't think that's how a governor should react."

At a Rutherford town hall meeting, Christie was confronted by a schoolteacher upset by his budget cuts to education. Herb Jackson, columnist for the *Bergen Record*, covered the event. "A largely friendly crowd of about 150 people turned out in a church gymnasium to hear Christie deliver a half-hour talk that trashed greedy public employee unions and state laws that handcuff local officials trying to control spending. He then opened the floor to questions. A few were softballs, including the declaration by Clara Nebot of Bergenfield that Christie is 'a god' to her relatives in Florida.

"But borough teacher Rita Wilson, a Kearny resident, argued that if she were paid $3 an hour for the 30 children in her class, she'd be earning $83,000, and she makes nothing near that. 'You're getting more than that if you include the cost of your benefits,' Christie interrupted. When Wilson, who has a master's degree, said she was not being compensated for her education and experience, Christie said: 'Well, you know then that you don't have to do it.' Some in the audience applauded,'" reported Jackson.

In west New York, an apparent stalker, who had attended several of the town hall events, confronted Christie about having plants in the audience to ask him questions that helped make him look good. Seemingly, this detractor's conspiracy theory was not that well thought out, and Christie seized upon the moment to respond. "You really, in front of this group, with all the problems we have in this state, you're wasting these people's times with a question on whether we plant questions in the audience? If I plant questions, why the hell did I call on you?"

The crowd roared with laughter as the embarrassed stalker sat back down.

Crowd Pleaser

Once Christie wraps up the Q&A, it's time for the grand finale. At the end of every medicine show comes the sale of the snake oil. The part of the act where the deal is consummated. Christie was smart enough to lace his snake oil with a flavoring of apple pie, Americana, and good old mom. He usually summed up his rant with the heart-rending deathbed story of his last encounter with his mother – the source of his mantra "nothing left unsaid." Legendary Notre Dame Football Coach Knute Rockne's pregame locker-room pep talk, the classic "win one for the Gipper" speech, couldn't hold a candle to the flames in the hearts of the audience that Christie's monologue lit.

The quintessential version of Christie's 'mom speech' was delivered at a town hall meeting in Clifton, New Jersey, on November 19, 2010. Christie really nailed it at that afternoon's hour-and-a-half session. He typically meanders into the touching story by first forming a bond with the crowd. "Listen, I said most of what I wanted to say in my comments before I took questions. And I said more than I probably should in response to the questions." The crowd giggles. "So, I'll end this way. One of the great things about being Governor of New Jersey is your interaction with the people that you serve.... For someone who is born and raised here, there is no greater honor that you could have ever given me than to give the chance over these four years to the lead the state that I love and has been my home my whole life. And, we understand that 'cause we're from New Jersey. We understand that things are tough. We understand that people are gonna have some good back and forth's. That we're not gonna leave a lot on the table. That we're not gonna leave a lot to imagination. And the person who for me is the quintessential New Jersey person was my mom."

Christie injects a short bio about his mom. "My mom was born in Newark, raised by a single mother. Helped to raise her two younger siblings from the time she was nine years old and her father was gone. And, never went to college. Worked her whole life as a receptionist. And, by the way, in one of the most ironic things you'll ever hear, was a member of the NJEA," (the teacher's union that Christie waged a constant war against). The crowd begins laughing. "Cause she was receptionist in a school system and they made her join the union," Christie adds sarcastically through a wry chuckle.

Christie now begins changing his tone. A serious demeanor befalls the Governor. "But this will tell you about New Jersey families, New Jersey people, and neighbors, and friends; and what we are to each other, and how we treat each other," he continues, about to offer his excuse for why he offends so many; and in so doing garners the crowd's indulgence.

"My mom passed away about six and a half years ago," Christie blurts out. The words slug the crowd like a sledgehammer. There is no more laughing now. There is only the dead silence that waits for the pin to drop. Christie next relates a somber story about when he was in San Diego, late in April 2004 attending a conference for federal prosecutors. He received an urgent call from his brother, Todd. Christie's mom, who was fighting an insurmountable battle against cancer, was suddenly at death's doorstep. Taking a turn for the worse, Sondra Christie was rushed to the hospital. While she lay in St. Barnabas Medical Center in Livingston, New Jersey, fading in and out of a coma, family members began to gather to offer their last goodbyes. Christie rushed back to New Jersey.

In one of her lapses from the grip of the coma, Christie explains, his mom was cognizant enough to recognize him. Christie then elaborates. "I sat down and my mother is kind of in and out of it for a little bit, but she recognized that it was me. And, she said to me, 'What day is it?'

"And, I said, 'it's Friday.'

"She said, 'What time is it?'

"And, I said, 'It's ten o'clock in the morning.'

"And, she said, 'What are you doing here?'

"I said, 'I'm here to visit you.'" Nervous giggles erupt ... the crowd is grasping at straws, hoping to escape from the unpleasant ending they sense will ensue.

"And, she said, 'Go to work.'

"And, I said, 'Mom, I'd rather spend the day with you, if you don't mind.'

"And, she said, 'GO TO WORK – That's where you belong!'

"I said to her, 'What, are you worried that you're not getting your taxpayer's money's worth today? I'll make up the time, don't worry about it. I'd rather stay here with you.'"

Christie, his voice beginning to tremble, tells the crowd that his mother then clutched his hand. Even the coldest shoulders of

Christie's detractors are warming at this point. Lumps begin filling the void of laughter that had just seconds earlier resonated in the throats of the crowd. Eyes begin welling with tears. Hands are fumbling for hankies and Kleenex to catch the occasional teardrop that streams down the side of a face. "And, she said to me, 'Christopher, go to work, it's where you belong. There's nothing left unsaid between us.'"

Like Rockne, Christie is about to tap the nerve and spike the adrenalin of the locker room. "That's New Jersey, there's nothing left unsaid between us. My mother sent me to work because that's the values she taught me. There was nothing left unsaid between us because she was Sicilian – so you know there was nothing left unsaid between us." The laughter resumes for a second, but Christie is quick to deliver his punch line.

"If you're wondering who I am, and where I came from, and why I'm doing this, and why I understand New Jersey the way I do, it's because of her, because she taught me don't leave things unsaid," Christie continues in his tribute. "She taught me: Be yourself today, and then tomorrow you won't have to worry about whether you got it right or wrong, and who you told what version of the truth to. You just have to be yourself everyday. That's what I'm gonna' be as Governor for every moment you give me the honor of being it. And, sometimes you'll agree with me, and sometimes you won't. Sometimes I'll anger you, and sometimes I'll delight you. Other times, I'm sure I'll frustrate you, but the one thing you'll know for sure is that I will always tell you exactly what I think, and you never will have to wonder where I stand."

At this point, Christie has them enraptured. Forget about the "you're an idiot" remarks and having war veterans tossed out of the events. Forget about the "vampire" insults or telling someone to leave their profession if they felt they were unfairly underpaid. Those confrontations were the red meat for the vultures in the crowd who already had their fill. The story about mom was the schmaltz for everybody else … *and how they loved it.*

After Christie told his mom's deathbed story with such impeccable emotion, all was forgiven. For Christie's critics it was a fatal distraction. Whatever the crowd might have taken prior offence to in the proceedings was now just water under the George Washington Bridge. Transformation was complete, and Christie had successfully added and christened countless more minions in his cause.

Rockne could not have done it any better.

"I guess we just can't expect to win 'em all. I'm going to tell you something I've kept to myself for years -- None of you ever knew George Gipp. It was long before your time. But you know what a tradition he is at Notre Dame ...

And the last thing he said to me – 'Rock,' he said – 'sometime, when the team is up against it -- and the breaks are beating the boys -- tell them to go out there with all they got and win just one for the Gipper ...

I don't know where I'll be then, Rock,' he said – 'but I'll know about it - and I'll be happy.'"

Chapter Fourteen

Nancy Reagan Launches Christie onto the National Stage

With the benefit of hindsight, Christie's life and career depict a man who was never content with his status in life. A burning ambition and voracious hunger for power and prestige have been the driving force throughout his life. As he oft times demonstrated, he has been willing to climb any mountain, as well as cross any line, in order to achieve his goal – a continuous rise to power. Bid Rig III is a testament to how far Christie was willing to go, even when the cost was counted in devastating human expense: suffering others to pay the piper for his success.

The National Stage: "One for the Gipper"

It was inevitable that Christie the Governor had to be President Christie. Learning from the scars of his disastrous grab for higher power after being elected Freeholder, Christie came to appreciate the value of biding his time. He demonstrated this by not engaging in the 2005 New Jersey gubernatorial election after Senator Jon Corzine announced he would run. Christie could almost taste it but he held back, having learned that timing is truly everything. In studying how he choreographed his career and used the U.S. Attorney's Office to pave the way for his 2009 election to Governor, one can see that everything being done was with an eye to stepping up.

Christie needed to get national attention, an entrée to the people and powerbrokers all over the country. In the fall of 2011, amidst the backdrop of the preliminary lead-up to the battle for the following year's 2012 GOP presidential primary campaigns, the political gods smiled down at Chris Christie. The New Jersey Governor landed an invitation from ex-First Lady Nancy

Reagan to give the keynote speech for a dinner at the Reagan Library. Someone had to be pulling piano-size strings for Christie to land as the headliner at a marquee event like this.

The timing was perfect, as an early series of debates between the Republican candidates vying for the following year's nomination showed the field to be lackluster. The competitors' eagerness for the prize was making the contest ugly early on. The GOP was a party splintering into two factions – the traditional conservative wing, further emboldened by the new Tea Party activists, and the establishment Republicans, or the old guard, who were seeking to take the party in a more moderate direction. The darling of the party, early on, became Businessman Herman Cain, whose "9-9-9" tax cut plan was wowing audiences everywhere, enabling the surprising frontrunner to win several early straw polls. Cain's performance was making the rest of the field start to sweat. Mitt Romney, Newt Gingrich, Rick Santorum, Texas Governor Rick Perry, and Congressman Ron Paul all began to unload on each other, turning off Republicans and the public-at-large as well. The GOP base was asking itself: *Is this the best we can do?*

Enter Chris Christie. Keenly aware of the dissatisfaction with the current field of candidates fighting for his party's nomination, Chris Christie had a to-die-for center stage spotlight at the Reagan Library dinner event. He seized the opportunity and delivered a knockout performance, using all the hokum that he had fashioned so well during his series of town hall meetings across New Jersey. He already had the recipe; all Christie and his wordsmiths needed to do was season the ingredients with spices that would suit a nationwide audience.

Christie opened by saluting President Reagan's vision and leadership in guiding the nation. Like a political chameleon, the moderate-leaning Christie morphed into a staunch conservative Reaganite. The speech was polished and exceptionally presidential. Whoever helped Christie put it together had in mind a larger audience and a motive bigger than simply addressing the listeners in the Simi Valley library that night.

"Today, the biggest challenge we must meet is the one we present to ourselves. To not become a nation that places entitlement ahead of accomplishment. To not become a country that places comfortable lies ahead of difficult truths. To not become a people that thinks so little of ourselves that we demand no sacrifice from each other. We are a better people than that; and we must demand a better nation than that," Christie philosophized.

In case someone wanted to know if he could be the one to lead his party and challenge Barak Obama, Christie left them with little doubt, quoting and mocking the eloquent speech that Obama had delivered as he burst on the stage of the Democratic National Convention in 2004, calling for the nation to unite.

"Now, seven years later, President Obama prepares to divide our nation to achieve re-election. This is not a leadership style, this is a re-election strategy. Telling those who are scared and struggling that the only way their lives can get better is to diminish the success of others. Trying to cynically convince those who are suffering that the American economic pie is no longer a growing one that can provide more prosperity for all who work hard. Insisting that we must tax and take and demonize those who have already achieved the American Dream. That may turn out to be a good re-election strategy for President Obama, but it is a demoralizing message for America. What happened to State Senator Obama? When did he decide to become one of the 'dividers' he spoke of so eloquently in 2004?"

Christie then turned his guns on the Congress, but still held President Obama ultimately responsible for neglecting his leadership role. "We watch a Congress at war with itself because they are unwilling to leave campaign-style politics at the Capitol's door.... And still we continue to wait and hope that our president will finally stop being a bystander in the Oval Office."

Much like the way his mom and apple pie speech brought tears to the eyes of his Jersey town hall crowds, Christie's closing brought tears to the eyes of some in the Reagan Library's intimate audience. He quoted, line for line, Reagan's powerful and moving farewell address, when the Gipper spoke glowingly, one more time, of the infamous Shining City on a Hill. "I've spoken of the shining city all my political life, but I don't know if I ever quite communicated what I saw when I said it. But in my mind it was a tall proud city built on rocks stronger than oceans, wind-swept, God-blessed, and teeming with people of all kinds living in harmony and peace, a city with free ports that hummed with commerce and creativity, and if there had to be city walls, the walls had doors and the doors were open to anyone with the will and the heart to get here. That's how I saw it and see it still."

Christie added his own interpretation of what the Gipper's speech meant to him, summing up his points as he very presidentially prepared to say goodnight. "That is American exceptionalism. Not a punch-line in a political speech, but a vision followed by a set of principled actions that made us the envy of the world. Not a re-election strategy, but an American revitalization strategy. We will be that again, but not until we demand that our leaders stand tall by telling the truth, confronting our shortcomings, celebrating our successes and, once again leading the world because of what we have been able to actually accomplish."

Christie let the thought soak in and then continued to his abrupt finish. "Only when we do that will we finally ensure that our children and grandchildren will live in a second American century. We owe them, as well as ourselves and those who came before us, nothing less. Thank you again for inviting me – God Bless you and God Bless the United States of America."

The speech and Christie's impeccable delivery earned him a standing ovation. For his encore, Christie engaged in an impromptu question and answer session with the audience. "You know how to tell the American people what they need to hear," a middle-aged mom, attending the speech with her daughter, commented. Then she brought the crowd to its feet a second time, as she implored Christie to reconsider his decision – for the umpteenth time – not to run for president, "I really mean this with all my heart. We can't wait another four years, I really implore you as a citizen of this country to, please sir, reconsider. Don't even say anything tonight, of course you wouldn't, go home and really think about it. Please sir, your country needs you."

Christie put on his humility act, as he responded to the woman's prompt. "I hear exactly what you are saying, and I feel the passion with which you say it and it touches me," he replied. "The fact of the matter is that anyone who has an ego large enough to say 'Oh, please, please stop asking me to be the leader of the free world, it is such a burden, if you could please just stop' – I mean what kind of crazy egomaniac would you have to be to say that? It's incredibly flattering. But at the same time, that heartfelt message that you gave me is not a reason to do it. That reason has to reside inside me. What I say is that I hear you. Please don't think ever for a second that I feel like I am so important in this world and I feel like what you are saying is a problem for me."

This was Christie at his best – twinkling like a diamond, a diamond being overvalued by the doting average Joe. The true flaw in all of this is that Christie was actually a weather vane, and his positions were being driven from whatever direction a favorable political wind was blowing.

Christie spoke of core values, but his core values were as hollow as the oath of office that he had sworn to uphold upon his appointment as United States Attorney; an oath of convenience not meaning. An oath he has seemed to debase. Christie spoke of beliefs, but his were always shifting to stay in step with wherever the popular opinion of the day was heading.

At home in New Jersey, Christie had to tip-toe around issues, continuously being challenged for his hypocrisy; but in other states – where people would not bother to check out the sincerity of what they were buying into – Christie could finesse his way around audiences and draw a national following. Far away from the place where he used the United States Attorney's Office as his political ward club, Christie could get away with it. He would con an entire party and Mitt Romney before he was done, but not everyone ...

Rush Limbaugh, the conservative sage, smelled something phony, and he let it be known to his audience of millions. Limbaugh warned fellow conservatives about Christie's Republican in Name Only (RINO) tendencies, including right after Christie's Reagan Library address. Christie could not sucker Limbaugh with his sound bites – El Rushbo looked for substance. Rush Limbaugh had done his homework on Chris Christie. Concerning Christie's speech, "I heard enough to send up a red flag or two," the prominent radio talk show host declared. He then offered his pragmatic observation.

"The Republican establishment is looking for anybody who can see to it that a conservative, a genuine conservative will not be nominated. 'But, Rush! But, Rush! Are you saying that Christie is not a conservative?' As far as the Republican establishment's concerned, yes.... Reagan was a conservative that worried the Republican establishment. Christie is not. Now, some people say that, 'Well, Christie's more conservative than you think, Rush. He's just governor of New Jersey. He has to say certain things. I mean, look at who the voting base is there. A bunch of lib Democrats. He's gotta work with a Democrat legislature in that state. He's a governor of a liberal state. He's gotta say some things to appease those people. So if he ever broke out of that you'd see the genuine full-fledged, 100% conservative Chris Christie.' OK, that's fine if that's what we want to do, roll the dice that that's what we're gonna get when he breaks free of New Jersey."

Chris Christie knew and always publically intimated that he was never getting into the 2012 presidential race. That position only caused susceptible throngs to further fawn over him and continue to beg him to run. He ate it all up. Christie knew that the timing was not right, and the risk was too great. First, no one was sure, just yet, if Obama could be taken down. Second, Christie risked pissing off Romney financial backers, supporters he would need whenever he decided to run for President, say in 2016, if the 2012 GOP nominee was unsuccessful. However, that didn't mean that Christie could not still ham it up and play to the public's fancy for his candidacy; in doing so it would help him build a future base of support for down the road. Christie took just that tack, right up until his endorsement of Romney, within weeks of the Reagan Library speech and a week after he confirmed he would not seek the GOP Presidential nomination in 2012.

Christie's move enabled him to become an early surrogate for Romney. He could travel the country and meet all the important people with whom a future candidate for the presidency would need to connect. In the interim, while waiting for his chance, Christie was actually beginning a 2016 presidential campaign under the guise of campaigning for Romney in 2012. Christie was out to pick up all the chits, markers, and IOU's that he could. Christie would then be in prime political shape to make a move on the presidency in 2016 ... now all he needed was for the eventual nominee, Mitt Romney, to lose.

Chapter Fifteen

Snubbing Romney and Embracing Obama

Picking up Chits

Dateline: West Des Moines, Iowa, December 7, 2011, Governor Chris Christie: "If you're looking for the candidate who agrees with you on everything, buy a mirror. What we need to be concerned about is not about being Republicans first, but being Americans first. It's up to us to save our country, and it starts in Iowa.... I guarantee you this, if Mr. Romney wins Iowa on January third, he is going to be the next President of the United States."

Dateline: Exeter, New Hampshire, January 8, 2012, Governor Chris Christie: "We can no longer put up with the most pessimistic man I've ever seen in the oval office, President Barack Obama."

Dateline: Elmhurst, Illinois, March 16, 2012, Governor Chris Christie "Governor Romney needs to show our party and our country that he's not only competing everywhere that he can win everywhere.... Mitt Romney's done it, he knows how to do it and he'll do it (in Washington.)"

Dateline: Richmond, Virginia, October 22, 2012, Governor Chris Christie: "The Constitution doesn't start off 'We the government' it starts off 'We the people....' Obama said you can't change Washington DC from the inside and that if that's what he truly believes, then why is he asking for another four years in office?... He's like a man wandering around a dark room, hands up against the wall, clutching for the light switch of leadership and he just can't find it, and he won't find it in the next 18 days."

By far, Christie was easily the most traveled sitting New Jersey Governor ever.

From coast to coast, and everywhere in-between, Chris Christie barnstormed the country hawking Mitt Romney for president like an Amway salesman on steroids. Christie was taking advantage of hobnobbing with the key GOP supporters and financiers that were vital to the success of any nominee for a presidential campaign – Christie in 2016? Besides Romney, Christie took the opportunity to campaign for and endorse a wide assortment of candidates for office, primarily governorships and United States congressional seats in both houses, who would forever be indebted to the New Jersey Governor. At the same time, though they would swear denials on stacks of Bibles, an unspoken strategy evolved amongst future aspirants for the oval office, including Christie – planning an option for the White House for 2016, just in case the unmentionable were to happen to the GOP standard-bearer.

Heading into the fall of 2012, the thinking was that if Romney were to lose the election to Obama, and Christie had his shot at the 2016 nomination, the only dilemma Christie would then face would be the dismal state of New Jersey's economic and employment conditions under his stewardship. Let alone the fact that the state budget was a ticking time bomb. Nonetheless, this was a drag-on to slay for another day. In the meantime, the pace of Christie stump appearances continued.

Christie reflected to Melissa Hayes of the *Bergen Record* about his criteria in stumping for candidates. "Christie said as vice chairman of the Republican Governors Association some of his endorsements were based on strategy, but others like... Drew Wrigley, who won reelection as North Dakota's lieutenant governor, and Pennsylvania Congressman Pat Meehan, are friends," Hayes reported. "I don't pick these upon who I think is going to win or lose. I pick them based upon the person and do I think they have some important things to say in the party, do I think their state is important to us – is there an important governor's race there that I want to make sure that there's strength in the ticket above and below it – so there's some strategic decisions that are made but it's not based upon can they win or can they lose, because you never know in these races, you just don't know," Christie commented.

Summing up his value to a candidate seeking election, Christie downplayed it. "I always say, I don't think endorsements mean as much as the people who are receiving the endorsement think they mean. You know they're really psyched when I come and I endorse them and say it makes a huge difference and I kind of wonder whether it really does. I think what it does is for the day it gets them a lot of attention from cameras and that's good for them."

However, it was never about Christie's value to a candidate. It was all about the successful candidate's future value for Christie … when the time was right. Christie did mention that his support had some other perks – the ability to draw money. "I tend to attract a crowd and they're willing to pay to hear me talk, so that helps them as well.… The money I raise helps to affect the races," he told Hayes. If Christie could raise money on behalf of others so far away from home, then he could raise money for himself and his own ambitions when the time came. That was the true value of his barnstorming tour.

In 2012, Christie campaigned for Utah Governor Gary Herbert and North Dakota Governor Jack Dalrymple, both re-elected, as well as Congressman Mike Pence who won his bid for the Indiana governor's office and North Dakota Congressman-elect Kevin Cramer. The big fish that Christie helped to land, though, was Charlotte Mayor Pat McCrory in North Carolina. McCrory took the Governor's seat away from the Democrats. "There's no more important a governor's race in America," Christie touted to a crowd at Catawba College in Salisbury. Christie also took McCrory's opponent, Lieutenant Governor Walter Dalton, to the woodshed. "You don't want to trade one failed administration for another failed administration. Dalton will raise the sales tax on you. You can take that to the bank." When McCrory's record as Charlotte Mayor was criticized, Christie would wittily deflect for him. "Isn't it ironic? All they do is criticize Pat McCrory's record in Charlotte, yet when Barack Obama had to pick a place for his convention, he chose Charlotte, North Carolina."

Other Christie endorsements would end up biting him on the hand, like his support of United States Senate candidate Richard Mourdock of Indiana. In one of those, *'tell me that he just didn't say that'* moments, Christie took heat when Mourdock, a Tea Party-backed candidate, while debating his Democratic opponent proclaimed, "I struggled with it myself for a long time, but I came to realize life is that gift from God. And I think even when life begins in that horrible situation of rape, that it is something that God intended to happen."

Christie's reaction was a dead giveaway that he was contemplating a presidential bid, and it demonstrated again how his spiel about never compromising principals and core beliefs was full of baloney. "Christie, who opposes abortion with exceptions for rape, incest and if the life of the mother is endangered, rejected Mourdock's comments today, though he stopped short of withdrawing his support for the U.S. Senate candidate. '(Christie) completely rejects Richard Mourdock's beliefs and views on this issue as expressed in (Tuesday) night's debate,' Michael Drewniak, a spokesman for the governor, said," the *Star-Ledger* reported.

Christie had no trouble withdrawing his support for another Tea Party-backed candidate, Todd Akin, when he advanced the same belief a few weeks earlier. "In that incident, Christie was quick to castigate Akin, calling his comments 'blatantly absurd' and saying he 'wouldn't campaign for a guy like Todd Akin,'" recalled the *Star-Ledger.*

What might have been behind the Christie double standard, demonstrated by his reluctance to walk away from Mourdock, was that Christie, thinking like a 2016 presidential candidate, did not want to alienate the Tea Party any further after having already dissed Akin. The Tea Partiers are well known for thrashing their opponents, including Republicans, whenever someone stands in the way of an issue about which they feel passionately. Christie could not afford another miscue with the Tea Party faction of the GOP, which he would one day have to deal with and coddle as a candidate for his Party's nomination.

Sometimes, the speaking engagements did not go over as smoothly as they were planned, such as the time in Iowa, when Christie was greeted by hecklers. Like showbiz, politics is tougher when performing before a live audience. As Christie spoke at a campaign stop in West Des Moines, just prior to the famous Iowa caucuses, about a dozen protesters confronted him. One of the arguments President Obama had stoked the political fires with was whether the wealthiest taxpayers in the nation were paying their fair share of overall taxes. Obama did not think so. He referred to them as the top one percent of the taxpayers in the country– the wealthiest people in America.

The antagonists began to shout, just as Christie spoke. "Mitt Romney and Chris Christie are part of the one percent! Put People First!"

For a moment, Christie must have thought he was back at one of his Jersey town hall meetings – he began to taunt and torture his tormenters. "You're so angry aren't you?" Christie mocked with sarcasm and scorn. "So angry, so terrible. Let them continue. Work it all out for yourselves. We're used to dealing with jokers like this in New Jersey all the time."

The crowd obliged Christie, continuing to shout their protest chants as they were escorted out of the event. Christie was not bothered – he was amused. "What was this – occupy West Des Moines?" Christie joked, referring to the Occupy Wall Street protests that were given birth in the famed New York City financial district. Christie was then quick to diagnose the shouters, putting his spin on their protest for the audience and the media in attendance. "They represent an anger in our country that Barack Obama has caused – a cynical Chicago ward politician who promises everything and comes to Washington and disappoints," he explained.

Christie was picking up in 2012 where he had left off during the country's midterm elections in 2010. The mid-term elections were Christie's first serious venture in campaigning beyond the borders of New Jersey. Christie, then too, had embarked on a whirlwind tour of the nation on behalf of Republican candidates for office. Christie's support helped to elect and re-elect several governors such as Susana Martinez in New Mexico, John Kasich in Ohio, and Tom Corbett in Pennsylvania. Christie also helped to elect and re-elect several members of the House of Representatives such as Michael Grimm in New York, Pat Meehan and Charlie Dent of Pennsylvania, and Robert Dold of Illinois. In his home Garden State, Christie helped to push Leonard Lance and Jon Runyan across the finish line.

It was most likely that Christie's 2010 political tour was the audition that served to help net his gig at the Reagan Library – like a vaudeville act finally landing an offer to play the Palace. After the Simi Valley speech, Christie was the hot commodity every Republican running for office wanted, but none more so than the candidates jockeying to be the GOP's presidential nominee. Christie's instincts pushed him to Romney, the candidate with the best-oiled organization and the most well-heeled financial backers – nice pieces to pick up if Romney's presidential bid fell apart.

Not only was Christie's clout able to land him on the most requested for appearances lists, but it enabled him to have influence with the Republican National Committee (RNC), which is the face and the voice of the GOP. They run the party, its conventions, and help to shape its platform. It is supposed to remain neutral in primaries, but if a candidate seeking the nomination has any friends in place, it could prove to be a strategic advantage. While many of Christie's potential adversaries for the future 2016 nomination contest were probably keeping just as brisk a pace in campaigning nationwide for other Republican candidates, Christie out politicked them – Michael DuHaime, one of Christie's chief strategists, was hired by the RNC in a senior advisory position. Christie now had someone on the inside and a leg up for 2016.

Another strategic advantage Christie had heading into 2016 would be his affiliation with the Republican Governor's Association, where he served in a leadership position. Governors are the most influential political entities in any given state – the titular leaders of their respective political parties. There were 30 sitting Republican Governors after the 2012 elections and Christie would certainly have the inside track for their support in a primary fight. Senators and Congressmen do not carry the sway of any state's chief executive. If Senator Marco Rubio were to be Christie's main challenge for the 2016 nomination, Christie would have the distinct political advantage, because of all the groundwork he had already laid down with fellow governors.

Christie was richer in worthy IOUs than any other marquee Republican.

The Veep Shuffle & Hitting the Keynote

When Mitt Romney secured the GOP nomination, the routine ritual of putting together the Republican National Committee program for the August convention in Tampa Florida ensued. Two key appointments would be made by Romney prior to the convention, the selection of the vice presidential nominee and the convention's keynote speaker. The backdoor lobbying commenced. There is always purposeful drama and plenty of leaks provided from the camp of the presidential nominee concerning the vice presidential nominee and keynote speaker considerations. The drama and leaks keep the public interested and the media focused on the campaign of the presidential nominee.

Early on, in October of 2010, having just won the first Tea Party straw poll as the preferential presidential candidate of choice,

Christie was emphatic that he was not running for president. When pressed about whether he might consider filling out the ticket as the veep, Christie indicated that he did not have the temperament to be a vice presidential candidate. Appearing on MSNBC's *Morning Joe*, Christie mused, "Can you see me as somebody's vice president? I mean, who would be that poor guy? You know, I just don't think my personality is necessarily suited for being number two."

Sometimes, whenever the vice presidential subject would ever come up, Christie would give his humble pie excuse. As he once told a crowd attending one of his town hall meetings in Haddon-field, New Jersey, "I had and have an obligation to the people of this state. And, to me it kind of feels like you're dating a woman for a while and you're really excited about it and then another really pretty woman walks into the room and she kind of makes the eye at you, like, hey, why don't you come over here? And, like if you bolt from the woman you're with for a while and you go over to the prettier one, what's that mean? Not good, not good in my mind, right?"

However, as crunch time for the veep selection moved ever so near, Christie's hunger pangs for power kicked in. Appearing on a late January of 2012 edition of NBC's *Meet the Press*, even before Romney had secured the nomination, Christie advertised for the job. "If Gov. Romney, who's going to be our nominee, picked up the phone and called me to talk about this, I love my country enough and I love my party enough to listen." Then Christie quickly disposed of his early statements to the contrary. "Everybody's misunderstood what I meant about saying being ready for president. I meant that, you know, being ready to leave the job that I had and being ready to run for president of the United States, with all that entails. I didn't want to do it, didn't feel ready to do it." It was all just one big "misunderstanding."

What might have caused Christie's change of heart is that he was unexpectedly fast becoming Romney's close political confidant. Romney, like the Jersey audiences who saw Christie perform at town hall meetings, was wowed by Christie's style and delivery. Christie could never have envisioned this happening, so it was now time to quickly rethink strategy. If he still had the same makeup of that school kid back in Jersey who was knocking on future Governor Tom Kean's door and asking, "How do I become a politician?" then he sure as hell was not going to let this opportunity slip by.

The easiest way to ascend to the presidency is from the vice presidency. History would be on Christie's side. If Romney won, and Christie wasn't his vice president, Christie's shelf life as a potential presidential candidate would rapidly expire. 2016 would be out the window, as Romney and his veep would stand for re-election, and for the time being, the ill state of affairs of New Jersey's economy and budget would seemingly saddle Christie with a tough re-election bid for the governorship. Even if all went well, Christie's next term would expire in 2017 – that would be three years away from the next opportunity to have a crack at the presidency in 2020. Christie was not waiting around; he could almost taste it.

Christie's competition for the vice presidential nomination would be Florida's United States Senator Marco Rubio, former Secretary of State Condoleezza Rice, and an assortment of Midwest candidates – which actually made the most sense, since Romney needed to build a Midwestern firewall and capture as many of these swing states as was possible, including Ohio. Those states were also healthy in Electoral College votes.

As early as April of 2012, Rubio began letting the field of potential GOP presidential nominees know that he was not interested in the second spot on the national ticket. Speaking to the media at an event sponsored by the *National Journal* at the University of Phoenix, the GOP's rising star stated, "I don't want to be the vice president right now or maybe ever, I really want to do a good job in the Senate. If in four to five years, if I do a good job as vice president – I'm sorry, as senator – I'll have the chance to do all sorts of things." Rubio then suggested his Senate colleague from the Midwest, Rob Portman of Ohio, as a "phenomenal choice," for the position.

Today, we all know that Wisconsin Congressman Paul Ryan was to become the vice presidential pick, but initially, it was Chris Christie who had won out. Two well-respected media outlets, known for their credible sources, *Politico* and the *New York Post* scoped out the behind-the-scenes drama that played out. *Politico's* Mike Allen and Jim VandeHei had an outstanding rapport with the Romney camp, as much as the Associated Press's Beth DeFalco, and the *Post's* and *The Jersey Sting* coauthor, Josh Margolin, had with the Christie camp. Apparently, Romney, always keen on Christie's grittiness, opted to select the New Jersey Governor as his running mate just before heading off to the London Olympics in

July of 2012. "Mitt liked him because he saw him as a street fighter," a Romney insider recalled, referring to Christie's style. "It's the kind of political mentality that Romney doesn't have, but admires. He wanted someone who could play the Chicago game [like Obama headquarters] on its own terms."

Politico further reported, "People involved in the selection process said the campaign believed there was no one who would be more adept and persuasive at delivering Romney's message. Advisers thought Christie would excel at retail campaigning among working-class voters. 'He'd be great anywhere there are ordinary white men,'" the official said. "'They would have loved him because here's this straight-talking, hard-charging, in-your-face guy, and he's a man's man. Ohio is the only battleground state where Mitt has a net negative gender gap – where his approval among men doesn't outweigh the president's approval among women. Chris Christie changes that.'"

As is typical in every campaign, from a mayor's election up to a presidential election, it is inevitable that staff will get in the way. Such was the case here. As a candidate who ran for numerous offices, I can attest to how frequently campaign higher-ups and even underlings can involve themselves, their personalities, and their personal whims in campaign matters that ultimately result in disastrous repercussions. *Politico* reported that during the rough early days on the primary trail, when Romney was not on such sure footing, Christie became the candidate's confidant. "During the long winter slog through the early contests, Christie spoke privately with Romney in long cell phone calls on the road. Romney liked Christie's fearless advice, unvarnished talk that he wasn't used to hearing from his cocoon of Boston advisers, many of whom had been with him since he was Massachusetts governor." For Christie to develop that kind of rapport with Romney had to drive the campaign's advisors up the wall with petty jealousy.

Staffers who feel pushed aside in a campaign with such high stakes will typically fight back. The backbiting began. "Some aides around Romney began to sour on Christie when he was late to a couple of events where they were appearing together. 'Chris is a sort of cavalier New York, New Jersey guy: 'If I'm a few minutes behind, I'll blame it on traffic,' said a person who knows him well. 'That's just who he is.' The tardiness rankled the by-the-book folks around Romney. As the vice-presidential selection ramped up, Christie was always at the top of the list, but always with an asterisk. Some Romney loyalists thought he was too much about himself," reported *Politico*.

Romney still wanted him ... but Romney staffers had other means by which not to make this happen, and somehow the decision for Romney to name his running mate was put off until after he returned home from traveling to the London Olympics. According to Margolin and the *New York Post*, Romney's advisors imposed a deal-killing ultimatum on Christie – if he wanted the second position on the ticket, he would have to step down as Governor. The Romney camp claimed, "Strict pay-to-play laws would have restricted the nation's largest banks from donating to the campaign – since those banks do business with New Jersey." Somebody had to really be working overtime on this one.

The highly efficient Romney aides had diagnosed two Securities and Exchange Commission rules that would pose a risk to the campaign's finances unless Christie resigned as Governor. "One rule, enacted in the mid-1990s, restricts Wall Street executives whose firms underwrite municipal bonds from making personal contributions of more than $250 to a governor running for federal office – or risk being banned from doing business in that state for two years." That would scratch the moola for Romney's campaign from banks such as Goldman Sachs, JP Morgan Chase, and Citibank, because they do business with New Jersey. "The second rule, enacted in 2010, limits pension-investment advisers from making campaign donations to a governor running for federal office." That would clip contributions of financial firms such as Morgan Stanley, Lazard and Wellington Advisors, because they also do business with New Jersey. Suddenly, unless Christie resigned his office, he was the candidate that Romney could not afford.

Back at Camp Christie, aides furiously tried to find loopholes in the laws that would allow Christie to remain as Governor and run for vice president. They were on thin ice. They must have been relying on the expertise of the former United States Attorneys who were now working for Christie in Trenton, after having so brutally misconstrued their own recusal guidelines when they prosecuted the Bid Rig III cases. None of the schemes that Christie's people came up with could satisfy Romney's campaign team. One thing for certain – Christie was not giving up the Governor's seat.

Christie had no time to re-think his position, because, without consultation, Romney announced that Wisconsin Congressman Paul Ryan would be his running mate. "Some Christie supporters were irritated to discover that the House budget chairman had been picked so long before the New Jersey governor had been told, meaning that he and other also-rans had remained as decoys. These supporters said at the time that Christie deserved more of a heads -up after being led on so strongly," *Politico* reported.

Any warm and fuzzy political relationship that Christie and Romney thought they had rapidly disintegrated. Political reality and hardball was all that would eventually be left between the two men. There was only one consolation prize left for Romney to offer Christie, an olive branch of sorts: the chance for Christie to deliver the keynote speech at the convention. Christie held his fire and issued a statement praising the selection of Ryan. But his Sicilian mother had taught him never to be disrespected, and he would have his revenge. But first he needed to shore up the consolation prize in order to keep hope alive for 2016.

On August 14, 2012, Governor Chris Christie was tapped by Romney to deliver the GOP convention's keynote address. Even his detractors in Romney's camp had to admit that the audiences loved his style in delivering a message. "The keynote speech is the highest profile spot for someone not accepting the party's presidential or vice presidential nominations. The slot has launched many political figures, most notably a little-known state senator from Illinois named Barack Obama in 2004. Four years later, he won the White House," the *Huffington Post* reported

Christie shared the sentiment of the *Huffington Post's* analysis – this was his time to shine and introduce himself to the nation for the 2016 campaign. Romney's camp, of course, wanted to screen the Christie speech, and they did, according to a Romney advisor quoted in *Politico*. "We told him that we thought there were more opportunities for him to put stuff in about Mitt, and he didn't take the hint." *Hint?* They could have dropped a grand piano on Christie and they still wouldn't have gotten his attention.

On the weekend before the speech, a scenario unfolded that even Mario Puzo could not have bettered. In Godfatherish style,

Christie delivered a message to the Romney camp in the form of a news leak that was dripped into the ears of the *New York Post's* Josh Margolin. Obviously, the source was from the Christie camp, and in order to make it to print, the story had to be confirmed by someone else. Margolin once covered Christie and the New Jersey statehouse on his old newsbeat at the *Star-Ledger* and his lead-in sentence fell upon Romney like the Sword of Damocles: "Gov. Chris Christie wasn't willing to give up the New Jersey statehouse to be Mitt Romney's running mate because he doubted they'd win, The *Post* has learned."

The *Post* leak was just a love tap. Christie was only warming up. Because the GOP convention was pushed back a day due to inclement weather, Christie shared the stage that night with Mitt Romney's wife, who delivered a memorable and moving speech about how loving a man her husband was. "Tonight I want to talk to you about love," Mrs. Romney intoned in her airless voice, after she had earlier, somewhat thoughtlessly, proclaimed 2012 "our turn."

Christie didn't reciprocate, thumping onto the stage moments later and tossing buckets of cold water on Ann Romney's words. "The greatest lesson Mom ever taught me, though, was this one: she told me there would be times in your life when you have to choose between being loved and being respected. She said to always pick being respected, that love without respect was always fleeting – but that respect could grow into real, lasting love," extracting excerpts from his standby "Mom's speech" that he had entertained so many town hall meetings with back home in New Jersey.

Christie rambled on, continuing to pay homage to himself. He obviously had no love lost for Romney, and even when it was time to hail the nominee, Christie could not resist the back-handed compliment. "If you're willing to stand up with me for America's future, I will stand up with you. If you're willing to fight with me for Mitt Romney, I will fight with you." Christie would not let the audience support Romney except through himself.

This was not the speech that anyone anticipated and the critics weighing in on the performance were not kind. The *Washington Post's* Chris Cillizza was prophetic: "Christie will take some [justified] criticism for spending 95 percent of his speech talking about himself and five percent talking about Mitt Romney. [And that's being generous]," he wrote.

"A prime-time belly-flop," *Politico* slammed.

"The most curious keynote speech I have ever heard.... For a moment, I forgot who was the nominee of the party," remarked Fox News's Chris Wallace, noting how long it took Christie to mention Romney, and then only seven times. "I thought it was a tremendous disappointment," commented Republican strategist Alex Castellanos.

"He doesn't mention Mitt Romney's name until the 16-minute mark," read the *New York Daily News* headline for the story covering Christie's speech. "Chris Christie accepts the nomination a bit early," wrote *Salon*. "Romney was almost an afterthought. There wasn't a personal line about Mitt. It was as though the two had never met," wrote Howard Kurtz of the *Daily Beast/Newsweek*. "This speech not only was a bad speech. I think this was one of the most remarkable acts of political selfishness I have ever seen," said MSNBC's Rachel Maddow "He waited 1,800 words into a 2,600-word speech to even bring [Romney] up."

Speaking before GOP delegates from the Pennsylvania and New Hampshire delegations on the morning after his veiled, "I wanna be the 2016 GOP nominee," speech, Christie tried to explain it all away. He blamed everything on Ann Romney, who he claimed spoke long enough about her husband so that "it freed me up – remember, she was supposed to be going Monday night and because of the hurricane, it was canceled – so instead both of us were on the same night." A few nights later, appearing on *The Tonight Show*, Christie tried to salvage himself from the disaster with contrived humor. Asked about the speech, Christie quipped, "it wasn't my finest hour – it wasn't even my finest hour-and-a-half."

Politico's analysis brought home the point about Christie's 2016 presidential campaign kickoff with humor, quoting a prominent GOP strategist: "If Democrats had a drinking game for every time he mentioned Romney, they all ended up sober [at] the end of the night." The *National Journal* said more bluntly, "Christie's prime time address seemed as much about positioning himself for 2016 and polishing his still developing national image."

The Romney camp noticed it too, "Several political figures close to Mitt Romney made acerbic comments to reporters, making clear they thought Christie laid an egg while also saying they didn't much care since Ann Romney was generally perceived as performing well. Several made eye-rolling references to what they regard as signs of the New Jersey governor's considerable ego: The number of self-references in his address and an entourage of aides who they believe is too obviously trying to promote Christie fever for the future rather than help Republicans in 2012," reported *Politico*.

Unbelievably, Chris Christie was not done yet ...

The Snub

As the 2012 presidential election campaign wound down in the final week of October, no one could have predicted the ending that would unfold. Mitt Romney had made up substantial ground and the race was tight – perhaps a dead heat. Romney had spent the entire campaign portraying President Obama as a polarizing force, a failed leader who was incapable of working with the other political side for the country's good.

Romney was quick to point out how, in contrast, while he served as Governor of Massachusetts with a Democratic dominated legislature, he frequently reached out across the aisle for the betterment of the state. Romney read the polling results very well – the people in the country were fed up with all the bickering and sniping in Washington. They wanted their leaders to stop fighting each other and start working together for the overall good of the nation.

It would take Chris Christie but a few short hours to completely destroy that perception. As Superstorm Sandy came roaring up the East Coast and hooked left, slamming into New Jersey, Christie, applying his mother's creed to not be disrespected, had a right cross of his own for the Romney campaign. As he toured the devastated Garden State with President Obama, he was about to give Romney the kiss of death. Mario Puzo used a christening as the backdrop for Michael Corleone's operatic vengeance in his famous novel *The Godfather*. Chris Christie would use the backdrop of a hurricane to serve up his version of unholy wrath. Or maybe he just knew a disaster when he saw one.

Christie mentioned Obama's name and praised him on national television during the Superstorm Sandy episode more times than he had ever mentioned Romney during his keynote address. "I thank the president for his telephone call and inquiring about how things are going here and I assured him that things were going well so far. He advised me to call him at any time that things were not going well. I appreciated the president's outreach today in making sure that we know he's watching this and is concerned about the health and welfare and safety of the people of the state of New Jersey," Christie fawned to the press.

The day after the storm, Christie took plenty of time off from handling the ongoing disaster and emergency, in order to do a whirlwind tour of national news shows. "It's been very good working with the president," he told MSNBC's *Morning Joe.* "He and his administration have been coordinating with us. It's been wonderful. The president has been all over this, and he deserves great credit. I've been on the phone with him, like I said, yesterday, personally three times. He gave me his number at the White House, told me to call him if I needed anything. And he absolutely means it."

Christie further echoed his warm sentiments towards the President on NBC's *Today* show, hailing him as "outstanding." This was a far cry from the President Obama that Christie had described just a few weeks earlier as "a man wandering around a dark room, hands up against the wall, clutching for the light switch of leadership, and he just can't find it."

On CNN's *Starting Point,* Christie continued his Obama monologues, even managing to work in the election: "I spoke to the President three times yesterday. He has been incredibly supportive and helpful to our state, and not once did he bring up the election. So if he's not bringing it up, you can be sure that people in New Jersey are not worried about that, primarily if one of the guys running isn't."

A few months later, Christie let the world know the skinny about some of his phone conversations with the President. Speaking to a group of Hyatt Regency executives, he elaborated on how he was able to get fuel to gas-starved service stations after the storm. "I said, 'Alright, I'll call the president.'" Christie begins to re-enact the call. "Mr. President, Hi, it's Chris. Remember yesterday when you told me if I needed anything to call you on this line? I need gas."

Christie then told the crowd that the President matter-of-factly asked him, "how much?" The animated Christie regaled his audience by telling them how he tactically stalled for time while his staff scrambled for an answer. "I'm sorry sir, you're breaking up." Christie said, at this point pantomiming someone with a poor cell phone connection. He was retelling the tale in the manner of an old Bob

Newhart comedic standup routine. "Did you ask how much gas I need?" Christie clarified, playing for more time.

Seconds later, Christie's staff fed him the answer, "12 million gallons."

"Mr. President, we've looked at the problem and we need 12 million gallons," Christie relayed to the President, who promised immediate action.

Christie related that five minutes later his cell phone rang, flashing "unknown." It was the President, Christie reported, deciding to ham it up for his audience, "Hey Chris, it's Barack." The President told Christie that the fuel was on the way.

Alas, in every administration, there is always someone who thinks they know better, and as *Star-Ledger* correspondent Jenna Portnoy would report, FEMA cancelled the delivery when they found out the gas would not be given out free. Christie broke into his Bob Newhart routine again, mimicking his follow-up call to Obama. "You're not going to believe this, but some idiot at FEMA ordered the gas trucks ... to be turned around because I wouldn't give it away for free," Christie recalled.

President Obama then brought FEMA Chief Craig Fugate in on a conference call, Christie recalled. "Craig what did I tell you when we were on the phone the other day as to Governor Christie?"

"Give him whatever he wants," Fugate replied, according to Christie. The Governor added that twenty minutes later the fuel trucks were rolling to New Jersey.

Appearing on *Fox and Friends*, when the co-host, Steve Doocy, brought up the election and asked whether Christie knew if Romney was scheduling a tour of the damage in New Jersey, Christie nearly took Doocy's head off. "I have no idea, nor am I the least bit concerned or interested," Christie barked. "I've got a job to do here in New Jersey that's much bigger than presidential politics, and I could care less about any of that stuff. I have a job to do. I've got 2.4 million people out of power. I've got devastation on the Shore. I've got floods in the northern part of my state. If you think right now I give a damn about presidential politics, then you don't know me."

A day later, the "I've got a job to do" Christie who had no time for "presidential politics" was doing his job right next to his new pal, Barack Obama. If you want to look presidential, stand next to the President; and Christie was now looking more Presidential than Romney was. Christie, so fond of helicopter rides, toured the devastated Jersey Shore with the President from high above in Marine One. Even Rush Limbaugh gave the tandem a buildup for their tour on his radio show. "New Jersey Governor Chris Christie has decided to play the role of a Greek column today for President Obama. Obama and Christie will tour the Jersey Shore."

The two men exited the helicopter at a hard-hit shore community to address the media. The tall and lanky Obama and the pudgy Christie looked a bit like Laurel and Hardy. United States Senators Menendez and Lautenberg joined the President and Governor, but Christie paid them little attention when taking to the podium to thank everyone. His disregard for the pair was evident.

Apparently, Christie and Obama had developed a great working relationship over the days leading up to and through the Superstorm event, and then on their helicopter ride. It was evident when they spoke to the media and the nation. "We spent a significant afternoon together surveying the damage up and down the New Jersey coastline; we were on Marine One together to be able to show the President that personally. I had an opportunity to see it, and we had an opportunity to discuss it at length," Christie began, leading off the press conference. "And then, going over to the shelter here, being able to meet with folks to have them see the President and his concern, and the concern that all of us have for making sure that things get back to normal as quickly as possible."

More bouquets. "He has worked incredibly closely with me since before the storm hit. I think this is our sixth conversation since the weekend, and it's been a great working relationship to make sure that we're doing the jobs that people elected us to do. And I cannot thank the President enough for his personal concern and compassion for our state and for the people of our state."

This was a very different President Obama from the one Christie had described earlier in the year: "A cynical Chicago ward politician who promises everything and comes to Washington and disappoints."

When the President took to the podium, he responded in kind. "The first thing I want to do is just to thank everybody who has been involved in the entire rescue and recovery process. At the top of my list, I have to say that Governor Christie throughout this process has been responsive; he has been aggressive in making sure that the state got out in front of this incredible storm."

Many media outlets referred to Obama's and Christie's new relationship as a "bromance." News analysts speculated upon what impact Christie's words and actions would have on the upcoming presidential election. The *Washington Times'* conservative columnist Henry D'Andrea wrote for his Halloween column, "Republican New Jersey Gov. Chris Christie and President Barack Obama have decided to take off the partisan costumes and go frolic around New Jersey collecting candy and enjoying each other's company. OK, well that's not exactly what is happening tonight with Christie and Obama, but it's a pretty good description of the sudden bromance that has resulted between the two, following the devastating Hurricane Sandy."

D'Andrea was not up for any political trick-or-treating, and he called Christie out. "Christie isn't fooling any of us; he might as well just come out and say, 'Hey look at me, Mr. Bipartisan! Vote Christie 2016.' Gov. Chris Christie should have, just like Bloomberg and Cuomo, helped New Jersey in every capacity he can, and even suggest that Obama not visit the state. Instead, Christie threw Romney under the bus and gave Obama the perfect photo-op that makes him look *presidential,* in the final days of the campaign. While there won't be a definite way to tell if Christie's sucking up to Obama is hurting Mitt Romney, it certainly is no place for a high-profile Republican governor to be in."

The *Washington Post's* columnist Jonathan Capehart speculated on the impact and influence of Christie's actions, "Working with Christie and the other governors affected by the megastorm, the president finally gets to stretch those bipartisan muscles that congressional Republicans refuse to let him exercise. And Christie's effusive praise of Obama after nailing him as someone groping for the light switch of leadership in a darkened room could prove invaluable. Christie's purrs for the president could possibly serve as the seal of approval for the few wavering swing-staters out there. As for Christie, well, there's nothing but upside for him. The first-term Republican governor of a blue state will get points for working with the president."

Another *Washington Post* columnist, Jena McGregor, saw Christie's actions as opportunistic. "It's possible Christie was doing his own bit of crisis politics, sounding bipartisan for whatever his political future holds."

A few days after the Obama-Christie tour, Mitt Romney prepared for a campaign event in Philadelphia, just a hop, skip, and jump from the Governor's Trenton, New Jersey office. The *Huffington Post* reported on yet another backhand Christie landed on Romney's candidacy. "New Jersey Gov. Chris Christie, who was effusive in his praise of President Barack Obama when the two leaders toured damage from Hurricane Sandy last week, turned down a request by Mitt Romney to appear with him at a rally on Sunday night in Pennsylvania, the *Huffington Post* has learned. Christie's decision will only add to questions among Republicans about what the governor – who is up for reelection a year from now – is thinking, and why he went out of his way to heap praise on the president, and then refused to appear with Romney." The Romney camp was obviously reeling. "You can't tell me that he couldn't have gone over there for a night rally," a Romney campaign source told *Huffington Post*. Despite his excuses that New Jersey's response to Sandy consumed his time, Christie decided to pour salt in an open wound by finding some time to yuk it up in a comedy skit on *Saturday Night Live.*

The Christie and Romney staffers were at war. Many Romney supporters felt, not unreasonably, that Christie's snubs were intentional. "Now Republican party bosses suspect Christie's momentary embrace of Barack Obama during the President's tour of devastated New Jersey this week was a deliberate snub to Romney," commented Hayley Peterson of (*Daily*) *Mail Online*. Christie returned the fire. "This is what happens when you get to the end of a campaign and it's unsure of the result. Those who fear they may be blamed if things don't go well try to look for other people to blame. As big as my ego is, not even my ego is that big that I would have that kind of effect on a national election," Christie snapped. "They're voting for Gov. Romney and Paul Ryan, not for me." After the election, there were more sour grapes and complaints about Christie. "'A lot of people feel like Christie hurt, that we definitely lost four or five points between the storm and Chris Christie giving Obama a chance to be bigger than life,' said one of Romney's biggest fundraisers, who requested anonymity to speak candidly," reported Philip Rucker of the *Washington Post* staff.

"There has been plenty of blame to go around after Romney's sizable defeat on Tuesday; an outcome that Republicans and Romney's campaign were quick to admit was a huge surprise. Christie has been a favorite scapegoat among Romney supporters who claim that the New Jersey governor's public praise of Obama's handling of Superstorm Sandy damaged Romney's campaign in its last days," the *Huffington Post* reported.

Christie hit back. "I did my job. I wouldn't call what I did an embrace of Barack Obama. I know that's become the wording of it, but the fact of the matter is, you know, I'm a guy who tells the truth all the time. And if the president of the United States did something good, I was gonna say he did something good and give him credit for it." Christie then gave himself a pat on the back. "But it doesn't take away for a minute the fact that I was the first governor to endorse Mitt Romney, that I traveled literally tens of thousands of miles for him, raised tens of millions of dollars for him and worked harder, I think, than any other surrogate in America other than Paul Ryan, who became his running mate."

The Christie & Obama 'bromance' story simply would not go away, and Christie continued to defend his actions. "My activity with President Obama was just another chapter in the leadership I've tried to show in this state, which is people care more about getting things done than they care about partisanship. And I'm going to continue to conduct myself that way." When asked what went wrong for Romney on election night, Christie deadpanned: "He didn't get enough votes. I'm not a pundit, I'm an office holder."

There was still to be one last communication between President Obama and his new friend. At a press conference after the election, Christie informed a gathering of reporters that he "reached out to President Barack Obama with a personal phone call to congratulate him on his re-election." Mitt Romney, the man Christie had campaigned with and raised money for, got a conciliatory e-mail, the governor said," according to the *Huffington Post*. "We didn't have a political strategy discussion, I said, 'Congratulations on your win last night, Mr. President,' and he said, 'Thank you.' Asked if he'd given Romney the same treatment, Christie said that he hadn't. 'No; we exchanged e-mails last night,' Christie said, according to Bloomberg. 'We haven't spoken on the phone yet.'"

In defeat, months later, Romney would remain magnanimous, taking sole responsibility for his loss. While not minimizing Christie's antics at the end of the election, he did not blame them on his loss. "I lost my election because of my campaign, not because of what anyone else did," he commented. Romney's loyal staff would take their own revenge – providing an unflattering depiction of Christie's role in the Romney campaign and a juicy version of his vetting for vice president. Mark Halperin and John Heilemann described the account in their book, *Double Down: Game Change 2012.*

The aftermath of the Superstorm and the election had taken its toll. Buried under the rubble that President Obama and Chris Christie had viewed on the Jersey Shore from high above in Marine One, were also the remnants of Mitt Romney's argument about Obama being incapable of reaching across the aisle. Christie helped to debunk all of that, and at the same time he helped to make himself look good as a prospective 2016 presidential candidate ... all at the expense of Mitt Romney. Then again, that *was* one Hell of a storm.

Chapter Sixteen

Eyes on the White House

The Wind and the Lying

The winds of Superstorm Sandy wrought devastation on New Jersey – a nationally declared disaster area with damages totaling approximately $30 billion. As the adage goes, "One man's garbage is another man's treasure." Just as sure as Bid Rig III had catapulted him into the governor's office, Superstorm Sandy would rescue Christie from his plight of having steered New Jersey into dire straits after just three years as Governor. Things were so bad, in fact, that there was a question of whether or not Christie would actually run for re-election, or instead opt to run for the presidency as a former governor. He could not chance sitting in the governor's office when Trenton's ticking budget time-bomb exploded.

Christie had helped set that bomb ticking when he halfheartedly enacted much-needed pension reforms. While he made sure public workers began to ante up their fair share for the benefits, Christie phased in the payments owed by the state over future budgets in order to claim that he had held the line on taxes. Under the next governor, the $1 billion payment due to fund pension debt would begin ballooning to $5 billon. To avoid raising the gas tax Christie kicked transportation funding costs down the road. He also planned to cut income taxes some $1.4 billion, mostly benefitting the wealthiest New Jerseyans, at the cost of cutting programs earmarked to assist the poorest. To make up for these shortfalls due the following year, New Jersey's budget would have to increase an estimated 14 percent.

Christie had not actually cut taxes; he merely put off costs and the higher taxes necessary to cover them into future year budgets. The *Star-Ledger* editors opined on how the public was being played, suggesting that Christie might be planning his exit strategy in order to run for the presidency. "But you can still see the tax-cut show. It's funny and entertaining. And Christie's shtick makes morbid political sense if his intention is to leave. Why would he want to stick around to clean up this mess? Why not leave the stage while the crowd is still cheering? If all goes well, they'll remember you as the guy who wanted to cut taxes," wrote the editors.

Another headache awaiting the next governor would be finding the funding necessary to deal with other New Jersey budget bleeders. The nonpartisan State Budget Crisis Task Force, headed by former Federal Reserve Chairman, Paul Volcker, and former New York Lieutenant Governor, Richard Ravitch, projected that New Jersey would have to increase the size of its budget an approximate 30 percent over coming years. The task force tagged the "skyrocketing" costs of the state's school funding and the escalating price tag for Medicaid as two of the culprits. The next governor would have to handle a string of budgets as if navigating a minefield.

Prior to the big bump in popularity Christie received from his masterful manipulation of the disaster wrought by Sandy, along with his mastery of the media coverage that followed, most pragmatic politicians thought Christie would not seek a second term as governor and instead shoot right for the presidency. "He's going to resign at the top of his game," stated Senator Ray Lesniak, a prominent New Jersey Democratic leader. "It's a no-brainer." In that way, as logic dictated, Christie could avoid all of the chickens that would be coming home to roost because of his piling up future debt in order to create for New Jerseyans the illusion that he had cut taxes: his self-proclaimed "Jersey Comeback."

Ross Baker, political science professor at Rutgers University, speculated to the media on Christie's political options given New Jersey's budget plight. "He can bail out. He can leave that problem to his successor. The most compelling reason not to run is that Christie is a man of modest means. He could follow the Sarah Palin route and become a political celebrity. He could write a book and have lots of autographing parties around the country. And that would give him exposure, so he'd still have the possibility of making a run in 2016."

Then, along came Sandy. Keenly aware of the media pummeling he took for bungling the 2010 Christmas week blizzard that paralyzed New Jersey while he skipped out of state for his Disney World vacation, this time Christie battened down the hatches. Unlike Governor Andrew Cuomo of New York and Mayor Michael Bloomberg of New York City, both of whom assumed command positions outside of disaster areas, in order not to divert resources and personnel away from storm victims, Christie did just the opposite.

When a president, governor, or mayor travels, especially into a disaster area, police and security personnel are required. Such staffing is often siphoned away from the personnel assisting victims of the disaster. Christie traveled directly into the heart of a number of the New Jersey disaster areas during the very crucial rescue and recovery period. At each stop, he would typically hold one of his endless parades of media updates. Someone made sure there were always an army of first responders and other police, fire, and medical personnel available to form a great photo op behind Christie when he spoke. It was shameless self-promotion.

During the crisis, Christie dedicated a good portion of his schedule to face-time on practically every major and minor news show. He never missed the opportunity to hug, hold, and reassure the dazed victims he came across while the cameras were rolling. The scenes played big everywhere. No one could question his sincerity at emotional moments like this, even if at the same time he also exploited the victims for a self-serving camera shot that would play well on the national news.

When President Obama decided to tour the sites, Christie hopped aboard Marine One and hammed it up even more. A shrewd politician, he knew that national polling indicated that the American public wanted their political leaders to work together. With the President as a co-conspirator, Christie served up a dish of bipartisanship for the entire nation to feed on during nightly newscasts. It was a stroke of genius.

Sandy was keeping the attention of New Jersey voters focused on the mess left behind on their beaches and off the mess in Trenton. State Senate president Stephen Sweeney said, "We gave the governor a jobs package. We gave him one. He vetoed it. And his job package is a hurricane. I guess he prayed a lot and got lucky a storm came." As the words slipped past his lips, Sweeney sensed the comment might be misunderstood and corrected himself in midsentence, "I shouldn't say that because that's – I apologize for saying it."

Christie's office and fellow Republicans pounced, wanting to take immediate advantage and rubbing Sweeney's nose in his words. An assortment of responses, calling Sweeney's statements "politics at its worst," "unconscionable," "absurd" and "extremely disturbing," followed.

They should have known that Sweeney was not one to hide. The Senator shot back, assuming a more diplomatic tack this time. "It's unfortunate that the governor has found time to exploit my misstatement, which I apologized for immediately. The truth of the matter is the chief politicizer of Sandy has been none other than Chris Christie. There is no better example of this than his appearance on *Saturday Night Live*."

The payoff for Christie would come in the days and weeks after the storm. Polling indicated that his popularity was skyrocketing to an unbelievable seventy-eight percent. The master media manipulator had done it again. Pollster Patrick Murray of Monmouth University Polling Institute called Christie "the perfect person for a crisis. Sandy was made for a personality like his to shine. He makes you feel like he's taking on the pain of all New Jersey."

Maurice Carroll, director of the Quinnipiac University Polling Institute, crunched his poll's numbers: "Gov. Christopher Christie never looked more like a 'Jersey Guy' than when he stood on the Seaside boardwalk after Sandy, and, just about unanimously, his New Jersey neighbors – Republicans, Democrats, Independents – applauded." There was even more good news inside the numbers for Christie; a near-unanimous ninety-five percent of those polled said he did a good or excellent job responding to Superstorm Sandy. The hugging, holding, and reassuring had paid off.

A Rutgers-Eagleton poll offered Mr. Popularity more of the same. The poll found that fifty-nine percent of New Jersey voters wanted Christie re-elected. Rutgers-Eagleton Poll's director, David Redlawsk, commented on his poll results, "The combination of leadership, empathy and bipartisanship shown by the governor during the crisis impressed most people and gave the governor a strong push into the 2013 campaign." Redlawsk also offered some caution to sober any drunken giddiness derived from the awesome numbers, "With a long time until Election Day, Sandy will become somewhat less of a factor. The realities of governing – including the budget and a host of other contentious issues – are likely to cool the governor's red-hot numbers over time. But Christie's leadership has given him a great deal of political capital to use over the next year."

Rutgers-Eagleton also asked voters to speculate on how Christie would fare against the suspected array of opposition Democratic candidates in the 2013 gubernatorial election. Amongst the cadre of Former Governor Richard Codey, Newark Mayor Cory Booker, Assembly Majority Leader Lou Greenwald, Senator Barbara Buono, and former State Democratic Party Chairman Tom Byrne, Christie pummeled his projected opponents in head-to-head matchups by double digits. Only Booker came close, trailing Christie by some nineteen points.

The Announcement

Christie wasted no time in taking his new favorability ratings out for a spin around the state. Running for Governor was back in the picture again. New Jersey's dire economic straits were no longer a problem. Sandy would afford Christie a convenient excuse to explain away New Jersey's anticipated financial cataclysm. There was also some $60 billion of federal aid approved for Sandy relief. Quietly, most likely on Marine One while he toured the disaster scenes with President Obama, Christie lobbied that the aid be dispensed in the form of Community Development Block Grants, ensuring that he would have a major say on how New Jersey's portion of the funding would be allocated. This meant that heading into an election year, Christie had billions of dollars of aid to play Santa Claus with, rewarding and punishing the naughty and nice list of towns that would, and would not, be favorable to his election chances.

Christie's ego was not going to allow him to step aside when, through the funneling of aid, his hand could help to sculpt the new landscape of New Jersey. This would be a monumental opportunity afforded no other Governor. On November 26, 2012, at one of his post-Sandy press conferences in Port Monmouth, New Jersey, he took the plunge, announcing his intention to seek re-election. This was to be Christie's launching pad for the presidency. "The public needs to know that I'm in this for the long haul. That the person who has helped to lead this through the initial crisis wants to be here to lead them through the rebuilding and restoration of our state and it would be wrong for me to leave now. I don't want to leave now. We have a job to do. I promised people when I made up my mind I'd tell you. So I made up my mind. So I'm telling you," he announced.

Within a month of the announcement, his campaign raised a record $2.1 million. Christie was determined to demonstrate to the nation that as a Republican governor in a Blue state, he could trample his Democratic opposition. That would give him the bragging rights to claim that he could do what neither of the past two GOP presidential nominees, McCain and Romney, could not – attract independent voters and pick off Democrat voters. The Republican establishment has been salivating for such a candidate.

Rider University political science professor, Ben Dworkin, saw the upside for Christie's decision to seek re-election. "A strong Christie victory in 2013 definitely sets him up for a run in 2016 for president," he observed.

Within days, as if it was choreographed, Christie was endorsed by the powerful Laborers' Union (LIUNA). The union's leader, Ray Pocino, rallied his troops behind the man who had earlier in the year given his workers gainful employment when Christie bailed out the stalled Revel Casino construction project by pledging $260 million in tax incentives to resurrect it. Despite Christie's gamble to rescue the casino, the project shortly afterward faced potential foreclosure and bankruptcy. The fact that Christie had also reappointed Pocino as a Commissioner of the Port Authority certainly did not hurt his chances in snagging the prestigious endorsement.

"A strong leader for a strong New Jersey. That's what we have in Governor Christie," the commissioner and labor leader declared to a mob of his members huddled in a laborer's training facility that had been converted from a former airplane hangar. "You have earned our support. You have earned the right to finish the job you have started. Justice. Honor. And Strength," Pocino intoned, quoting the union's motto. "It may as well be Gov. Christie's campaign slogan, because he has every one of those traits."

Christie was pumped. The approval rating that he was riding, courtesy of Sandy, was holding the campaign road just fine. "I am not in this race for re-election just for the hell of it. We are in this thing to win and win big, and that's what it's all about. I'm willing to fight with you if you're willing to fight with me," he declared. "I doubt I'll have many better days than the day I was endorsed by the Laborers' of North America." As for his Democrat opposition, which the early polls showed he would crush, Christie assumed a cavalier posture. "I have no idea who I'll be running against, and frankly I don't care," he quipped. Weeks later the *Star-Ledger* reported, "he won't be satisfied unless he trounces the opposition by a bigger margin than any Republican in a generation. 'I'll consider that a raging success and a historic success,' he said. 'I'd consider that to be a real affirmation of my time in office and my vision for the future.'"

In responding to the labor union endorsement, the State Democratic Party Chairman, Assemblyman John Wisniewski, offered a pragmatic comment, "The endorsement by NJ LIUNA of Governor Chris Christie's campaign for re-election was probably set in stone when the governor reappointed Ray Pocino as a Commissioner of the Port Authority."

It didn't take long for Christie's decision to seek re-election to alter the course of his suspected Democrat opposition. The Democratic candidate who polled the best and conceivably had the best chance to take him on, despite trailing by substantial double-digit numbers, Newark Mayor Cory Booker, chickened out. The *Star-Ledger's* columnist Tom Moran called Booker's decision, "the punt heard around the world." He then offered a dead-on analysis. "The decision to punt, Booker insists, was all about Newark. He needs another year to finish work in his beloved adopted city. 'It's about purpose, and not position,' he says. Don't believe it. This was no more complex than the decision to step aside when a bulldozer is rumbling your way." Though running away from the Christie challenge, Booker also announced that he would explore running for the United States Senate seat that was then occupied by incumbent Frank Lautenberg.

Christie's numbers were awesome and, no matter where he went, all New Jersey's political world was his stage. The *Star-Ledger's* Tom Moran described the Christie mystique, "And here is the really remarkable part of the story: He's doing all this while the state's miserable economy is lagging well behind the nation's and the regions. While the state's foreclosure crisis is among the worst anywhere. While the property tax burden has gone up thanks to reductions in rebates." Moran pondered the phenomenon. "It's probably a mix of more earthly things. He is the best communicator since Bill Clinton, with a keen eye for emotional punch."

"I can't figure it out," Patrick Murray, the director of the Monmouth University Polling Institute, told Tom Moran. "I've tried. I've polled all the things that should be his Achilles' heel." Moran explained Murray's thoroughness in probing the magic numbers: "He asked about property taxes and found that most people are furious. But they blame the school board, the mayor, or the Legislature. Anyone but Christie. He asked about jobs. Remember that Christie predicted a jobs boom would follow his hard line against tax hikes and taunted Connecticut Gov. Dannel Malloy when he raised taxes there. Turns out Connecticut is doing much better than Jersey. 'People say jobs are Washington's problem, not his,' Murray found."

Sandy's winds also blew Christie to the front of the pack of probable contenders for the 2016 GOP's presidential nomination. The *Star-Ledger* reported that a Fairleigh Dickinson University PublicMind poll heralded Christie as besting a field of prominent candidates the likes of Senator Marco Rubio of Florida, Louisiana Governor Bobby Jindal, Jeb Bush and Rick Santorum.

Christie and his likely toughest competitor, Rubio, topped the favorability rankings among those surveyed. Christie posted 55 percent favorability to Rubio's 46 percent. "Although early, these numbers are good news for those who are already perceived favorably by a majority or near-majority of those familiar with the candidate," Krista Jenkins, a political scientist and director of the poll, said in a news release," the *Ledger* reported. Focusing on the attraction of voters to Christie, Jenkins further stated, "The governor's appeal is likely based on his call for bipartisanship during his high-profile speech at the Republican convention, as well as the praise he had for President Obama in the days after Hurricane Sandy."

In the wake of those astronomical polling numbers, Sandy became the gift that just kept on giving. In the first few days of 2013, Congress was slated to vote on the package of bills committing financial aid to the northeast states massacred by Superstorm Sandy. The appropriations measures were competing for time with the "fiscal cliff" stage show that had been held over on Capitol Hill. The melodrama was played out like a bad movie serial of yesteryear with the predictable nail biting and last minute rescue staged by politicians to make themselves look good in the eyes of the public. Apparently, Speaker of the House John Boehner was exhausted from stage-managing the fiscal cliff production, because he failed to post the aid bills for the suffering millions trying to recover in the wake of the storm. More likely, Boehner needed to trade off the delay on the aid package for votes on the fiscal cliff agreement with Tea Party house members who were critical of the Sandy bills.

Storm of Discontent

The failure to call the aid package to the floor for a vote went over about as well as another hurricane. A superstorm of criticism swept out from representatives of both parties whose constituents had just been shoved into the deep freeze by the delay. Leading the charge was none other than Chris Christie, who attributed the cause of the delay to "toxic internal politics," and who once more had the chance to play to the poll numbers and assume the role of Mr. Nonpartisan. Declaring that Sandy victims were being treated "like pawns on a chessboard," Christie placed Boehner in his cross-hairs, climbed upon his soapbox, and fired away:

"It's absolutely disgraceful. This used to be something that was not political. Disaster relief was something that you didn't play games with, but now in this current atmosphere, everything is a subject of one-upsmanship, everything is a possibility, a potential piece of bait for the political game. It is why the American people hate Congress. It's why they hate them....

"There's only one group to blame for the continued suffering of these innocent victims – the House majority and their speaker, John Boehner. This is not a Republican or Democratic issue. Natural disasters happen in red states and blue states, in states with Democratic governors and Republican governors. We respond to innocent victims of natural disasters not as Republicans or Democrats but as Americans. Or at least we did, until last night. Last night, politics was placed before our oath to serve our citizens. For me, it was disappointing and disgusting to watch. Last night, the House of Representatives failed that most basic test of public service, and they did so with callous indifference to the suffering of the people of my state....

"Americans are tired of the palace intrigue and political partisanship of this Congress, which places one-upsmanship ahead of the lives of the citizens who sent these people to Washington, D.C., in the first place. New Jerseyans and New Yorkers are tired of being treated like second-class citizens. New York deserved better than the selfishness we saw on display last night. New Jersey deserves better than the duplicity we saw on display last night. America deserves better than just another example of a government that has forgotten who they are there to serve and why. Sixty-six days and counting. Shame on you. Shame on Congress."

President Obama could not have said it any better.

Christie told Mike Symons of Gannett news that Boehner had refused to return four phone calls the Governor had placed to the Speaker once he learned that the bills were pulled from the voting session. Finally, a day later, Boehner spoke to the irate Governor. Asked about his chat with the Speaker of the House, Christie expressed his frustration, "I'm not going to get into the specifics of what I discussed with John Boehner today. But what I will tell you is: There is no reason for me at the moment to believe anything that they tell me, because they've been telling me stuff for weeks and they didn't deliver."

While some might feel that Christie's response was over-the-top rhetoric, for someone eying the 2016 GOP presidential nomination, it was a measured tactical response. There was sparse criticism from fellow Republicans for his rebuke of the Party's Congressional Speaker and its caucus. "Personally I think he went a little overboard," said Steve Duprey, a former New Hampshire GOP chairman and onetime John McCain presidential adviser, commenting to *Politico*. "I don't blame Gov. Christie for being frustrated [and vocalizing it] ... but I think he was overblown in his criticism of the speaker given what else was going on." Asked for the Governor's response, the Christie camp was in keeping with Christie's vintage character. "He doesn't give a shit what people think."

Knowing how well Christie and his handlers read the polls; it was hard for them not to notice that Congress's most recent approval rating were hovering around 11 percent. In fact, lice and rats had a better reputation nationwide. With Boehner portrayed as an obstructionist in Washington, Christie knew that picking on the unpopular Speaker of the House would only serve to make himself look good. Furthermore, Boehner is not believed to be one of the GOP leaders that would be supportive of Christie in a 2016 presidential nomination contest and, even if he were, with congress at an 11 percent approval rating, he could prove to be a liability.

Additionally, Christie's numbers-crunchers would understand that Boehner was from Ohio (always a key state in Presidential politics), note that Romney lost Ohio, and thus assess Boehner's political stock as nil.

Also, the Tea Party wing, the group that Christie would have his toughest time winning over, were also ticked at Boehner, although for other reasons. The Tea Party was angry and blasting Boehner for caving to the Democrats over the fiscal cliff farce. Christie knows that, and by not criticizing the compromise (which he stayed silent on), he could still extract some benefit from disgruntled members of the party, because he went so far in demonizing Boehner. Christie's unsubtle attack on Boehner was a calculated political strategy designed to make Christie look good to the far right and it did. His already astonishing favorability ratings soared into the stratosphere.

Ironically, a few months later, a charity established by New Jersey First Lady Mary Pat Christie for assisting victims of the superstorm would come under the same criticism Christie was doling out. The *Asbury Park Press* reported that the fund "has raised more than $32 million so far. But four months after the superstorm, none of that aid has reached storm victims yet."

The First Lady defended the charity and claimed, "I have taken excruciating steps to make sure that we give the money out in a really judicious way." But as the *Asbury Park Press* noted, her justification, "comes on the heels of the pointed barbs her husband, Gov. Chris Christie, has hurled at the Federal Emergency Management Agency and Speaker of the House John Boehner, among others, for what the governor sees as inexcusable delays in helping the state's residents, businesses and communities still reeling from the Oct. 29 storm. Christie famously had called Congress' holdup of Sandy relief 'disgusting.'"

Mary Pat Christie also appointed an inexperienced executive director for the fund (her former chief of staff and director of protocol), at a salary of $160,000. In response to the criticism, Mrs. Christie announced that $1million, three percent of the funds collected, would be issued in grants within days. The gesture did not sit well with a least one disgruntled storm victim, quoted by the *Press*. "That's absolutely 100 percent unacceptable, because we want help yesterday," said Liaguno-Dorr, of Middletown, who is still battling her insurance company over the destruction of her Union Beach restaurant, Jakeabob's Bay. 'She's the governor's wife. If anybody can push it through, she can,' she said. 'Let's move it.'"

An upset donor to the fund also e-mailed a complaint to the newspaper regarding their story. "When my wife and I were moved to give $500 to the fund, it was out of compassion and efforts to do something for the devastated families and small businesses," Little Silver resident Patrick wrote in an e-mail to the *Press*. "To read this spin control coming from Mrs. Christie when people are still suffering is a disgrace. I feel that we were duped with false promises about our donation and feel a deep sense of sorrow for those who need the aid most."

When the New Year kicked in, it was time for Christie to deliver the annual State of the State address. Sandy dominated every paragraph of the speech, and keeping in tune with what polling showed the public was clamoring for, Christie shared credit with the legislature for simplistic successes that he built up because he needed to show that he could work across the aisle, an important quality for 2016. One got the sense that Christie was auditioning the new town hall routine for the year ahead.

He even worked in another tug-on-the-heartstrings moment in case the stories about he and his mom were wearing thin.

This time he would prey on his audience's emotions and their susceptibility for the plight of children. Christie builds his story like Steven Spielberg sets up a scene. "As I walked around the parking lot of the fire department in Port Monmouth in one of the days soon after Sandy had laid waste to so much of our state, I saw so many of the scenes that I had come to expect in the aftermath of the storm. Neighbors helping neighbors. Food being prepared for the hungry. First responders helping the homeless."

'Ginjer' Bread Man

With the stage set, Christie brings out the star of his tale. "Then I met nine-year-old Ginjer. Having a 9-year-old girl myself, her height and manner of speaking was immediately familiar and evocative. Having confronted so many crying adults at that point I felt ready to deal with anything. Then Ginjer looked at me, began to cry and told me she was scared. She told me she had lost everything; she had lost her home and her belongings. She asked me to help her."

The eyes of the audience in the Statehouse Assembly Chamber begin to well up with tears as Christie introduces himself into the story's mix. "As my eyes filled with tears, I took a deep breath and thought about what I would say to my Bridget if she said the same thing to me. If she had the same look on her face. If she had the same tears in her eyes. I asked her where her mom was and she pointed right behind her. I asked her if her dad was okay. She told me he was. So I told Ginjer, you haven't lost your home; you've just lost a house. A house we can replace, your home is with your mom and dad. I hugged her and told her not to cry – that the adults are in charge now and there was nothing to be afraid of anymore."

Christie glances off to his left, down towards the dignitary seating area in the well of the assembly hall. You didn't have to be Jeanne Dixon to know what would happen next. "Ginjer is here today – we've kept in touch – she has her own cell phone and she gave me the number – and Ginjer I want to thank you for giving voice to New Jersey's children during Sandy and helping to create a memory of humanity in a sea of despair. You are a special, special girl. Thank you for coming today."

All eyes fall upon a cute young girl seated between her sobbing mother and New Jersey's First Lady. Christie then pounces down from the elevated lectern (you could tell there was no true spontaneity here) and saunters over to Ginjer. He bends over and plants a soft kiss on her cheek, hugging her long enough for every camera to preserve the moment for history – the fulfillment of a public relations specialist's dream. Another moment in time to ratchet the favorability numbers further up the polls.

Once again, the road to Christie's fortunes had been paved by the misfortune of others. One of the most devastating natural disasters in U.S. history, Superstorm Sandy, saved him … for a while.

Chapter Seventeen

The Re-election

Loyal Opposition

Literally, every move made and every word spoken in the year in which a governor faces re-election is done with an eye toward that election. The same could be said for the opposition. As Governor Christie continued to ride the wave of popularity that came courtesy of Superstorm Sandy, New Jersey Democrats assumed the unenviable task of trying to stop the juggernaut that threatened their political existence. If Christie's expected November victory came with coattails, long entrenched elected Democratic officials were in harms way.

The brave Alpha Dem's, who would typically trample one another in attempting to become the party's standard-bearer in a gubernatorial election, suddenly suffered from a mass outbreak of cold feet. After Cory Booker became the first to bail, a succession of other prominent Democrats quickly followed suit. Typically, a politician's decision to make a challenge would be based on simple arithmetic: assessing the strengths and weaknesses of the opposition, and what a campaign might cost to overcome that opposition. This wasn't too hard for any political strategist worth their salt to figure out.

One by one, Former Acting Governor and State Senator Dick Codey, Senate President Stephen Sweeney, and Congressman Bill Pascrell withdrew their names from consideration. This time, the Jersey 'Political' Boys were like gentlemen on the Titanic: offering the party standard-bearer's seat to women first. Senator Barbara Buono, who had bravely tossed her bonnet into the ring early on, but couldn't attract substantial support or momentum until the scent of fear gripped the men in the party, was the beneficiary of the unmanly lack of nerve. Those seeking to preserve their political hides were more than willing to let Buono, a State Senator who got pushed aside in the Senate reorganization after the 2009 elections, slip her political neck into the Christie re-election noose.

Buono formally kicked off her campaign in early February, declaring, "Leaders lead and real leadership means hearing the voices of the other New Jersey. The hardworking men and women who've been unemployed or underemployed for years, and who've gotten nothing – nothing – but sound bites and empty promises from a governor who seems more intent on courting his right-wing base than tending to the needs of the middle-class and working poor."

Despite her sincerity and sterling capabilities as a candidate, right out of the gate, Senator Buono was trailing Christie by a staggering thirty-seven percentage points in a head-to-head Quinnipiac Poll. Outside of her District and home base, nobody knew her. Considering there are approximately three-quarter million more registered Democratic than Republican voters in New Jersey, the numbers were astonishing. Christie was actually capturing almost as many Democratic voters as Buono. The numbers would make potential supporters and donors tempted to set sail with Buono's campaign feel as though they were walking a gangplank shortly after they boarded.

Another clique of Democratic officials decided to skip the gangplank and instead merge into a Conga line of cross-party support for Christie, the prominence and numbers of which had not been seen in New Jersey history. By the middle of June 2013, twenty-seven elected Democrats (including twelve Democratic mayors) had endorsed Governor Christie for re-election. Among the entourage of Democratic party figures were State Senator Brian Stack, Essex County Executive Joe DiVincenzo, Essex County Sheriff Armando Fontoura, Orange Mayor Dwayne Warren, Paterson City Council President Anthony Davis, Long Branch Mayor Adam Schneider, Harrison Mayor Ray McDonough and all eight members of the Harrison City Council, and Sea Bright Mayor Dina Long.

Another grouping of labor organizations, which typically supported Democratic candidates, also bolted from tradition and joined the Christie Conga line. These early defections were yet another death knell for Senator Buono's doomed campaign.

Of all his support from the ranks of Democrat Party mayors and typically Democratic-leaning organizations, the curious circumstances surrounding Belleville Mayor Raymond Kimball's endorsement of Christie would hint of scandal. The *Star-Ledger* reported that despite being left unscathed by Superstorm Sandy, Belleville was the beneficiary of six million dollars of the Federal funding dedicated to help communities recover from the hurricane. In fact, the money was being used to support the construction of a senior citizen housing complex conceived years before Sandy was ever a blip on weather radar screens. Not one Belleville resident was displaced by Sandy.

Mayor Kimball met with Christie in late April of 2013, afterwards remarking to the press that he was going to endorse Christie. "I think the governor is going to help the town of Belleville with certain projects we need," Kimball added. Christie's gift of funding for the project and a groundbreaking followed shortly after Kimball and Christie's initial meeting. Within weeks of the funding announcement, Kimball delivered his public endorsement for the Governor in the November election.

The *Star-Ledger* Editorial Board labeled the pool of Sandy relief dollars as Christie's "political slush fund" utilized for helping his own campaign agenda. "What it points to is the need for further inquiry into how Sandy funds were part and parcel of the governor's campaign for reelection," State Senator Raymond Lesniak commented, adding, "And how they were misused for political purposes rather than going to those who really in need."

The Storm of Scandal

An issue that Democrats quickly seized upon and played to the hilt was an evolving scandal regarding Christie's handing out of an exorbitantly priced no-bid contract for debris cleanup in the wake of Superstorm Sandy to a contractor steeped in political connections. As we know, Christie had plenty of experience with costly no-bid contracts from his days when voting for them as a freeholder or handing them out in the form of deferred prosecution monitoring agreements as United States Attorney.

One of the sharpest investigative reporters to ply the trade, the *Star-Ledger's* Jarrett Renshaw, hunted down the story like a bloodhound. In the wake of the storm, cleaning up the devastation as quickly as possible remained a daunting task for the hardest hit New Jersey communities. In fairness to the Christie Administration, they were dealing with an emergency and catastrophe of epic proportions and attempting to be proactive in handling it. Garbage and debris was piling up by the minute and if the state and local government intended to comply with time-costly bidding laws, those piles of garbage and debris were only going to pile higher.

The story being peddled for public consumption by Christie's Administration was that in order to help local governments cope with the disaster promptly and maximize FEMA expenditures, they were providing them a mechanism to work around public contract bidding laws by engaging the experienced Florida firm, AshBritt. New Jersey did so by co-opting a Connecticut state contract executed with AshBritt. The state contract allowed AshBritt to bring in unlicensed subcontractors to assist in removing debris and waived New Jersey administrative fees to the tune of a quarter-million dollars. AshBritt was in position to land some $100 million worth of local government contracts in New Jersey.

Behind the Christie Administration's cover story lay some troubling facts. Apparently, AshBritt was charging practically double for hauling debris compared to other firms. The facts also show that another contractor, Ceres Environmental Services, warned the state about AshBritt's "unreasonably high" rates. It also turned out that the decision not to bid out disposal contracts could actually jeopardize federal reimbursement to the state and local governments for the services they already paid.

It turned out that AshBritt's Washington D.C. lobbyist firm, BGR Group, was founded by former Mississippi Governor Haley Barbour, who, Christie publically admitted, had recommended AshBritt. According to the *Asbury Park Press*, "When Barbour was chairman of the Republican Governors Association, the group spent $7.5 million on Christie's 2009 gubernatorial race."

AshBritt has contributed some $136,000 to the Republican Governors Association. A few months after the contract award, Ed Rogers, the head of the BGR Group, hosted a fundraiser in Virginia to benefit Christie's 2013 gubernatorial campaign. Speaking about Barbour in 2012, Christie stated, "If it wasn't for Haley Barbour, I wouldn't be governor of New Jersey. A guy like that who was with you when not only wasn't there anybody on the bandwagon, there wasn't a bandwagon, you remain incredibly indebted to somebody like that."

Renshaw's investigation uncovered even more: some familiar faces were aiding and abetting AshBritt in their pursuit of local government contracts. Ocean County Republican Party Chairman George Gilmore, who delivered a 71,000-vote plurality to Christie in the 2009 gubernatorial election, and mysteriously dropped off the radar screen of confidential informant Solomon Dwek and Bid Rig III prosecutors during their pursuit of Assemblyman Daniel Van Pelt, was contracted by AshBritt to assist the efforts in Ocean County.

Gilmore's law firm had contracts with a slough of local governments in Ocean County, and New Jersey law prohibited his lobbying on behalf of AshBritt to those local governments that employed his law firm. Yet, some of those towns, Seaside Heights and Jackson Township, had contracts with AshBritt.

Miraculously, the Ocean County Board of Freeholders, where Gilmore certainly held sway, agreed to pay cleanup costs upfront for Ocean County towns if they were under contract with AshBritt. This brainstorm was claimed to be the idea of Ocean Country Administrator Carl Block, a friend of Gilmore's. When questioned by Jarrett Renshaw, Block acknowledged that Gilmore spoke to him about AshBritt, but maintained that the strategy for approaching the towns was his idea. Gilmore brushed off questions by stating, "Due to a confidentiality clause, I cannot comment."

Even Solomon Dwek would have been hard pressed to contrive this elaborate a ruse.

The Associated Press reported that Gilmore "says he played no role in county towns' decisions to hire a debris contractor that used him as a consultant." This still left unanswered the questions as to just what AshBritt hired Gilmore to do and why there was practically a military secrecy concerning his role.

As expected, the Democratic legislature wanted the matter investigated and prepared to do so. "Taxpayers have a right to know why a company that is charging in some cases nearly twice as much as other companies is working in the state," stated Senate President Stephen Sweeney. The legislature convened a joint State Senate and Assembly Oversight Committee to examine the circumstances.

On a snowy afternoon in March, the legislature kicked off its investigation. The perception of the hearings from the vantage point of Republican legislators was that they were "nothing more than a political dog-and-pony show" staged by the Democrats. The Democratic composition of the committee consisted mostly of legislators who happened to be in hotly contested elections in the fall. It also happened that Christie's gubernatorial opponent, Senator Barbara Buono, was a pre-existing member of the committee.

The guests of honor for the Committee's initial hearing were the officers from the AshBritt firm that was the focus of the controversy. Most of the legislative panel's questioning was redundant and initially seemed like a fishing expedition. AshBritt's CEO, Randy Perkins, was so robust and skillful in testifying that even though he unintentionally dropped clues as large as elephant squat concerning potential untoward conduct regarding New Jersey's hiring of his firm, they somehow defied the laws of physics and flew over the heads of the oversight committee. Perkins further went out of his way to take repeated potshots at the *Star-Ledger,* obviously upset with what he felt was the paper's unfair characterization of AshBritt in its coverage.

In her turn at bat, Buono got to the heart of the matter "On its face, it appears to me that the administration went out of its way to give a lucrative no-bid contract to a connected out-of-state firm at double the price," she asserted.

Perkins mater-of-factly took issue with Buono's conclusion. His strategy was to shield the company with what he inferred was FEMA's approval for the New Jersey AshBritt contract. "Before our contract was signed by the state of New Jersey – this is fact, back to checking the facts – the lead counsel, the head counsel for FEMA … and the federal government, prior to us starting work, signed off on the contracting process that the state of New Jersey was using. They blessed it, they anointed it and the state signed it."

The *Star-Ledger's* Jarrett Renshaw tried to confirm Perkins' assertion with FEMA, "There was no blessing of the contract," Lars Anderson, Director of Public Affairs, said. "Neither the administrator nor the chief counsel 'approve' contracts entered into by state or local governments." Anderson's assertion lasted as long as it took for Christie's people to contact FEMA officials. The *Star-Ledger* then reported, "FEMA advised the state it could proceed with the AshBritt contract but warned it would be 'subject to usual review' to determine if the rates were fair."

What became painfully obvious after more than three hours of testimony was that AshBritt testified that their *first* contact with the state of NJ was in a call placed to mid-to-upper level employees in the Attorney General's office (Charles McKenna). With all of the "consultants" that AshBritt had on board, the testimony does not seem to make much sense. If you are trying to nail down a contract in the face of fierce competition and limited time, you try to reach decision-makers or people as high up the ladder in the Administration as possible. Further, that account conflicts with the account already given by Christie and Haley Barbour. That is why the early press accounts of both Haley Barbour and Chris Christie confirming that "Christie had said AshBritt was recommended to him by Barbour," make AshBritt's explanation shaky. The Barbour-to-Christie approach makes more sense: this sounds more in line with how AshBritt would have gone after NJ's business.

What most likely happened is that Barbour lobbied Christie for the contract. Barbour was most likely then directed to have AshBritt's personnel reach out to McKenna and the AG's office – the buffers and fixers. Here the discussion could have gone along the lines of the AG's office explaining to AshBritt about New Jersey's contracting laws and seeing what could be worked out. That is when the suggestion by AshBritt to piggyback the Connecticut contract could have come up, as AshBritt had testified. Therefore, it is plausible that the decision to hire AshBritt could have been made by Christie prior to AshBritt contacting the AG's office, or before Christie ever knew about the Connecticut contract.

The crucial question is, when Christie and Barbour had their discussion, *had an emergency already been declared* to pre-empt contracting laws and give the state's executive officers the power to do so? If it had not, then Christie could not have legally directed the hiring of AshBritt, nor put into motion the actions for doing so.

When Perkins was asked at the hearing about an earlier FEMA statement disputing his prior testimony, he didn't back off. He said he would love to come back and testify with FEMA director Craig Fugate so he could verify his account. Meanwhile, United States Senator Tom Coburn, a Republican fiscal conservative from Oklahoma and the party's ranking member on the United State Senate Homeland Security and Oversight Committee reviewing the federal aid doled out for aiding states damaged by Sandy, stated that he was "troubled by the cost of the subcontractors used by ... AshBritt."

The AshBritt contract was not the only one that would come under media scrutiny. When the Christie Administration announced their intention to privatize the operation of the New Jersey Lottery, Rhode Island-based company, GTECH, teamed up with a New York company, Scientific Games, to become the sole bidders for the contract that could net the firms millions of dollars. The hurdles for achieving privatization apparently seemed daunting enough for the companies to engage the help of lobbyists. Two months after the bidding process closed, there was still no indication of whether the Christie Administration would move forward and award the project.

According to an investigative news story by the *Bergen Record's* Michael Linhorst and Melissa Hayes, the companies had plenty of star power to bring the privatization to fruition. According to its lobbying expenditures, the firm hired Wolff & Samson to lobby on its behalf. "David Samson, one of its founding members, led Christie's transition team when he was elected governor in 2009. Samson, who served as state attorney general in 2002 and 2003, was also counsel to Christie's campaign. He serves now as the chairman of the Port Authority, a post filled by Christie.... It is the bond counsel to the New Jersey Economic Development Authority, and it provides legal services to NJ Transit and other state departments."

The firm also hired Mercury Public Affairs. "Mercury Public Affairs has been hired by GTECH to handle its public relations. Mike DuHaime, the chief strategist for Christie's re-election campaign, is the head of Mercury's public affairs operations in New Jersey. DuHaime declined to comment other than to confirm the relationship."

The GTECH and AshBritt contract recommendations and awards were reminiscent of the conduct of the United States Attorney's Office in awarding no-bid deferred prosecution monitoring contracts when Christie was United States Attorney for New Jersey.

A related controversy that was triggered by Superstorm Sandy revolved around a portion of the federal aid dispatched to New Jersey – some $23 billion in federal funds utilized to help revive the state's economy. The money was earmarked by the state to promote tourism in an attempt to attract back the hordes of visitors and vacationers to the Jersey Shore. The state's tourism promoters decided to cast Christie and his family as the stars of television commercials that would air around the nation. There was precedent for the tactic, dating back to Governor Tom Kean, whose 'NJ and you, perfect together' slogan was the basis of an advertising campaign that he starred in during the 1980s.

The theme of the ads was that New Jersey was rebounding, with critics panning them saying they should have featured shore residents and businesses. Obviously, Christie's presidential aspirations would be greatly enhanced by the promotion and it would not cost him a dime. Christie's spokesperson called his casting a "creative decision" and hailed the Governor as "uniquely qualified" for the role. The *Star-Ledger* Editorial Board saw otherwise. They lambasted the decision.

"Given Christie's presidential ambitions, is it any surprise that he'd use federal relief dollars to splash his face all over TV in New York, Pennsylvania, Maryland and Canada – in addition to ads in print, on the radio and Internet? Sure, governors have appeared in tourism ads before. But not in campaigns this big, when the competing need was so dire. When former Governor Thomas H. Kean launched his series of ads, it was a $3 million project. Pocket change compared to this Christie propaganda. But until then, people all up the East Coast will be forced to watch Christie feed his staggering ego at the expense of Hurricane Sandy victims. Has he no shame?"

The Election Year Budget Ploy

Christie's election year budget was a no-brainer – crafted to be as uncontroversial as possible. The Governor stepped up to the Assembly Chamber's pulpit on February 26, 2013 and delivered the budget address. Knowing that Democrats would be looking to skewer him at the drop of a hat, Christie presented a budget that offered them little to savage him with, and gave himself plenty to crow about in order to woo centrist voters already polling in his favor. In fact, given the perplexing contradiction confronting Christie (his need to appear moderate to secure re-election in New Jersey and at the same time to appear conservative enough to remain in the pecking order for a GOP presidential nomination) the budget hit the mark for the Governor.

Christie exploited his celebrity and gave a masterful presentation recital for his budget. It was a Jekyll & Hyde performance, as Christie navigated a tightrope between appeasing moderate New Jerseyans and national conservatives. As astute *Star-Ledger* columnist Tom Moran concluded, "he did what incumbents always do during an election year: He moved to the middle to capture the strategic ground where New Jersey elections are won and lost." Moran further predicted that, "Next year, with an eye to the presidential race in 2016, he'll do the same move in reverse. Look for tax cuts as the Big Idea in his 2014 budget speech."

Christie proposed a $32.9 billion budget that increased spending about $1.27 billion from the previous year's proposal. Fiscal conservatives may never know that Christie had actually increased spending contrary to their principles, because of his cunning ability to pull the wool over the public's eye and, in this case, even the legislatures.

Christie purposefully compared the increase to his predecessor, former Governor Jon Corzine's 2008 budget's spending increase. "In total, the budget I am submitting to you today provides $32.9 billion in state spending. While we are meeting the needs of our people in this budget, we are doing it by spending less than the state spent in fiscal year 2008. Let me repeat that for you. Six years later, a budget that still spends less," the Governor stated in perfect Christiespeak. Then he accentuated his point with a punch line: "Where else is this happening in America?"

Christie managed to siphon off approximately $392 million dollars from the current year's budget by failing to credit homeowners' property tax bills with their state rebate credits. Instead of funding the credit in April, so the cost would be covered by the current budget, he deferred it to August, so the proposed budget would cover the funding. The most controversial savings and injection of revenue into the proposed budget was Christie's acquiescing to Obamacare, a move that could put a crimp in his 2016 GOP presidential nomination ambition.

Echoing his mantra, "I will make all my judgments as governor based on what is best for New Jerseyans," Christie opted to sign New Jersey onto a program that expanded Medicaid to more than 300,000 in New Jersey and effectively would save the state some $227 million in the proposed budget and even more in future year budgets. In an un-Reaganlike moment, Christie caved in on his supposedly conservative philosophy and cashed in on the controversial expansion of the social health care program. Christiespeak would have to engage in full gear.

"Let me be clear, I am no fan of the Affordable Care Act. I think it is wrong for New Jersey and for America. I fought against it and believe, in the long run, it will not achieve what it promises. However, it is now the law of the land," Mr. Hyde declared. A few seconds later Doctor Jekyll uttered, "expanding Medicaid by 104,000 citizens in a program that already serves 1.4 million, is the smart thing to do for our fiscal and public health." Then Mr. Hyde pivoted back around: "If that ever changes because of adverse actions by the Obama Administration, I will end it as quickly as it started."

Of course, not forgetting how nationwide polling determined that the American people were clamoring for their elected officials to work together to solve the country's problems, Christie rattled off a number of accomplishments that he and the Democrat-controlled legislature shared. Doctor Jekyll smoothed over any animus that stood between him and the lawmakers. "The people of New Jersey have trusted us. They have put their faith in us to come together.... It's truly remarkable what we have accomplished in these last three years.... Let's work on a bipartisan basis."

Mr. Hyde then had his choice moments in the speech, kicking the Democratic legislature in the teeth by regurgitating the past and blaming them for practically everything that had gone wrong for New Jersey. "Those who were supposed to be responsible for controlling taxes and spending before we came to office fundamentally deceived the people of our state. They said yes to everything – yes to higher taxes. Yes to more spending. We must not return to that era of recklessness and deceit." Christie, without mentioning her, was landing a backhand smack on Barbara Buono, who was the New Jersey Senate Budget Committee Chair when the matters he spoke about transpired.

Mr. Hyde would lash out further, again seemingly targeting Buono without mentioning her name, "And one message to those naysayers and perpetual cynics who refused to fund the pension on their own watch and opposed our reforms to protect the monied special interests: our citizens are fortunate that your type of politics is dying in Trenton. Our pension system is alive as a result."

Christie then threw down the gauntlet, sticking his finger in the Democrats' eyes and hinting to what might become one of his potential campaign strategies. First he blasted them for striking down the income tax cut he wanted in the current year's budget, then he sounded a warning: "It is clear to me that on this subject we simply disagree. I believe New Jerseyans are overtaxed. Many of you in this chamber repeatedly vote for tax increases. So, let me be direct with you – I have compromised and offered your plan for tax cuts. You have reneged on your promise to me and the people of New Jersey. I will not shut down the budget process to continue this argument; the people's business and our least fortunate citizens' needs are too vitally important in the aftermath of Sandy. But, if you change your mind and concur with my conditional veto, my Administration will figure out how to pay for this long overdue tax relief. If you do not, I am content to let the voters decide this in November."

The Democratic response to the speech was underwhelming – the equivalent of a teenage girl at a pajama party walloping Christie with a pillowcase full of feathers. The Governor's strategy of implementing portions of Obamacare and not cutting spending on his opposition's pet programs gave them very little to complain about. His adversary, Senator Buono, gave what seemed to be a campaign-scripted response. "The governor likes to portray himself as a moderate. He's far from it," she observed. The comment could only serve to help ingratiate Christie to conservatives who might have been leery about his moderate positions.

By fully funding the State's commitment to its pension liability and paying down debt, Christie also de-fanged many of the newspaper editorial boards that had savaged him for failing to do so in the last budget he presented. Team Christie proved once again how they were head and shoulders above Democratic strategists in setting Trenton's political pace.

Subsequent to his budget address, Christie stated that he would make a tax cut the focus of his re-election campaign. By proposing so, the shrewd Governor would again be putting the Democrats in a bind. According to *Star-Ledger* reporter Jenna Portnoy, Christie "repackaged a tax cut plan that state Senate President Steve Sweeney (D-Gloucester) proposed last year, with a few changes. The proposal would give households earning up to $400,000 an income tax credit equal to 10 percent of their property tax bill over four years. The cut is capped at $1,000 a year and is for bills less than $10,000."

Christie was trying to put Democrats immediately on the defensive in an election year. "If I win, then I want the people's tax cut right after the election," Christie proposed. At the end of the day, Christie's popularity caused Democrats to go belly-up and hand him practically everything he wanted. It was the easiest passage of a budget Christie has had so far.

Celeb Phenom

From the Barbara Walters December 2012 television special to cohosting the *Today* show in May 2013, Christie's celebrity filled the television airwaves, sprinkling his brand on Jimmy Fallon's late-night show numerous times and, of course, his memorable *Saturday Night Live* appearance. Christie's appearances also included a prominently aired interview with Brian Williams for NBC's *Nightly News* and a *Rock Center* segment.

Christie could not chance restricting himself to the gubernatorial re-election campaign if he harbored thoughts of taking a shot at the White House. He would have to take advantage of every opportunity that presented him with the prospect of a national audience. His exploits during Superstorm Sandy gave him a segment on Barbara Walters' annual television special, *10 Most Fascinating People.* The interview took an unexpected twist, focusing on a subject matter Walters obviously felt could be a detriment to Christie – his obesity.

"OK, governor, I feel very uncomfortable asking this question when I'm sitting opposite you, but you are a little overweight," Walters opened.

"More than a little," Christie quipped.

"Why?"

"If I could figure that out, I'd fix it," Christie quipped again.

"There are people who say you couldn't be president because you're so heavy," Walters said, cutting to the heart of the matter.

"That's ridiculous. I mean, that's ridiculous. I don't know what the basis for that is," Christie protested, as a serious demeanor befell him. Barbara Walters moved the conversation elsewhere.

In January of 2013, Christie landed on the cover of *Time* magazine. The cover story was a positive piece positioning Christie as the potential savior of the GOP. The exposé by Michael Crowley inferred that, "Christie may now be America's most popular politician." Despite the favorable spin, the cover photo was less than flattering – an almost mug-shot style photo of Christie with the words

"THE BOSS" emblazoned across it. Christie inferred on the Don Imus radio program that the picture made him look like a "mob boss." Christie teased that, "I'm reporting *Time* magazine to the, like, anti-Italian defamation league. I mean, look at that thing. It says 'boss' underneath it." *Time* further branded Christie, two years in a row, as one of the magazine's Top 100 influential people in the world – sharing the leaders category with twenty other prominent world political officials.

Time was but the tip of the iceberg. Between the magazine exposé and a scheduled cameo appearance on Michael J. Fox's new primetime television show in the fall, Christie was on a celebrity publicity roll. In early February of 2013, Christie would be given the opportunity of a lifetime. The frequent brunt of fat jokes courtesy of *The Late Show* host David Letterman, Christie snagged an invite to appear on the show and being a good sport consented to appear, where he confessed that Letterman was his favorite late-night talk show host. Again, the topic of Christie's weight would sandbag the interview, but this time Christie was the initiator of the banter, in an attempt to diffuse the issue of his obesity as an obstacle for him to land the presidency.

Strolling on the stage of the Ed Sullivan Theater to the sounds of his rock music hero Bruce Springsteen's *Thunder Road* being played by the CBS Orchestra under the direction of Paul Shaffer, Christie was greeted by Letterman and quickly sat on the guest chair. Christie reached into his jacket pocket, pulled out a jelly doughnut and bit into it. The unexpected stunt brought down the house. A split-second later, Christie brought the house down again as he deadpanned, "I didn't know this was going to be this long."

That turned the conversation immediately onto the topic of his obesity. The *New York Post* had reported that, "Christie has struggled with his weight for decades. He sometimes jokes about it, while other times, it's a sensitive topic. Insiders said it was the only thing keeping the straight-talking executive from higher office."

After the Barbara Walters interview, Christie's weight was fair game. Letterman poked and prodded, but only uncovered the fact that Christie wasn't at all shy in talking about his weight. The Governor confessed that he strove to lose weight like lots of other Americans. He humanized his condition. Christie stressed that his weight had not yet presented a health threat to him, backing his assertions by citing perfect blood pressure, cholesterol, and blood sugar levels. "I'm basically the healthiest fat guy you've ever seen in your life," Christie quipped.

Christie told Letterman that his fat jokes did not bother him. "If the joke is funny, I laugh, even if it's about me." Pulling out a stack of index cards from another jacket pocket unoccupied by a doughnut, Christie told Letterman that he had jotted down some of the comedian's jokes that he considered his favorites. He then mimicked Letterman delivering a Christie joke, "Celebrity birthday today – Chris Christie turned 50. He blew out the candles on his cake, and he wished for another cake."

The conversation turned serious for a bit as Letterman praised Christie for stepping up and taking on Congress for stalling Superstorm Sandy relief bills during the fiscal cliff crisis. Then Christie got his chance to elaborate on his criticisms of Washington, drawing sustained applause from the *Late Show* audience. Before the show was over, Christie showcased his sense of humor again, reaching into another jacket pocket and pulling out another jelly doughnut to chomp down on. He had diffused the weight issue magnanimously.... At least for a few hours ...

The Weight

The day after his Letterman appearance, as if on cue, a former White House doctor who served President Clinton and both Bushes, Connie Mariano M.D., appeared on CNN news shows and sounded the alarm. She exclaimed that she was "worried Christie may have a heart attack," and that she feared he "may have a stroke." She continued to elaborate. "I will bet he has some kind of issue. He probably has incredible stamina and that's great, but you wonder what his blood pressure must be like, whether he has sleep apnea at night." She framed his condition as a disease and then even offered Christie some political advice. "If he can get the obese vote, he's got it. He can feel compassion, but he can also be a great example for people to conquer this. There are ways to do it.... And if he can overcome this disease, he deserves the White House. The thing that's holding him back, I'll be honest, is his weight."

Christie did not bother to take the advice and instead took aim. He wasn't going to allow the good doctor to ruin his Letterman debut. Pressed by reporters for a comment on Doctor Mariano's assessment, at a Superstorm Sandy related conference in Sea Girt the next day, the governor weighed in with an opinion of his own. "This is just another hack who wants five minutes on TV." Christie was only warming up. "I find it fascinating that a doctor in Arizona who's never met me [and] never examined me ... could make a diagnosis from 2,400 miles away. She must be a genius. My children saw that last night. It's completely irresponsible." He then added that his twelve year-old daughter asked him bluntly, "Dad, are you going to die?"

At another press conference in Union Beach the same day, Christie softened his tone and attempted to identify with the average person concerning his obesity. "I'm making the best effort I can, and sometimes I'm successful and sometimes I'm not. And sometimes periods of great success are followed by periods of great failure. That's just the way it's worked for me for probably the last 30 years of my life."

The weight issue obviously struck a nerve, because unbeknownst to even his closest friends, ironically on President's Day weekend, Christie stealthily signed himself into the NYU Langone Medical Center where he underwent lap-band stomach surgery, a medical procedure that inserts a silicone tube around the stomach to restrict the amount of food a person can eat at one time and making them feel fuller, faster. The procedure was successfully covered up by Christie's handlers, and only made public by Christie himself, exclusively to the *New York Post,* in early May of 2013.

Christie said, "I've struggled with this issue for 20 years. For me, this is about turning 50 and looking at my children and wanting to be there for them." He denied that his status as a political celebrity had anything to do with his decision. "It's so much more important than that," he said, capitalizing on his ability to morph the coverage by the media.

However, the political inference for the medical procedure was obvious, as the *New York Post* reported. "Insiders said it was the only thing keeping the straight-talking executive from higher office. Despite Christie's denials, political fund-raisers say that the surgery is a clear sign that he's going to join the 2016 race – and will do whatever it takes to win. 'This means he's running for president. He's showing people he can get his weight in control. It was the one thing holding him back,' a top political donor told *The Post.*"

Patrick Murray, Director of Monmouth University Polling, was sought out to weigh in with his reading of Christie's surgery. "Despite assuring the *New York Post* the underlying reason for the weight-loss surgery was his family, not the presidency, Christie knows full well his weight is an issue, Murray says. 'It's just something that you can't avoid in terms of conversation about his qualifications for being president,' Murray said. 'He's one that understands that,'" PolitickerNJ reported.

State Democratic Chairman, Assemblyman John Wisniewski saw it both ways. "I take him at his word that he did it for his kids. But obviously everyone has pointed out ... that would be a major impediment in a national campaign, his weight. He might be getting a twofer here, taking care of his health and getting ready for a presidential campaign," he told the *Star-Ledger*.

The War Chest

The key to any campaign is of course the ability to finance it. Without money, a candidate for statewide office is literally stuck in the mud. Christie's celebrity and nationwide stature served him well. His stumping for the election of candidates across the country would pay back big dividends for him. After undergoing his lap-band surgical procedure, Christie embarked on a coast-to-coast fundraising tour that netted him more than $6.2 million in just May of the election year.

Christie kicked off the fundraising at the Palo Alto home of Facebook CEO Mark Zuckerberg. Home Depot founder Kenneth Langone and hedge fund manager Stanley Druckenmiller hosted a New York City fundraiser that was projected to raise Christie a half-million dollars. Christie also extended his California gold digging to events in Los Angeles, La Jolla, and Santa Barbara according to correspondent Jenna Portnoy, who covered Christie for the *Star-Ledger*. The AshBritt lobbyist, Ed Rogers, also hosted an event for Christie in his McClean, Virginia home. Ron Kauffman, a former advisor to Mitt Romney and unsuccessful 2010 Massachusetts gubernatorial candidate Charles Baker sponsored a fundraising event for Christie in Boston. Christie also scheduled fundraising pit stops in Palm Beach, Florida and Edina, Minnesota.

When all was said and done, the $6.2 million put Christie in the record books. PolitickerNJ reported that the donations represented money that had poured into Christie "from some 14,000 donors in all 50 states." Christie's close friend and one of his chief fundraisers, Bill Palatucci, claimed that, "14,000 donors has never been done before in gubernatorial politics."

While primarily engaged in raising funds for his re-election campaign, Christie didn't ignore his need to attract donors for a potential presidential run. Clearing the air with Mitt Romney provided Christie with an invitation to speak at a gathering of such potential donors at an event sponsored by the former GOP presidential candidate, "Experts and Enthusiasts", in Park City, Utah. Jenna Portnoy further reported that, "The conference – sponsored by Solamere, the venture capital firm co-founded by Romney's oldest son, Tagg – gives Christie another opportunity to expand his national donor base. 'For whatever you say about Romney, he had a tremendous fundraising network,' said a Republican familiar with his presidential campaign. 'Those people are loyal to him and there's no question Christie could use their help.' Several of the wealthy donors who pressed Christie to seek the 2012 GOP presidential nomination jumped over to Team Romney once Christie made it clear in October 2011 he wasn't running."

As Christie's campaign money talked, supporters of his Democratic opponent, Senator Barbara Buono, walked. In early May, *Star-Ledger* correspondent Jarrett Renshaw reported that "Democratic gubernatorial candidate Barbara Buono's campaign war chest is so skimpy she may not generate enough contributions to secure all of her public matching funds for the primary or general election."

Christie's awesome 25-point lead in the polls was translating into a weapon itself. Renshaw's story captured the political sentiment in the early election season well, "'Christie is an intimidating figure,' said a top Democratic operative who is not associated with the Buono campaign. 'People are afraid that their names will be out there and his team will seek revenge.' Another top Democratic lobbyist put it more bluntly: 'People don't want to back a loser.'"

Christie's State Attorney General's Office also created a problem for Senator Buono's fundraising expectations, by bringing a never before tried prosecution of New Jersey's Election Law Pay-to-Play provisions to fruition. In Bid Rig III fashion, prosecutors criminalized bidding conduct that was routinely accepted as legal in the state's "Fair and Open" contracting system. The prosecutors used diverse local pay-to-play laws, termed by the New Jersey Comptroller as unenforceable, in order to charge criminal fraud. A procurement report of the NJ Office of the State Comptroller entitled, 'Weaknesses in the Pay-to-Play Law's "Fair and Open" Contracting System', which was issued September 15, 2011, found that "Given the absence of a challenge mechanism, fair and open's 'requirements' are, in practice, essentially advisory." Christie's Attorney General disregarded the Comptroller's opinion and treated the convoluted requirements as gospel.

The Comptroller further cited the disparities among the State pay-to-play restrictions and local governments, and the disparity amongst local governments themselves. Against this backdrop, the Attorney General's office again ignored the NJ State Comptroller's warning and initiated a questionable criminal prosecution against one of the state's most prominent engineering firms, Birdsall Services Group.

The prosecution sent chills down the spines of New Jersey corporations that typically raised money for candidates through their employee base. The prosecution put a severe crimp in campaign donations from corporate employees that typically would have been given to gubernatorial and legislative candidates. Christie could afford the cut-back as he was flush with more than six million dollars and access to unlimited out-of-state sources. Buono's campaign, on the other hand, needed every dime it could come across.

The Balancing Act

With one eye towards a presidential run and the other focused on the re-election campaign, Christie was faced with a dilemma unlike those confronted by any other typical politician. New Jersey is a Blue state, but the key to winning a GOP presidential primary election was to be staunchly conservative. The dilemma: being able to walk the tightrope between these two extremes and not damage your chances for accomplishing both goals. Christie went left when deciding to accept federal monies to increase the Medicaid roles through provisions of the Affordable Care Act, but the alternative, to leave money on the table that New Jersey sorely needed, cut him slack with the middle-of-the-road crowd.

After the school shooting tragedy in Newton, Connecticut, gun control activists throughout the nation jumped on a bandwagon and led what conservatives felt was an assault against the right to bear arms and the Second Amendment. The national spotlight fell upon Christie as an alleged conservative running a a Blue state with a progressive thinking electorate.

Christie offered a unique plan, which drew a muted response from those on opposite sides of the issue. He advocated strongly for tougher penalties to curtail gun trafficking, curtailing straw-man purchasers who buy guns for criminals and allow guns to fall into the hands of minors. He further proposed banning future sales of .50-caliber rifles. Christie also advocated expanding mental health screenings and treatment, and placing restrictions on violent video games.

Bergen Record columnist, Charles Stiles, offered a logical interpretation of Christie's proposal. "His 50 "common sense" recommendations appear also to be a strategy to protect his political future by offering up just enough new restrictions and penalties to satisfy New Jersey's pro-gun control voters without alienating the Second Amendment purists whom he'll have to woo if he runs for the Republican nomination for president in 2016.... And if Christie jumps into the 2016 race, he will have to run a gantlet of Republican primaries in pro-gun states in the South and the West. He can't afford to be seen as a gun-control activist from a blue New Jersey. If anyone has any doubts, Friday's report put them to rest."

In March of 2013, Christie was snubbed by the Conservative Political Action Conference (CPAC). Christie, a prominent national Republican who fared well in presidential polling, was uninvited to address its conference. The snub would benefit Christie among Democratic voters, some of whom he would need to win over for his gubernatorial re-election, and also independent voters he would need on his side for both the gubernatorial election and any future presidential race. It allowed Christie to continue the mantra that Washington is dysfunctional because both political parties refuse to work with each other. In public and on talk shows he was always making the point that he identified himself as a fiscal conservative.

But true conservatives in the GOP were soon to become just as disenchanted with other party hopefuls for the 2016 presidential nod when many of them supported the bipartisan immigration bill, which ultra-conservatives frowned upon. (Marco Rubio sponsored the bill and Rand Paul initially supported it but then backed off).

The conservatives were finding many faults with the Republican Party and realized a newfound sense of comfort with the policies of the Tea Party. The best thing that could happen to Christie was for conservatives, who looked upon him as a left-leaning Republican, to bolt the GOP in favor of the Tea Party. Then, the likes of Karl Rove and others, who were warning that if the GOP didn't move towards the center it would be doomed, could purge the party and introduce a more moderate voting faction into GOP primaries that would be to Christie's benefit. They would even go so far as to bite the hand that fed them and demonize conservative talk radio.

By late July of 2013, Christie's strategy and careful balance of his high-wire act showed signs of paying off. A Quinnipiac Poll showed him the as the sole GOP contender who could take the White House, including up against Hillary Clinton. No other GOP presidential nominee hopeful could come close to Clinton.

Christie's October Surprise in June

When his nemesis, United States Senator Frank Lautenberg, passed away in early June of 2013, Christie pulled off a truly diabolical scheme to help secure his re-election bid. Because Lautenberg's death occurred before the 2013 June primary, a number of New Jersey election laws were triggered that gave Christie several scenarios for filling the vacant Senate seat. Christie could have appointed a replacement until the 2014 term election for the seat. He could have scheduled the election on the same day as the November general and gubernatorial elections, allowing the elected state committee members of the Republican and Democratic parties to pick the nominees, or he could schedule a special election, which would trigger a primary election as well, sometime before the November elections.

With Christie anxious to blow out his opponent in the gubernatorial election, and perhaps sweep some legislative seats to victory on his coattails as well, there were some imminent dangers looming in allowing the Senate election to fall on the same date as the November general elections. First and foremost, Christie would no longer have top billing on the ballot; the senate candidates would. Since the popular Cory Booker was the odds-on favorite to become the Democrat nominee, there was the possibility of pulling out an unusually high number of Democrats who might just vote down the line and cripple Christie's chances.

As *New York Times* correspondents Kate Zernike and David M. Halbfinger pointed out, "Mr. Christie has made clear that he does not just want to win re-election; he wants to win by an enormous margin, one that would allow him to sell himself to his party as a rare Republican presidential candidate who can win even in blue states. So he has worked to avoid appearing on the same ballot as Cory A. Booker, a Democrat and the popular mayor of Newark, who has said he will run for Mr. Lautenberg's seat and who might have drawn more young and black voters to the polls for Mr. Christie's Democratic challenger."

Politically, the best move for Christie would be any other option that kept the United States Senate's race off the November ballot. In conformance with political wisdom, Christie announced that he would be calling a special election to fill Lautenberg's seat. But that too posed a dilemma. The Office of Legislative Services estimated the costs of the special elections to be approximately $19 million, and as the *Star-Ledger* editorial board noted, Christie was the same governor "who opposed early voting by citing the extra costs." Not to mention that the Assembly Budget Committee Chairman Vincent Prieto would be calling him out on his costly decision in light of New Jersey's grim fiscal picture. "The governor needs to decide whether the state is broke or flush with cash, because he can't have it both ways. I don't know how he can argue with a straight face that we have no money to help the working poor or provide low-income women with access to health care and then throw away millions of dollars to protect his own political interests."

It was time for Christie to employ his reliable charm school approach and try and win with spin. He decided to conjure up the bogeyman and frighten the electorate, seizing on the perfect foil for his argument: politicians whom he knew the general public detested. "I will not permit the insiders and a few party elites to determine who the nominee of the Republican Party and the Democratic Party will be," Christie barked. "I don't know what the cost is, and I quite frankly don't care. I don't think you can put a price tag on what it's worth to have an elected person in the United States Senate."

With Christie riding a more than seventy-percent approval rating, the public didn't seem to mind at all. His decision roiled only the *Star-Ledger* editorial board, which opined, "There is no legitimate reason to hold two separate elections, and the reason he's doing it is purely self-serving. He calculates that more Democratic voters will show up and cast ballots against him if a popular Democratic candidate like Newark Mayor Cory Booker is on the ballot as well. Given the big lead the governor has already, the greed here is striking: He apparently wants to run up his margin of victory as a credential for his 2016 presidential campaign."

To cut short any further media outrage over his "self-serving stunt," Christie quickly named his Attorney General, Jeffrey Chiesa, as the interim replacement. The move drew little criticism. If all worked out well, the Democrat's fight over the senate in their primary would distract attention away from the gubernatorial election and, likewise, Christie's opposition. It was likely that there would be a fall-off of staunch Democratic voters in November after already voting in the October special election – and that would suit Christie's purposes just fine.

Victory and Moving On

The Christie strategy worked to perfection. The two elections, within weeks of each other, killed voter turnout in both, mostly in Democratic strongholds. Cory Booker won his Senate seat by a closer margin than expected. Christie, despite a record low turnout for a New Jersey gubernatorial election, trampled Barbara Buono by more than twenty percentage points, impressively garnering a shade over sixty percent of the ballots cast. Despite the landslide victory, Christie had virtually no coattails and could not pick up any legislative seats in the New Jersey Assembly or Senate.

Christie's critics seized on this victory to play down the shellacking he gave the Democrats, but they failed to remember that most of the Democrats in closely contested legislative districts were actually praising Christie in their own ads, citing chapter and verse of how they worked with Christie in the spirit of bipartisanship. They tied themselves to Christie and actually used his coattails across the ballot to help themselves at the expense of Barbara Buono.

The decision of the Republicans in the Assembly and Senate to run separate campaigns through their committees negated the help that Christie's popularity could have provided them. The more they highlighted themselves instead of Christie, the less likely they were to ride the Governor's coattails. There would be hell to pay for those lackluster campaigns that bruised Christie's political prestige. Despite the fact that the son of his popular political mentor Governor Tom Kean, Senator Tom Kean, Jr., was the Republican Senate minority leader in charge of those campaigns, Christie apparently gave a wink and a nod for an attempt to dethrone him from his leadership position.

Kean Jr. had boasted the Republicans would win five additional seats. "We picked up zero. How could I be excited about that," Christie later commented in an awkward defense of the coup attempt. The vengeful move seemed much like the treatment that Christie had bestowed upon Mitt Romney during the waning days of the 2012 Presidential campaign: the payback to Romney's staff for leading the charge in dumping Christie as the national ticket's vice presidential candidate.

Unlike Romney, Kean Jr. survived. Christie misread the character of the legislators who worked with the Senate Minority Leader; they stayed faithful to Kean and kept him in power, in opposition to the Governor's wishes. Then again, history has proven that loyalty is one of the characteristics Christie knows little about, and therefore stabbing his mentor in the back by politically deposing his son was just political business as usual.

Former Governor Tom Kean publically displayed his contempt for Christie's actions. He explained Christie's potential motives, to which many political insiders had subscribed, to columnist Charles Stile of the *Bergen Record*, who reported them. "'I don't know what the motivation was, what the giveback was,' Kean said, echoing suspicions that Christie may have cut a deal with the Democratic Senate president, Stephen Sweeney, to remove his son from power. Sweeney and Kean Jr. have been locked in a bitter political feud, which reached a boiling point this fall when Kean Jr. financed an aggressive campaign to defeat Sweeney. But Sweeney has developed a friendship with a far more powerful Republican – Christie. Over the past four years, Sweeney has collaborated with Christie on big-ticket items, such as health and pension benefit reform. Christie will need Sweeney's help if he is to have any chance of building on that "bipartisan" record in a second term. Seen through that lens, Sweeney may be more valuable to Christie than Kean Jr."

Stiles further elaborated on Christie's lack of character. "The episode raises another question about whether Christie's ambition trumps loyalty – an issue that dogged the governor when his post-Sandy embrace of President Obama was seen by some supporters of Republican Mitt Romney as an act of betrayal."

The Coincidences of Chris Christie's Career

A mentally incompetent felon, Solomon Dwek, is offered the plea deal of the century; and then compromises Christie's political opposition for the purpose of advancing Christie's personal political agenda.

A United States Attorney's Office influenced by the promise of jobs acted as if it were a political ward club for Christie's gubernatorial campaign. As former United States Senator Frank Lautenberg stated, "It is shocking to learn that a former deputy to Chris Christie was conducting a political campaign within the U.S. Attorney's Office. It was particularly distressing that this raw political agenda came into an office...and Ms. Brown went so far as trying to bring political campaign objectives into the planning of law enforcement actions."

The same US Attorney's Office illegally pour hundreds of thousands of dollars into an unauthorized sting of candidates in local elections, causing the corruption of those election results and the disenfranchisement of tens of thousands of voters.

The same United States Attorney's Office blazed a trail of political prosecutions that crippled New Jersey Democratic strongholds, and seemingly manipulated the Bid Rig III sting as a boost that helped secure the governor's chair.

The same United States Attorney's Office handed out no-bid million-dollar contracts to his soon-to-be Christie campaign contributors and then overlooked the criminal conduct of public officials who would be vital for Christie securing the Republican gubernatorial nomination and then election.

As Governor, Christie had a penchant for manipulating disasters, such as Superstorm Sandy, to cobble his Governor's persona into that of a mythical political hero and audaciously used first responders, in the midst of an emergency, for the purpose of serving as a backdrop for his press conferences.

As governor, Christie employed ruthless cunning and cold-hearted nerve to throw supporters and allies to the wolves after they took bullets for him [Commissioner of Education Brett Shundler, Mitt Romney, and Senate Minority Leader Tom Kean.]

Christie's resilience in surviving these political traumas rested in his chameleon celebrity. Christie secured his re-election victory and within months was the favorite to win the 2016 GOP Presidential nomination. His precarious abuse of the United States Attorney's Office had already secured for him a governorship. He was well on the way to his ultimate coup – winning the Presidency of the United States.

Then the bottom fell out.

Christie's addiction to power and self-gratification will ultimately do him in. The Bridgegate episode that opened this book may well be his Waterloo, perhaps because it was an incident that everyone could relate to. We've all been stuck in traffic, and we have all cursed those responsible for the gridlock. The other scandals that Christie escaped were too complex and over the head of the average Joe, but everyone can identify with what happened to the residents of Fort Lee and the commuters on the George Washington Bridge for those four days in September 2013, after Christie's office ordered the traffic lanes closed.

The depth of duplicity by the highest ranking public officials in State government had everyone in the nation questioning the sanity of Christie and his administration. If that wasn't bad enough, Christie then chose to raise the ante. In his arrogance, he convinced himself that he could talk his way out of the mess, proceeding to hold an almost two-hour press conference that the *Star-Ledger* characterized as "a Broadway show of lies."

In perhaps a last ditch effort to cling to glory, Christie tried to rely on his celebrity again to save him. In the midst of the Bridgegate crisis, he even made an appearance at Howard Stern's 60th birthday party to hobnob with celebrities that, perhaps, his own mind told him he was on a par with. But that act was over, lying to the public was too much to overcome.

The people who believed him and were let down by such a phoney baloney now see only the shell of Christie's former public persona – a man living in the fantasyland of his own narcissism, pretending to himself that all the world is lying and only he is telling the truth. Now we see, not a straight-talking tough guy, but a man who came close to the highest office in the land acting like a sociopath.

As his cadré of apparent co-conspirators look for deals with prosecutors and the ugly truth of their deeds continues to leak out and prove Christie a liar, all he has left to do is wait for indictment or impeachment. If he can muster any integrity at all from a public service career that has been completely devoid of that quality to date, then perhaps he may spare New Jerseyans any further embarrassment and simply resign.

Chris Christie never really heeded the prophetic words of his mother, "Be yourself today, and then tomorrow you won't have to worry about whether you got it right or wrong and who you told what version of the truth to."

In the end, Chris Christie could not escape the truth. No one ever does.

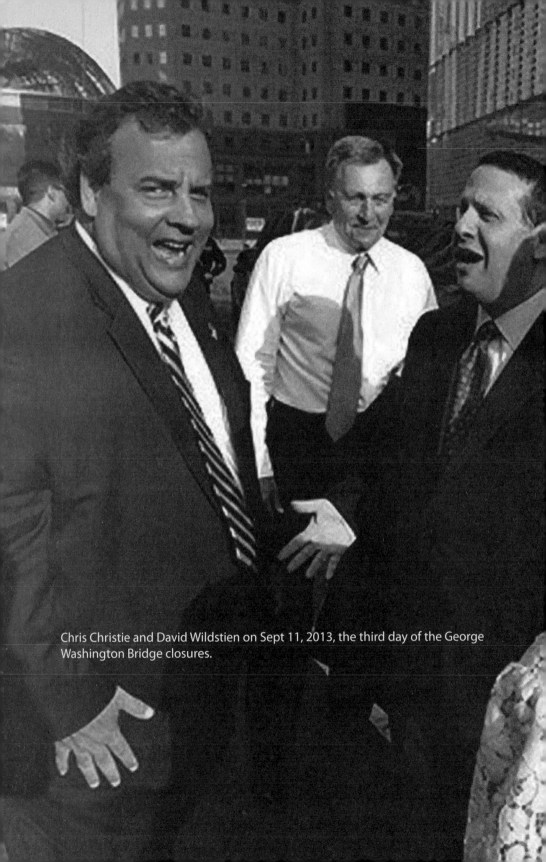

Chris Christie and David Wildstien on Sept 11, 2013, the third day of the George Washington Bridge closures.

Afterword

The Tragedy of Politics as Usual

Chris Christie is a politician reared in the philosophy that it is unimportant to believe in what you say, so long as the public believes it. His greatest asset is not what he does or does not stand for, but how well he can captivate and entertain the electorate with his persona. The American public is a born sucker for this P.T. Barnum circus-style of politics.

Like another demagogue of yesteryear, Senator Joseph McCarthy, Christie mastered the tactic of exploiting people's fears as a weapon against his political enemies. In the process, Christie destroyed the reputations, lives, and careers of innocent individuals who merely served as stepping-stones for the advancement of his career. Like McCarthy, Christie has used many a public official and people with lesser platforms than his as his personal scapegoats-cruelly demonizing and saddling them with blame to cover for his own blunders.

McCarthy exploited the fear of Communism, using his office and a Senate Committee to inflame public passions against his political opponents, and destroyed many good people in the process. Christie's tools were the public's contempt for their own officials, his willingness to abuse his office by further stirring that contempt, and then aiding and abetting the unjust prosecutions (and persecutions) of his political opposition for his own and others' personal and political agendas.

The Fourth Estate, in the person of Edward R. Murrow, stopped McCarthy, but the decline in the caliber and intestinal fortitude of journalism today allowed Christie's conduct to continue unchecked, until Bridgegate. His flair for showmanship enabled him to manipulate the truth and any crisis for his own benefit. He has successfully pulled the wool over many an eye.

Unlike his convenient hero, Ronald Reagan, Christie's politics are not based on nor engrained in principles and values; they are poll-driven and constantly changing to accommodate the whims of the voters in the shadow of the next election. Reagan was driven by his own moral compass, whether one agrees or disagrees with his actions. At the core of Christie's beliefs is a weathervane pointing in the direction of the prevailing political winds.

In the Gallup Poll's annual 2011 President's Day survey, Ronald Reagan was chosen as the greatest American President; besting Lincoln, Clinton, Kennedy, Washington and FDR. Is it any wonder why, in evidence of such polling, Christie would choose Reagan as the leader he claimed to want to emulate. For many Americans, Reagan is the most recent connection to a seemingly extinct breed: patriotic heroes. Love or hate the man, there was not a phony bone in Reagan's body. Christie's sincerity is as rare as hen's teeth. He has consistently held truth to be a commodity to exploit for his personal benefit. Edward Tamm saw the real Christie when he sued him for libel after he defamed Tamm in order to win his election to the Morris County Board of Freeholders. "He'll do anything to get elected. He'll say anything, do anything."

Christie's politics, especially on social issues such as birth control and gun control, are more the philosophy of a conservative Democrat than a Republican; that positioning is what has helped to keep him in play in a Blue state such as New Jersey. Political chameleon that he is, whenever he travels outside of New Jersey, where people don't know him and only have the perception of Christie that was crafted by his handlers, he adapts to the political surroundings. With his considerable political theatre skills, Christie knows how to wow the audience, standing for everything they think they want even though, in the end, he will "say anything, do anything."

The staus quo sees the wealth of the nation in the caliber of its leaders as opposed to the character of its people.

If the American People continue to misplace the notion of what represents our nation's wealth or where it can be found, they will continue to fall victim to the tragedy of "politics as usual" and those who thrive in its seductive stew.

In a final message to his countrymen, a New Jersey Governor who successfully ran for President, Woodrow Wilson, brilliantly defined the true source of our wealth:

"The vitality of America lies in the brains, the energies, the enterprise of the people throughout the land; in the efficiency of their factories and in the richness of the fields that stretch beyond the borders of the town; in the wealth which they extract from nature and originate for themselves through the inventive genius characteristic of all free American communities.

"That is the wealth of America, and if America discourages the locality, the community, the self-contained town, she will kill the nation. A nation is as rich as her free communities; she is not as rich as her capital city or her metropolis.

*"The amount of money in Wall Street is no indication of the wealth of the American people.*That indication can be found only in the fertility of the American mind and the productivity of American industry everywhere throughout the United States. If America were not rich and fertile, there would be no money in Wall Street. If Americans were not vital and able to take care of themselves, the great money exchanges would break down.

"The welfare, the very existence of the nation, rests at last upon the great mass of the people; its prosperity depends at last upon the spirit in which they go about their work in their several communities throughout the broad land. In proportion as her towns and her country-sides are happy and hopeful will America realize the high ambitions which have marked her in the eyes of all the world."

Today's politicians have misunderstood President Wilson's vivid perspective of our nation's wealth – distorted by the Christie phenomena and America's gullibility for politics as usual, which can best be explained thusly: Sometimes people are so thirsty for leadership that they will even drink sand. Out of desperation, they will allow the hollow words of their leaders to suffice for too few deeds. Look at the shape of our beloved Country. We fail to examine the character of the people who ask for our trust; then we blindly turn it over to them all too willingly. Where is the due diligence?

Americans remain profoundly disappointed with the caliber of their leaders...but they still don't get it. Our current society is teetering dangerously close to fulfilling the ominous warning of another American President, Abraham Lincoln: "America will never be destroyed from the outside. If we lose our freedoms, it will be because we destroyed ourselves."

Election after election, we vote for change, more change, followed by even more change; never realizing that not until we change our perspective for choosing leaders, can we finally bring down the curtain on the tragedy of politics as usual.

Instead of blaming the leaders that we elect, such as the likes of Chris Christie, for being who they are and doing what they do, we should be mindful of Cassius's words to Brutus in Shakespeare's immortal line from Julius Caesar: "The fault, dear Brutus, lies not in our stars, but in ourselves."

Buona Fortuna, U.S.A.!

Chapter Notes

Foreword

STAR-LEDGER

Hoboken mayor stands firm as Christie's office refutes claim over sandy aid by Kelly Heyboer & Ryan Hutchins January 20, 2014.

Chris Christie faces the wrath of a scorned friend by Tom Moran February 2, 2014.

In Super Bowl 2014 spotlight, Chris Christie muddles through bridge scandal fallout by Jenna Portnoy and Mark Mueller February 2, 2014.

Chris Christie ramps up travel plans as scandals continue by Jenna Portnoy February 4, 2014.

UPDATED: Timeline of Port Authority's George Washington Bridge controversy by Christopher Baxter January 13, 2014.

Chris Christie's Port Authority appointee David Samson's judgment defended amid scandals by Jenna Portnoy January 30, 2014.

Bridge scandal: Chris Christie knew about lane closures. Wildstein's lawyer says by Christopher Baxter January 31, 2014.

Hoboken Mayor Dawn Zimmer alleges Chris Christie's office withheld Sandy aid over development deal by Christopher Baxter & David Giambusso January 18, 2014.

Former prosecutor accuses Christie administration of corruption in NJ court by Salvador Rizzo January 29, 2014.

Hoboken development at center of latest Christie allegations was rejected by city by Stephen Stirling January 18, 2014.

Amid federal probe into N.J.'s Sandy ads, Jersey Shore mayors weigh in on campaign by Erin O'Neill January 13, 2014.

Chris Christie bridge scandal: Documents show Port Authority chairman blasting executive director by Steve Strunsky January 10 2014.

Bridgegate fallout: Chris Christie apologizes in wake of bridge scandal, fires top aide by Ted Sherman & Steve Strunsky January 9, 2014.

BERGEN RECORD

Governor Christie's brother invested in real estate near new PATH station in Harrison by Craig McCarthy January 29, 2014.

EMS responses delayed by GWB lane closures in what Fort Lee mayor calls 'absolute power corruption' by Linh Tat January 8, 2014.

NEW YORK TIMES

Christie Linked to Knowledge of Shut Lanes by Kate Zernike January 31, 2014.

The Quashing of a Case Against a Christie Ally by Michael Powell October 10, 2013.

Editorial Board: The Bully Was a Dupe by Editorial Board January 8, 2014.

Top Christie Staff Sought to Disrupt Traffic as Revenge by Kate Zernike January 8, 2014.

ASBURY PARK PRESS

'Bridgegate' documents show fight over ending of lane closures by John Schoonjongen January 11, 2014.

HUFFINGTON POST

Chris Christie's Top Aide Linked To Traffic Jam Payback Against Democratic Mayor by Amanda Terkel January 8, 2014.

Chris Christie Denies Knowledge of Bridge Payback Scheme by Amanda Terkel January 8, 2014.

NBC NEWS

Christie acknowledges federal subpoena by Michael O'Brien February 4, 2014.

NJ.COM

U.S. Attorney subpoenas Christie campaign and GOP State Committee over bridge scandal by Darryl Isherwood.

CORRESPONDENCES

Letter from Attorney Alan L. Zegas to The Port Authority of New York and New Jersey regarding David Wildstein's legal bills January 31, 2014.

Chapter One

DAILY BEAST

Chris Christie: Call Me, Mitt by Peter J. Boyer Jun 18, 2012 1:00 AM EDT.

SALON

What Chris Christie is really afraid of by Steve Kornacki March 4, 2011.

NEW YORK TIMES

For N.J. Candidate, First Ethics Push Was Brief by David M Halbfinger August 17, 2009.

NEW JERSEY MONTHLY

New Jersey Nasty by Gabriel Sherman October 19, 2009.

UNITED STATES DEPARTMENT OF JUSTICE

District of New Jersey Office Report 2002-2008 by Christopher J. Christie, U.S. Attorney.

Chapter Two

UNITED STATES DEPARTMENT OF JUSTICE

District of New Jersey Office Report 2002-2008 by Christopher J. Christie, U.S. Attorney.

UNITED STATES OF HOUSE OF REPRESENTATIVES JUDICIARY COMMITTEE

Majority Staff, Allegations of Selective Prosecution in Our Federal Criminal Justice System. Prepared for Chairman John Conyers, Jr. April 17, 2008.

BLUE JERSEY NEWS BLOG

Chris Christie: Caught in The U.S. Attorney Web of Lies by huntsu August 3, 2007.

NEW YORK OBSERVER

Prosecutor Makes a Meal of N.J. Senate Race by Jason Horowitz October 16, 2006.

See Chris Christie Skate by Steve Kornacki August 13, 2009.

NEW YORK TIMES

Usually on Attack, U.S. Attorney in Newark Finds Himself on Defensive by David Kocieniewski February 13, 2008.

TPMMUCKRAKER

Feds Probing Dem Sen. Relationship to Former Aide by Paul Kiel November 1, 2007.

THE ASBURY PARK PRESS

Capitol Quickies: Menendez responds to Probe's Closure by Raju Chebium October 25, 2011.

STAR-LEDGER

Editorial: Chris Christie's subpoena on Senator Menendez during an election was a mistake by Editorial Board October 24, 2011.

Fed tell Sen. Menendez 2006 probe now closed... by Mark Mueller October 23, 2011.

Chapter Three

NEW YORK TIMES

For N.J. Candidate, First Ethics Push Was Brief by David M Halbfinger August 17, 2009.

Usually on Attack, U.S. Attorney in Newark Finds Himself on Defensive by David Kocieniewski February 13, 2008.

Ashcroft deal Brings Scrutiny in Justice Dept. by Philip Shenon January 19, 2008.

In Testy Exchange in Congress, Christie Defends His Record as a Prosecutor by David Kocieniewski June 26, 2009.

Money for Nothing by Editorial April 16, 2005.

ASSOCIATED PRESS

N.J. GOP gubernatorial candidate Chris Christie's deferred prosecution agreements by Associated Press June 25, 20009.

STAR-LEDGER

Congressman criticizes monitoring deal for Ashcroft by John Martin November 21, 2007.

GOP candidate Chris Christie agrees to testify before Congress on federal monitoring contracts by Claire Heininger June 19, 2009.

$52 M-plus payday for Christie's old boss by John Martin November 20, 2007.

UNITED STATES DEPARTMENT OF JUSTICE

Letter from Craig S. Morford, Acting Deputy Attorney General March 7, 2008.

KOMISAR SCOOP BLOG

Former U.S. Attorney Chris Christie, GOP Candidate for NJ Governor, gets $ from IDT, NJ telcom investigated by Justice Dept. for bribing Haitian officials by Lucy Komisar October 22, 2009.

FACTCHECK.ORG BLOG

Corzine on Christie: Contracts for Cronies by Analysis July 13, 2009.

Chapter Four

NEW YORK TIMES

Showdown Looming Over McGreevey Fund-Raising Inquiry by David Kocieniewski March 16, 2006.

Lurid Charges Hit Top Donor to New Jersey Governor by Ronald Smothers July 14, 2004

A Governor Unindicted, but Implicated by David Kocieniewski July 9, 2004.

GEORGETOWN JOURNAL OF LEGAL ETHICS

Prosecutorial Discretion: What's Politics Got to Do with It? By Sandra Caron George Volume 18 Number 3 Summer 2005.

STAR-LEDGER

Gov. Corzine wants GOP challenger Chris Christie to explain Rove talks by Michael Rispoli August 13, 2009.

Chapter Five

JERSEY JOURNAL

Editorial: Accusations against GOP nominee need full scrutiny June 19, 2012.

Solomon Dwek grilled on the Ten Commandments in Beldini corruption trial by Michaelangelo Conte February 1, 2010.

ASBURY PARK PRESS

Dwek gets six years in prison, $22.8 million restitution by Jeanne Mikle October 18, 2012.

STAR-LEDGER

Infamous federal informant Solomon Dwek is sentenced to 6 years, must pay $22.8M by Ted Sherman October 19, 2012.

Former Sheriff's nomination to N.J. Superior Court in jeopardy over FBI files by Matt Friedman October 23, 2012.

Gov. Christie prods Dems to hold hearing on judicial nominee Joseph Oxley by Jenna Portnoy October 23, 2012.

N.J. senator wants Solomon Dwek to appear before committee to explain foreclosure tipoff claims by Matt Friedman June 13, 2012.

FBI informant Solomon Dwek headed back to prison after his bail is revoked by Ted Sherman June 28, 2011.

Corruption probe informant Solomon Dwek back behind bars after lying to the FBI by Ted Sherman June 29, 2011.

FBI informant Solomon Dwek is mentally ill, his attorney says by Ted Sherman October 8, 2012

FBI informant Solomon Dwek gets 6 years in prison for role in $50M fraud scheme by Ted Sherman October 18, 2012.

Infamous federal informant Solomon Dwek is sentenced to 6 years, must pay $22.8M by Ted Sherman October 19, 2012.

NEW YORK TIMES

Rabbi Convicted of Sexual Abuse Is Freed Bail Pending Appeal by Ronald Smothers October 12, 2012.

Editorial: Rampant Prosecutorial Misconduct by Editorial Board January 4, 2013.

WALL STREET JOURNAL

Christie's Senate Fight by Heather Haddon August 20, 2012.

POLITICKERNJ

Christie defends Oxley judicial nomination in face of Dem resistance by Minhaj Hassan October 23, 2012.

Larsen, Eric / *ASBURY PARK PRESS* / Dwek tells of meeting with Van Pelt, Ocean County GOP Chief / May 6, 2010.

VOS IZ NEIS? NEWS BLOG / Copying *ASBURY PARK PRESS* / Dwek Accuses Long Branch City Prosecutor Fixed Traffic for the Jewish Community / October 9, 2010.

FBI 302s
Solomon Dwek debriefing August 8, 2006 by SA William B. Waldie.
Alfonso Santoro debriefing September 23, 2009 by SA Waldie & Brogan.

USA v. ANTHONY SUAREZ trial transcripts
Volume 5 October 7, 2010 5.38-5.45, 5.50-5.121, 5.150-5.201.
Volume 4 October 8, 2010 [2.193 – 2.196].

USA v. DANIEL VAN PELT
Criminal Complaint executed July 23, 2009, Page 228 – 234.

USA v ALFONSO L. SANTORO

USA v. KENNETH R. OLSEN order of the court
Dissent by Chief Judge Alex Kozinski, United States Court of Appeals for the Ninth Circuit December 10, 2013.

FBI OTHERWISE ILLEGAL ACTIVITY AUTHORIZATION
Case 270D-NK-114696 February 23, 2007.
Case 270D-NK-114696 May 15, 2007.
Case 270D-NK-114696 August 6, 2007.
Case 270D-NK-114696 November 21, 2007.
Case 270D-NK-114696 February 12, 2008.
Case 270D-NK-114696 August 8, 2008.

THE JERSEY STING by Ted Sherman and Josh Margolin
Pages 36-37, 70-71, 80-81, 84-95, 100-101, 168-173.

COURT DOCUMENTS
Solomon Dwek Forensic Evaluation by Jerome Rubin, Ph.D. issued August 10, 2011.

Chapter Six

NEW YORK TIMES
Why This Scandal Matters Editorial May 21, 2007.

ASBURY PARK PRESS
Gov. nominates Holmdel man for Supreme Court by Michael Symons December 11, 2012.

BERGEN RECORD
The Political State: Michele Brown leaving as Christie appointments counsel, will head EDA by Juliet Fletcher July 25, 2012.

STAR-LEDGER
Merkt says Christie ally offered him job in campaign to stay out of GOP gubernatorial race by Chris Megerian May 7, 2009.

Democratic lawmakers seek probe of alleged offer to keep GOP candidate from race by Chris Megerian May 8, 2009.

Karl Rove and Christie discussed N.J. governor run while serving as U.S. Attorney by Michael Rispoli August 12, 2009.

Gov. Corzine wants GOP challenger Chris Christie to explain Rove talks by Michael Rispoli August 13, 2009.

Federal prosecutor Ralph Marra joins N.J. Sports and Exposition Authority as top lawyer by Star-Ledger Staff February 18, 2010.

Former federal prosecutor named head of N.J. Division of Consumer Affairs by Christopher Baxter April 18, 2012.

EDA chief steps down; authority to reorganize executive structure by Tom De Poto July 25, 2012.

EMPTYWHEEL BLOG

Chris Christie, Former U.S. Attorney, Claims He's Still "Got" Federal Prosecutors, Talked with Them about State Jobs by emptywheel August 19, 2009 [Christie speech at West Windsor on February 28, 2009].

ZACHARY FINK BLOG

Christie Faces Reporters by Zachary Fink August 25, 2009.

MAIN JUSTICE

Post Tagged "U.S. Attorney's Office for the District of New Jersey" by MAIN JUSTICE January 8, 2010 through January 14, 2011.

UNITED STATES OF HOUSE OF REPRESENTATIVES JUDICIARY COMMITTEE

Majority Staff. Allegations of Selective Prosecution in Our Federal Criminal Justice System. Prepared for Chairman John Conyers, Jr. April 17, 2008.

DOCUMENTS

New Jersey Election Law Enforcement Commission [contribution reports] Chris Christie 2009 gubernatorial campaign contributions from staff of the United States Attorney's Office for the District of New Jersey.

Chapter Seven

STATE AND FEDERAL LAWS & GUIDELINES

The United States Code of Federal Regulations 28 USC 528.

United States Attorneys' Manual (USAM) USAM 3-27-260, USAM 9-27.260, USAM 3-27-260 [Recusals], USAM 9-27.260 [Initiating and Declining Charges-Impermissible Considerations].

The United States Code of Federal Regulations 5 USC 7323 [Political activity prohibitions].

The United States Code of Federal Regulations 28 USC 530B [Ethical standards for attorneys for the Government].

The New Jersey Court Rules of Professional Conduct New Jersey RPC 8.4. [Misconduct].

The Attorney General's Guidelines Regarding the Use of FBI Confidential Human Sources [pages 34 – 36].

FBI Domestic Investigations and Operations Guidelines [excerpts].

FBI 302s

Jack M. Shaw debriefing July 22 & 27, 2009.

Dennis Jaslow debriefing August 5, 2009.

USA v. ANTHONY SUAREZ trial transcripts

Volume 6 October 8, 2010 [6.158 – 6.169 & excerpts from evidentiary hearing].

BID RIG III TAPE TRANSCRIPTS

Excerpt from 2/16/09 meeting @ Casa Dante Restaurant, Jersey City, N.J. between Solomon Dwek and Ed Cheatam.

Excerpt from 2/17/09 meeting @ Casa Dante Restaurant, Jersey City, N.J. between Solomon Dwek, Ed Cheatam, and Jack Shaw.

Excerpt from 2/25/09 meeting @ Perkins Restaurant, Staten Island, N.Y. between Solomon Dwek and Ed Cheatam.

BID RIG III CRIMINAL COMPLAINTS

Excerpts from USA v. Serrano, King, Catrillo, Webb-Washington, [M.Manzo, Castagna, Jaslow], [Cammarano & Schaffer], [Elwell & R. Manzo], [Smith & Greene], Cardwell, [Shaw, Cheatam, Beldini], Kenny, and [L. Manzo & R. Manzo] criminal complaints executed July 23, 2009.

USA v Michael Manzo, Dennis Jaslow and Joseph Castagna executed July 23, 2009.

STAR-LEDGER

Former head of N.J. community affairs quietly cleared of wrongdoing after two-year investigation by Star-Ledger Staff October 7, 2011.

Braun: Former N.J. Assembly Speaker Joseph Doria survives the "slings and arrows" by Bob Braun October 19, 2011.

THE JERSEY STING by Ted Sherman and Josh Margolin

Pages 118-119, 250-251, 259.

HUDSON REPORTER

Lunch hour for "Buddy" by Al Sullivan March 20, 2011.

JERSEY CITY INDEPENDENT

L. Harvey Smith on trial, Day Eleven: Closing Statements by Matt Hunger February 6, 2013.

UNITED STATES SUPREME COURT

Robert L. McCORMICK, Petitioner v. UNITED STATES

500 U.S. 257, 111 S.Ct. 1807, 114 L.Ed.2d 307.

No. 89-1918. Argued Jan. 8, 1991. Decided May 23, 1991.

Chapter Eight

STATE AND FEDERAL LAWS & GUIDELINES

The Attorney General's Guidelines Regarding the Use of FBI Confidential Human Sources [pages 30 – 40].

FBI Domestic Investigations and Operations Guidelines [excerpts].

FBI OTHERWISE ILLEGAL ACTIVITY AUTHORIZATION

Case 270D-NK-114696 February 28, 2009 [excerpts].

OFFICE OF THE INSPECTOR GENERAL REPORT

The Federal Bureau of Investigation's Compliance with the Attorney General's Investigative Guidelines, September 2005 [pages 7 – 9, 103, 104, 106].

USA v. ANTHONY SUAREZ trial transcripts

Volume 6 October 8, 2010 [6.1 – 6.157].

Volume 12 October 19, 2010 [12.190 – 12.200].

USA v. LOUIS MANZO

Opposition brief to request for attorney fees, April 16, 2012.

Chapter Nine

STATE AND FEDERAL LAWS & GUIDELINES

United States Attorneys' Manual [Criminal Resource Manual 2404].

USDOJ DISTRICT OF NEW JERSEY U.S. ATTORNEY'S OFFICE
Press Release July 23, 2009 [bidrig0723.rel].

WIKIPEDIA
Compilation of Polling Results for 2009 N.J. Gubernatorial Election.

HARPER'S MAGAZINE
Manure for the Garden State by Scott Horton August 19, 2009.

BLOOMBERG NEWS BLOG
Corruption Bust May Aid Christie Bid Against Corzine [Update 2] by Terrence Dopp July 24, 2009.

BERGEN RECORD
A body blow to Corzine's reelection by Charles Stile September 7, 2009.

NEW YORK DAILY NEWS
Corruption arrests in N.J. hurt Corzine election bid, thrill GOP by David Salon July 25 2009.

NEW YORK TIMES
Corruption Case a Blow to Corzine's Campaign by David M. Halbfinger & Davis Chen July 25, 2009.

STAR-LEDGER
Arrests shine spotlight on an unknown crime fighter by Josh Margolin August 1, 2009.

JERSEY JOURNAL
[Political Insider] Menendez will feel heat from new gov by Agustin Torres November 5, 2009
[Political Insider] It's a chilly Massachusetts wind blowing on Menendez by Agustin Torres January 23, 2010.

PolitickerNJ
Corzine is Not Corrupt – But The Corruption Scandal Dooms His Campaign by Alan Steinberg July 23, 2009.
Marra defends his office's response to Corzine campaign's FOIA requests by max Pizarro August 12, 2009.

DAILY KOS NEWS BLOG
NJ – Gov: Are "Christie's" U.S. Attorney's Stonewalling the Corzine Campaign? By Steve Singiser August 22, 2009.

THE JERSEY STING by Ted Sherman and Josh Margolin
Pages 254 – 257, 325,326.

Chapter Ten

UNITED STATES v. LOUIS MANZO [select court documents]
Second Superseding Indictment returned July 8, 2011 [excerpts] page 13.
District Court Opinion dismissing charges May 18, 2010 [excerpts] page 18.
District Court Opinion dismissing charges February 17, 2012 [excerpts] page 58.
Transcripts of Proceedings March 23, 2010 [excerpts] page 60.

USA v. KENNETH R. OLSEN order of the court
Dissent by Chief Judge Alex Kozinski, United States Court of Appeals for the Ninth Circuit December 10, 2013.

BID RIG III TAPE TRANSCRIPTS

Excerpt from January 7, 2009 meeting @ Union City, N.J. between Solomon Dwek, Dennis Jaslow, and Maher Khalil [Tape 2265NT].

Excerpt from March 24, 2009 phone conversation between Solomon Dwek and Maher Khalil [Tape 2399].

FBI 302

Ronald A. Manzo debriefing January 5, 2012 by SA S. McCarthy.

CORRESPONDENCES

Letter from U. S. Senator Frank Lautenberg to Department of Justice October 21, 2009.

JERSEY JOURNAL

Political Insider: Credit Manzo's unwillingness to go along by Agustin Torres May 19, 2010.

STAR-LEDGER

Acting U.S. Attorney Ralph Marra faces internal ethics probe by Katherine Santiago August 18, 2009.

ASSOCIATED PRESS

Acting U.S. Attorney Ralph Marra faces internal ethics probe by AP August 18, 2009.

NEW YORK TIMES

Candidate for New Jersey Governor Apologizes for Failing to Report Loan by David M. Halbfinger August 19, 2009.

Christie May Have Gotten Improper Aid by David M. Halbfinger October 20, 2009.

Editorial: Rampant Prosecutorial Misconduct by Editorial Board January 4, 2014.

POLITICKERNJ

Congressman calls for federal investigation of Christie by Max Pizarro August 18, 2009.

Marra says complaint is 'wholly trumped up' by Editor August 25, 2009.

In letter to Holder, Pallone makes his case against Marra by Matt Friedman August 26, 2009.

JUSTICE INTEGRITY PROJECT

Court Slaps Feds Again For Christie-Era NJ Prosecutions by Andrew Kreig February 2011.

TPMMUCKRAKER BLOG

Did Christie Politicize U.S. Attorney's Office? By Zachary Roth October 20, 2009.

Chapter Eleven

DOCUMENTS

New Jersey Election law Enforcement Commission contribution recording – Chang H. Kwong August 11, 2009.

Governor Chris Christie's inauguration speech January 18, 2010.

STATE AND FEDERAL LAWS & GUIDELINES

United States Attorneys' Manual 1-4.410 restrictions on all Employees.

STAR-LEDGER

Gov. Chris Christie compromises independent judiciary by denying tenure to Justice John Wallace by Editorial Board May 4, 2010.

Gov. Christie nominates two for state Supreme Court, including gay African-American mayor by Star-Ledger Staff January 23, 2012.

Moran: In a war of wills, Supreme Court nominee Kwon was a casualty by Tom Moran March 23, 2012.

N.J. Superior Court judges beware: Gov. Christie may be after you by MaryAnn Spoto May 7, 2012.

The latest victim of Christie's sharp tongue: a budget chief he nicknamed 'Dr. Kevorkian' by Megan DeMarco May 24, 2012.

Gov. Christie pushes Sen. Sweeney's tax cut plan in speech to AARP by Salvador Rizzo June 7, 2012.

Gov. Christie signs $31.7B budget with spending cuts by Salvador Rizzo June 29, 2012

Failed Christie court nominee gets Port Authority job by Steve Strunsky July 27, 2012

Moran: Five things the rest of America doesn't know about Chris Christie by Tom Moran August 19, 2012.

Gov. Christie tells Wall Street that N.J.'s surplus may be lower by Jarrett Renshaw September 15, 2012.

N.J. takes another financial hit as Standard & Poor's lowers state's credit outlook by Jarrett Renshaw September 19, 2012.

N.J. unemployment rate rises to 9.9 percent, highest in 3 decades by Jarrett Renshaw September 20, 2012.

Editorial: In Gov. Christie's latest rant against Dems, a clue to his future by Editorial Board September 30, 2012.

Utilities head, military veteran named Gov. Christie's latest Supreme Court nominees by Matt Friedman & Salvador Rizzo December 11, 2012.

ASBURY PARK PRESS

Sweeney says relationship with Christie has changed by Jason Method July 6, 2011.

Capitol Quickies: Lautenberg criticizes Dems for cooperating with Christie by John Schoonejongen September 6, 2012.

Gov. nominates Holmdel man for Supreme Court by Michael Symons December 11, 2012.

NEW YORK TIMES

New Tangle In Battle Over Court In Trenton by Richard Pérez Peña January 3, 2011.

Christie and Democrats Agree to Truce Over Court Seat by Richard Pérez Peña May 2, 2011.

Legislative Panel Rejects 2nd Christie Pick for State Supreme Court by Kate Zernike & Nate Schweber May 31, 2011.

BERGEN RECORD

N.J. Supreme Court nominee's family tied to illegal deposits by Charles Baxter [Star-Ledger] January 29, 2012.

PoliTickerNJ

Labor, Lautenberg, state lawmakers rally against Christie, public sector cuts; governor's office dismisses methodology of 'dubious' study by Bill Mooney October 3, 2012

Hanna and Christie co-authored deferred prosecution paper by Daryl R. Isherwood December 10, 2012.

NEW JERSEY PUBLIC RECORD

Dems Slam Christie Over Spending in NJ Budget Battle by Bob Hennelly June 13, 2012.

Chapter Twelve

NEWJERSEYNEWSROOM.COM

Ousted education chief Schundler blames Christie and Bagger for Race to the Top missteps that led to his firing by Tom Hester Sr. September 1, 2010.

Sen. Weinberg accuses Gov. Christie of insensitivity toward battered women by Tom Hester Sr. April 14, 2011.

BERGEN RECORD

Teachers take off the gloves by Patricia Alex April 10, 2010.

Christie urges media to 'take the bat' to Senator Weinberg on pension issue by Elise Young April 13, 2011.

ASSOCIATED PRESS

Bad Blood between Gov. Christie, U.S. senator by Angela Delli Santi April 20, 2012.

STAR-LEDGER

N.J. teachers' union apologizes for Bergen office's 'humor' about Gov. Christie's death by Lisa Fleisher April 9, 2010..

N.J. Gov. Christie kills Hudson River tunnel project, citing taxpayers woes by Star-Ledger Staff October 8, 2010.

New Jerseyans make the most out of blizzard of 2010 by Star-Ledger Staff December 28, 2010.

Gov. Christie praises his administration for work done after blizzard, chastises mayors for local effort by Ginger Gibson December 31, 2010.

Brett Schundler had to go; education commissioner was out of sync with his boss by Editorial Board August 27, 2010.

Gov. Christie's helicopter rides raise ire of Democratic lawmaker by Star-Ledger Staff June 1, 2011.

Christie refuses to reimburse N.J. for traveling by helicopter to see son's baseball game by Statehouse Bureau Staff June 1, 2011.

Democrats line up to blast Gov. Christie for helicopter ride to baseball game by Statehouse Bureau Staff June 2, 2011.

Unrepentant Gov. Christie says he wants to end the drama, writes check for $2151 for helicopter travel by Ginger Gibson June 2, 2011.

Gov. Chris Christie accuses N.J. teachers' union of 'using students like drug mules' in school elections by Claire Heininger April 19, 2010 [updated on October 13, 2011].

Gov. Chris Christie fires schools chief Bret Schundler by Statehouse Bureau Staff by Statehouse Bureau Staff August 27, 2010 [updated on October 13, 2011].

N.J. Gov. Chris Christie's new bullying target: Sen. Richard Codey's family, friends by Editorial Board December 15, 2011.

Black leaders: Gov. Christie needs history lesson after linking civil rights to gay marriage vote by Matt Friedman January 26, 2012.

Calling opponents 'numbnuts.' Christie refuses to back down from gay marriage comments by Statehouse Bureau Staff January 31, 2012.

Chris Christie says no to N.J. gay marriage bill, would agree to strengthen civil union law by MaryAnn Spoto February 18, 2012.

Editorial: In Gov. Christie's latest rant against Dems, a clue to his future by Editorial Board September 30, 2012.

Gov. Christie says foreclosure aid fell short by Jenna Portnoy October 2, 2012.

Justice Albin warns of political threat to N.J. judges' independence by Salvador Rizzo May 17, 2013.

TIMES OF TRENTON

Opinion: N.J. Gov. Chris Christie's foul-tempered, foul-mouthed ways show disrespect by Thomas P. Ryan [guest opinion column] July 21, 2012.

THINKPROGRESS

Gov. Christie Vastly Exaggerated Costs To Justify Scuttling Important Infrastructure Project by Pat Garofalo April 10, 2012.

VIDEO CAFÉ

Chris Christie urges reporters to 'take the bat' to 76-year-old widow April 14, 2011.

MEDIAITE

NJ Governor Confronts Reporter Over His "Confrontational Tone" by Frances Martel May 14, 2010 [story and video].

DAILYMAIL.COM

'Are you stupid?' New Jersey Governor Chris Christie berates reporter for being an 'idiot' and storms out of press conference by Louis Boyle July 2, 2012.

HUFFINGTON POST

Chris Christie Blows Up At Jersey Shore Heckler by Molte Reilly July 6, 2012

Chris Christie Goes On Attack Against reporter At Press Conference by John Celock September 25, 2012.

YouTube

Christie Blows Up at Heckler While Eating Ice Cream [David Pakman Show & TMZ].

Chapter Thirteen

BERGEN RECORD

N.J. Gov. Chris Christie defends cuts, promotes tax cap in Rutherford by Herb Jackson May 25, 2010.

ASSOCIATED PRESS

Town halls become hallmark of NJ gov's tenure by Beth DeFalco April 15, 2012.

STAR-LEDGER

Former Navy SEAL booted from Gov. Christie town hall after heated exchange by Jenna Portnoy March 9, 2012.

Gov. Chris Christie compares Democrats to vampires at town hall by Jenna Portnoy June 19, 2012.

PHILADELPHIA INQUIRER

Christie's town halls a formula that works by Matt Katz March 10, 2011.

TOWNSQUARE NEWS NETWORK

Town Halls Become Hallmark of Chris Christie's Tenure by Townsquare News Network April10, 2012.

HUFFINGTON POST

Chris Christie Cuts Down Town Hall Questioner (Video) December 7, 2011.

YouTube

Governor Christie: Nothing Left Unsaid.

UNIVERSITY OF NOTRE DAME ARCHIVES
Knute Rockne's "Win One for the Gipper" Speech.

Chapter Fourteen

NEW YORK TIMES
The Caucus: After Speech, Christie Revels in Pleas to Run by Jennifer Medina September 28, 2011.

NEW YORK POST
One for the Gipper by Josh Margolin & Carl Campanile September 28, 2011.

USA TODAY
Chris Christie supports Mitt Romney for president by Jackie Kucinich October 12, 2011.

DAILY CALLER
Chris Christie's Reagan Library Speech [Full Text] September 27, 2011.

RUSH LIMBAUGH SHOW
Monologue: Analysis of Chris Christie's Speech September 28, 2011.

Chapter Fifteen

NEW YORK POST
Christie chose NJ over Mitt's VP role due to fears that they'd lose: sources by Josh Margolin & Beth DeFalco August 27, 2012.

WASHINGTON TIMES
Is Chris Christie's bromance with Obama hurting Romney? By Henry D'Andrea October 31, 2012.

WASHINGTON POST
Chris Christie says he would consider being Mitt Romney's vice president by Aaron Blake January 22, 2012.
Christie stumps for Romney in Illinois by Dan Balz March 16, 2012.
On Leadership: In superstorm Sandy, Gov. Chris Christie praises Obama's crisis leadership by Jena McGregor October 30, 2012.
Obama and Christie: A bromance of convenience by Jonathan Capehart October 31, 2012.
Romney donors unload campaign staffers, Christie by Philip Rucker November 8, 2012.

NEW YORK TIMES
The Caucus: Christie Stumps for Romney at Iowa Event by Susan Saulny December 7, 2011.

NEWS & OBSERVER
NJ Gov. Christie goes on attack for McCrory by Jim Morrill September 13, 2012 [modified on September 21, 2012].

DAILY NEWS
N.J. Gov. Chris Christie: Not my fault that Mitt Romney lost! By Kenneth Lovett November 7, 2012.

EXAMINER.COM
Gov. Christie praises Obama's leadership amidst Sandy by Jonathan Harris November 1, 2012.

STAR-LEDGER

Top spot for Gov. Christie could be GOP Convention keynote speech; allows room for future in White House, N.J. by Jenna Portnoy June 17, 2012.

Full text of Gov. Christie's keynote speech by Statehouse Bureau Staff August 28, 2012 [excerpts].

Senate candidate endorsed by Christie says pregnancy from rape 'something that God intended' by Jenna Portnoy October 25, 2012.

Christie thanks Obama for federal resources, rebukes shore stragglers by Jenna Portnoy October 28, 2012.

Christie slams Romney staffers, who he says questioned his loyalty to GOP ticket by Jessica Calefati November 6, 2012.

Christie gives hospital executives an inside look at life during Sandy by Jenna Portnoy January 26, 2012.

A 2016 presidential preview? Mitt Romney invites Chris Christie to speak to major donors by Jenna Portnoy April 27, 2013.

BERGEN RECORD

Christie reflects on wins, loses of candidates he endorsed by Melissa Hayes November 12, 2012.

HUFFINGTON POST

Chris Christie Denied Mitt Romney Request To Appear At Campaign Event Days Ahead Of 2012 Election by Huffington Post November 6, 2012.

Chris Christie Called Obama To Congratulate Him, Offered Mitt Romney Condolences Over E-mail.

Mitt Romney Reflects On Election Loss In First Interview Since Then March 3, 2013.

POLITICO

Chris Christie: No vice presidential run in 2012 by Meredith Shiner October 20, 2010.

Chris Christie's flop at the GOP convention by John Harris & Tim Mark August 29, 2012.

Hurricane Sandy 2012: Chris Christie heaps praise on Obama by Kevin Robillard October 30, 2012.

Exclusive: Chris Christie was Mitt Romney's first choice for VP by Mike Allen & Jim VandeHei November 3, 2012.

RAW STORY NEWS BLOG

Christie praises Obama, doesn't 'give a damn' about Romney photo op by David Edwards October 30, 2012.

DAILYMAIL.COM

Is THIS why Chris Christie was so loving toward Obama? New Jersey Governor was Romney's FIRST choice as VP and was bitter when Mitt Romney suddenly changed his mind by Hayley Peterson November 3, 2012.

WNYC – FM

It's A Free Country news blog: Endorsement Report Cards: How Palin, Bloomberg and Christie's Picks Fared by Stephen Nessen, Stephen Reader, Sarah Kate Kramer, Sarah P. Reynolds December 7, 2012.

Yahoo! NEWS

Rice, Christie and Rubio top VP polls, but Rubio insists he won't be Romney's running mate in 2012 by Holly Baily April 19, 2012.

Chris Christie Stumps for Mitt Romney in Richmond, Virginia by Samuel Gonzales October 22, 2012.

CROOKS AND LIARS NEWS BLOG

Rush Limbaugh Attacks Chris Christie For His "Man-Love" Of Obama by John Amato November 1, 2012.

KTBB.COM [News-Talk-Sports on the Web].

Decision 2012 [News & Opinion on the Road to the White House]: NJ Governor Chris Christie stumps for Romney in NH January 10, 2012 [video link].

Chapter Sixteen

BERGEN RECORD

Hurricane-force blast by Gov. Christie by Ken Serrano & Michael Symons January 2, 2013.

Christie raises $2 million for re-election bid by Melissa Hayes January 3, 2012.

ASBURY PARK PRESS

Capitol Quickies: Sweeney says Christie "prayed a lot and got lucky" Sandy hit, then apologizes by Michael Symons January 7, 2013.

Watchdog: Hurricane Sandy New Jersey Relief Fund has raised $32M, doled out $0 by Shannon Mullen March 12, 2013.

Christie defends wife's charity; donor critical of delays by Shannon Mullen March 12, 2013.

WALL STREET JOURNAL

Christie: Proposed Sandy aid would cover NJ costs by Associated Press December 10, 2012.

PoliticKerNJ

'We're going to win big;' Christie revels in Laborers endorsement by Max Pizarro December 18, 2012.

STAR-LEDGER

Hedge fund's risky ties to Revel casino shine light on N.J.'s investing habits by Jarrett Renshaw September 10, 2012.

Editorial: In Gov. Christie's latest rant against Dems, a clue to his future by Editorial Board September 30, 2012.

Moran: Will Christie seek a second term? By Tom Moran November 4, 2012.

Gov. Christie on running again: 'I'm in this for the long haul' by Matt Friedman November 27, 2012.

Report: N.J. will be hard-pressed to fund pensions, education in coming years by Salvador Rizzo December 13, 2012.

Chris Christie the favorite among 2016 Republican presidential candidate, poll shows by December 18, 2012.

Christie begins re-election campaign with endorsement from major labor union by Jenna Portnoy December 19, 2012.

Moran: Cory Booker ducks fight with Gov. Christie by Tom Moran December 21, 2012.

Fiery Christie lashes out at Boehner, House Republicans for denying vote on Sandy relief by Matt Friedman January 3, 2013.

Christie looks ahead to big victory in 2013, reflects on how Sandy changed him by Jenna Portnoy January 6, 2013.

Full text of Chris Christie's 2013 State of the State address by Statehouse Bureau January 8, 2013.

Sweeney: Gov. Christie 'prayed a lot' and 'got lucky' when Hurricane Sandy hit by Matt Friedman January 8, 2013.

Moran: Gov. Christie's magic still strong despite N.J.'s miserable economy by Tom Moran January 9, 2013.

POLITICO

Chris Christie 'straight talk' grates GOP right by Maggie Haberman January 4, 2011.

HUFFINGTON POST

Chris Christie Approval Rating Hits 72 Percent by Ariel Edwards-Levy November 27, 2012

Mary Pat Christie Hasn't Given out Any of Her Sandy Charity's $32 Million: Report by Eleanor Goldberg March 11, 2013.

RUTGERS EAGLETON INSTITUTE OF POLITICS

Christie Re-election Support Soars In Sandy Aftermath, Rutgers-Eagleton Poll Finds [press release accompanying polling results] November 27, 2012.

Chapter Seventeen

WASHINGTON POST

Christie raises $6.2 million, holds huge fundraising edge by Aaron Blake May 6, 2013.

ASBURY PARK PRESS

Analysis: Christie's address walked political line by Michael Symons February 26, 2013.

Watchdog: Christie's political connections to the Sandy 'cleanup network' by Bob Jordan February 27, 2013.

Christie on the road again seeking donations by Bob Jordan March 6, 2013.

GOP defends choice of AshBritt, despite cost by Bob Jordan March 8, 2013.

Newspaper: Odd math jacks up Sandy tab by Shawn Boburg May 1, 2013.

Watchdog report: AshBritt didn't pad travel fees in cleanup May 2, 2013.

CPAC snub makes a winner of Christie by Bob Ingle March 2, 2013.

BERGEN RECORD

Lottery hopeful ratchets up lobbying, spending $180,000 and seeking help from Christie allies by Michael Linhorst & Melissa Hayes March 11, 2013.

Stile: Christie's gun plan plays it safe politically by Charles Stile April 23, 2013.

Stile: Former Governor Kean cools on Chris Christie by Charles Stile November 12, 2013.

PoliTickerNJ

Christie on Clinton's former physician: A 'hack' looking for five minutes of fame by Mathew Arco February 6, 2013.

Christie's weight is 'something that you can't avoid' in seeking White House, Murray says by Matthew Arco May 7, 2013.

Long Branch mayor Schneider formally backs Christie by Max Pizarro June 17, 2013.

Quinnipiac: Christie best GOP candidate against Clinton by PolitickerNJ Staff July 22, 2013.

Wisniewski: we may subpoena Baroni, Wildstein by Bill Mooney December 9, 2013.

POLITICO

Hillary Clinton and Chris Christie to headline event by Maggie Haberman May 2, 2013.

PHILADELPHIA INQUIRER

Democrats begin to question Christie's strength: Sandy by Mark Katz March 8, 2013.

Chapter Notes

ASSOCIATED PRESS
GOP leader denies influence in NJ debris deal by AP March 19, 2013.

NEW YORK POST
Christie reveals secret stomach surgery to lose weight by Tara Palmeri & Beth DeFalco May 7, 2013.

NEW YORK TIMES
Christie Decides on October Vote for New Senator by Kate Zernike & Davis M. Halbfinger June 4, 2013.

TIME (magazine)
The Boss by Michael Crowley January 21, 2013.

The 100 Most Influential People in the World by Ginjer Doherty April 29 / May 6, 2013.

STAR-LEDGER
Chris Christie tells Barbara Walters he isn't too overweight to run for president by Jenna Portnoy December 12, 2012.

Christie says he looks like a mob boss on Time Magazine cover by January 9, 2013.

Politically connected Florida firm gets Sandy cleanup contract by Jarrett Renshaw January 13, 2013.

Barbara Buono kicks off campaign for N.J. governor with rally in New Brunswick by Matt Friedman February 2, 2013.

Christie shares doughnut with David Letterman on late-night talk show by Jenna Portnoy February 4, 2013.

Christie weight worries former White House doctor by Jenna Portnoy February 6, 2013.

Head of lobbying firm hired by AshBritt will host Christie fundraiser by Jenna Portnoy February 7, 2013.

Florida cleanup firm's political ties sweep across N.J. by Jarrett Renshaw February 15, 2013.

Christie's ambitious fundraising schedule takes him to New York City and across country by Jenna Portnoy February 20, 2013.

Poll: Christie's approval rating still sky high by Matt Friedman February 20, 2013.

Christie unveils $32.9B N.J. budget that expends Medicaid, covers pension payment by Jenna Portnoy February 26, 2013.

Chris Christie's 2013 budget: Full text of the governor's speech by Star-Ledger Staff February 26, 2013.

Moran Column: In Christie vs. Buono, it's the champ by a knockout by Tom Moran February 27, 2013.

Firm offered cheaper rates to clean up after Sandy, but Christie stuck with AshBritt by Jarrett Renshaw & Chris Baxter February 28, 2013.

FEMA 'blessed' Christie's decision to award no-bid contract, AshBritt head says by Jarrett Renshaw March 9, 2013.

Top Republican on U.S. Senate oversight panel questions N.J. Sandy debris removal costs by Jarrett Renshaw March 20, 2013.

Christie says tax cut will be focus of re-election campaign by Jenna Portnoy April 18, 2013.

'This is Bono': Christie's wife receives a celebrity voice message by Jenna Portnoy April 24, 2013.

A 2016 presidential preview? Mitt Romney invites Chris Christie to speak to major donors by Jenna Portnoy April 27, 2013.

Buono's money woes threaten campaign, cause a change of mind by Jarrett Renshaw May 5, 2013.

289

Christie's quiet decision for Lap-Band surgery explodes into public eye by Jenna Portnoy May 8, 2013.

Federal Sandy relief dollars inflate Christie's ego: Editorial by Star-Ledger Editorial Board May 19, 2013.

Christie's self-serving stunt: Editorial by Editorial Board June 5, 2013.

Christie's cameo on 'The Michael J. Fox Show' may be too much for N.J. voters by Jenna Portnoy July 22, 2013.

Chris Christie holds early lead for 2016 Republican presidential nod, new poll shows by Brent Johnson November 29, 2013.

Christie-Buono race draws record low turnout for N.J. governor's election by Star-Ledger Staff November 7, 2013.

Chris Christie cruises: Governor coasts to second term with big win over Barbara Buono by Jenna Portnoy November 6, 2013.

Christie speaks about his rift with Tom Kean Sr. by Darryl Isherwood December 2, 2013.

Christie's officials are hiding something in Bridge-gate: Editorial Star-Ledger Editorial Board December 5, 2013.

Port Authority official resigning over GWB lane closure controversy by Steve Strunsky December 8, 2013.

Christie used funds for senior complex in town where mayor endorsed him by Matt Friedman January 28, 2014.

Chris Christie should resign if bombshell proves true: Editorial by Editorial Board January 31, 2014.

Christie used Sandy money as political slush fund, evidence shows (Editorial) by Editorial Board January 30, 2014.

NEWSMAX

Star-Ledger: if Christie Lied, He Should 'Resign or Be Impeached' by Cathy Burke January 31, 2014.

CBS TELEVISION

The Late Show with David Letterman February 4, 2013.

ABC TELEVISION.

Barbara Walters' 10 Most Fascinating People December 12, 2012.

MSNBC.

Rachel Maddow: Dubious traffic jam shows signs of politics December 9, 2013.

WIKIPEDIA

2013 NJ gubernatorial election results from various sources.

HUFFINGTON POST

Chris Christie Administration in a Jam Over Charges of Using Busiest U.S. Bridge in Political Payback by Amada Terkel [Associated Press] December 10, 2013.

STATE OF NEW JERSEY OFFICE OF THE STATE COMPTROLLER

Procurement Report: Weakness in the Pay-to-Play Law's "Fair and Open" Contracting System by A. Matthew Boxer September 15, 2011.

Afterword

GALLUP

Politics: Americans say Reagan is the Greatest U.S. President by Frank Newport February 18, 2011.

Bibliography

ABC Television: *Barbara Walters' 10 Most Fascinating People*. December 12, 2012.

Alex, Patricia. Bergen *Record*: "Teachers take off the gloves." April 10, 2010.

Allen, Mike & Jim VandeHei. *Politico* Exclusive: "Chris Christie was Mitt Romney's first choice for VP." November 3, 2012.

Amato, John. *Crooks And Liars,* news blog: "Rush Limbaugh Attacks Chris Christie For His "Man-Love" Of Obama." November 1, 2012.

Arco, Mathew. PolitickerNJ: "Christie on Clinton's former physician: A 'hack' looking for five minutes of fame." February 6, 2013.

   PolitickerNJ: "Christie's weight is 'something that you can't avoid' in seeking White House, Murray says." May 7, 2013.

Associated Press–*Wall Street Journal*: "Christie: Proposed Sandy aid would cover NJ costs." December 10, 2012.

Associated Press [Uncredited]: "Acting U.S. Attorney Ralph Marra faces internal ethics probe." August 18, 2009.

Associated Press [Uncredited]: "GOP leader denies influence in NJ debris deal." March 19, 2013.

Associated Press [Uncredited]: "N.J. GOP gubernatorial candidate Chris Christie's deferred prosecution agreements." June 25, 2009.

Baily, Holly. *Yahoo! News*: "Rice, Christie and Rubio top VP polls, but Rubio insists he won't be Romney's running mate in 2012." April 19, 2012.

Balz, Dan. *Washington Post*: "Christie stumps for Romney in Illinois." March 16, 2012.

Baxter, Charles. *Star-Ledger:* "The Record - N.J. Supreme Court nominee's family tied to illegal deposits." January 29, 2012.

Baxter, Christopher. *Star-Ledger*: "Former federal prosecutor named head of N.J. Division of Consumer Affairs." April 18, 2012.

Star-Ledger: "Bridge scandal: Chris Christie knew about lane closures, Wildstein's lawyer says." January 31, 2014.

Star-Ledger: "Hoboken mayor Dawn Zimmer alleges Chris Christie's office withheld Sandy aid over development deal." January 18, 2014 [David Giambusso cowriter].

Star-Ledger - Updated: "Timeline of Port Authority's George Washington Bridge controversy." January 13, 2014.

Bid Rig III Criminal Complaints
Excerpts from USA v. Serrano, King, Catrillo, Webb-Washington, [M. Manzo, Castagna, Jaslow], [Cammarano & Schaffer], [Elwell & R. Manzo], [Smith & Greene], Cardwell, [Shaw, Cheatam, Beldini], Kenny, and [L. Manzo & R. Manzo] criminal complaints executed July 23, 2009.

Bid Rig III Tape Transcripts
Excerpt from 2/16/09 meeting @ Casa Dante Restaurant, Jersey City, N.J. between Solomon Dwek and Ed Cheatam.
Excerpt from 2/17/09 meeting @ Casa Dante Restaurant, Jersey City, N.J. between Solomon Dwek, Ed Cheatam, and Jack Shaw.
Excerpt from 2/25/09 meeting @ Perkins Restaurant, Staten Island, N.Y. between Solomon Dwek and Ed Cheatam.
Excerpt from January 7, 2009 meeting @ Union City, N.J. between Solomon Dwek, Dennis Jaslow, and Maher Khalil [Tape 2265NT].
Excerpt from March 24, 2009 phone conversation between Solomon Dwek and Maher Khalil [Tape 2399].

Blake, Aaron. *Washington Post*: "Chris Christie says he would consider being Mitt Romney's vice president." January 22, 2012.

Washington Post: "Christie raises $6.2 million, holds huge fundraising edge." May 6, 2013.

Boburg, Shawn. *Asbury Park Press*: "Newspaper: Odd math jacks up Sandy tab / May 1, 2013.

Boxer, Matthew A. [NJ State Comptroller]: "State Of New Jersey Office Of The State Comptroller Procurement Report: Weakness in the Pay-to-Play Law's "Fair and Open" Contracting System." September 15, 2011.

Boyle, Louis, *Dailymail.Com*: "'Are you stupid?' New Jersey Governor Chris Christie berates reporter for being an 'idiot' and storms out of press conference." July 2, 2012

Boyer, Peter J. *Daily Beast*: "Chris Christie: Call Me, Mitt." Jun 18, 2012 .

Braun, Bob. *Star-Ledger*: "Braun: Former N.J. Assembly Speaker Joseph Doria survives the "slings and arrows." October 19, 2011.

Star-Ledger: "Former N.J. Assembly Speaker Joseph Doria survives the 'slings and arrows.'" October 19, 2011.

Burke, Cathy. *Newsmax-Star-Ledger*: "If Christie Lied, He Should 'Resign or Be Impeached.'" January 31, 2014.

Calefati, Jessica. *Star-Ledger*: "Christie slams Romney staffers, who he says questioned his loyalty to GOP ticket." November 6, 2012.

Capehart, Jonathon. *Washington Post*: "Obama and Christie: A bromance of convenience." October 31, 2012.

CBS Television: *The Late Show with David Letterman*. February 4, 2013.

Celock, John. *Huffington Post*: "Chris Christie Goes On Attack Against reporter At Press Conference." September 25, 2012.

Chebium, Raju. *Asbury Park Press*: "Capitol Quickies: Menendez responds to Probe's Closure." October 25, 2011.

Chris Christie's inauguration speech: January 18, 2010.

Christie, Christopher J., U.S. Attorney: United States Department Of Justice, *District of New Jersey Office Report.* 2002-2008.

Conte, Michaelangelo. "Solomon Dwek grilled on the Ten Commandments in Beldini corruption trial." February 1, 2010.

Crowley, Michael. *Time (*magazine): "The Boss." January 21, 2013.

D'Andrea, Henry. *Washington Times*: "Is Chris Christie's bromance with Obama hurting Romney?" October 31, 2012.

De Poto, Tom. *Star-Ledger*: "EDA chief steps down; authority to reorganize executive structure." July 25, 2012.

DeFalco, Beth. *Associated Press*: "Town halls become hallmark of NJ gov's tenure." April 15, 2012.

Delli Santi, Angela. *Associated Press*: "Bad Blood between Gov. Christie, U.S. senator." April 20, 2012.

DeMarco, Megan. *Star-Ledger*: "The latest victim of Christie's sharp tongue: a budget chief he nicknamed 'Dr. Kevorkian.'" May 24, 2012.

Doherty, Ginjer. *Time (*magazine): "The 100 Most Influential People in the World." April 29 / May 6, 2013.

Dopp, Terrence. *Bloomberg News Blog*: "Corruption Bust May Aid Christie Bid Against Corzine [Update 2]." July 24, 2009.

Edwards-Levy, Ariel: *Huffington Post*: Chris Christie Approval Rating Hits 72 Percent." November 27, 2012.

Edwards, David. *Raw Story* news blog: Christie praises Obama, doesn't 'give a damn' about Romney photo op." October 30, 2012.

Emptywheel blog. "Chris Christie, Former U.S. Attorney, Claims He's Still "Got" Federal Prosecutors, Talked with Them about State Jobs." August 19, 2009 [Christie speech at West Windsor on February 28, 2009].

FactCheck.org Blog. [Uncredited analysis]: "Corzine on Christie: Contracts for Cronies." July 13, 2009.

FBI Otherwise Illegal Activity Authorization Report, Case 270D-NK-114696. February 28, 2009 [excerpts].

Fink, Zachary. *Zachary Fink Blog*: "Christie Faces Reporters." August 25, 2009.

Fleisher, Lisa. *Star-Ledger*: "N.J. teachers' union apologizes for Bergen office's 'humor' about Gov. Christie's death." April 9, 2010.

Fletcher, Julie. *Bergen Record*: "The Political State: Michele Brown leaving as Christie appointments counsel, will head EDA." July 25, 2012.

Friedman Matt & Salvador Rizzo. *Star-Ledger*: "Utilities head, military veteran named Gov. Christie's latest Supreme Court nominees." December 11, 2012.

Friedman, Matt. PolitickerNJ: "In letter to Holder, Pallone makes his case against Marra." August 26, 2009.

Friedman, Matt. *Star-Ledger*: "Barbara Buono kicks off campaign for N.J. governor with rally in New Brunswick." February 2, 2013.

Star-Ledger. "Christie says he looks like a mob boss on *Time Magazine* cover." January 9, 2013.

Star- Ledger, Poll: "Christie's approval rating still sky high." February 20, 2013.

Star-Ledger: "Black leaders: Gov. Christie needs history lesson after linking civil rights to gay marriage vote." January 26, 2012.

Star-Ledger: "Fiery Christie lashes out at Boehner, House Republicans for denying vote on Sandy relief. January 3, 2013.

Star-Ledger: "Former Sheriff's nomination to N.J. Superior Court in jeopardy over FBI files." October 23, 2012.

Star-Ledger: "Gov. Christie on running again: 'I'm in this for the long haul.'" November 27, 2012

Star-Ledger: "N.J. senator wants Solomon Dwek to appear before committee to explain foreclosure tipoff claims." June 13, 2012.

Star-Ledger: "Christie used Sandy funds for senior complex in town where mayor endorsed him." January 28, 2014.

Star-Ledger: "Sweeney: Gov. Christie 'prayed a lot' and 'got lucky' when Hurricane Sandy hit." January 8, 2013.

Garofolo, Pat. Thinkprogress: "Gov. Christie Vastly Exaggerated Costs To Justify Scuttling Important Infrastructure Project." April 10, 2012.

George, Sandra Caron. *Georgetown Journal Of Legal Ethics*: "Prosecutorial Discretion: What's Politics Got to Do with It?" Volume 18 Number 3, Summer 2005.

Gibson, Ginger. *Star-Ledger*: "Gov. Christie praises his administration for work done after blizzard, chastises mayors for local effort." December 31, 2010. *Star-Ledger*: "Unrepentant Gov. Christie says he wants to end the drama, writes check for $2151 for helicopter travel." June 2, 2011.

Giambusso, David [Christopher Baxter co-writer]. *Star-Ledger*: "Hoboken mayor Dawn Zimmer alleges Chris Christie's office withheld Sandy aid over development deal." January 18, 2014.

Goldberg, Eleanor. *Huffington Post*: "Mary Pat Christie Hasn't Given Out Any Of Her Sandy Charity's $32 Million." March 11, 2013.

Gonzales, Samuel. *Yahoo! News*: "Chris Christie Stumps for Mitt Romney in Richmond, Virginia." October 22, 2012.

Graves, Lucia. *Huffington Post*: "Mitt Romney Reflects On Election Loss In First Interview Since Then." March 3, 2013.

Haberman, Maggie. *Politico*: "Chris Christie 'straight talk' grates GOP right." January 4, 2011.

   Politico: "Hillary Clinton and Chris Christie to headline event." May 2, 2013.

Haddon, Heather. *Wall Street Journal*: "Christie's Senate Fight." August 20, 2012.

Halbfinger, David M. & Davis Chen. *New York Times*: "Corruption Case a Blow to Corzine's Campaign." July 25, 2009.

Halbfinger, David M. *New York Times*: "Candidate for New Jersey Governor Apologizes for Failing to Report Loan." August 19, 2009.

   New York Times: "Christie May Have Gotten Improper Aid." October 20, 2009.

   New York Times: "For N.J. Candidate, First Ethics Push Was Brief." August 17, 2009.

Harris, John & Tim Mark. *Politico*: "Chris Christie's flop at the GOP convention." August 29, 2012.

Harris, Jonathan. *examiner.com*: "Gov. Christie praises Obama's leadership amidst Sandy." November 1, 2012.

Hassan, Minhaj. PolitickerNJ: "Christie defends Oxley judicial nomination in face of Dem resistance." October 23, 2012.

Hayes, Melissa. *Bergen Record*: "Christie raises $2 million for re-election bid." January 3, 2012.

   Bergen Record: "Christie reflects on wins, loses of candidates he endorsed." November 12, 2012.

Heininger, Claire. *Star-Ledger*: "GOP candidate Chris Christie agrees to testify before Congress on federal monitoring contracts." June 19, 2009.

   Star-Ledger: "Gov. Chris Christie accuses N.J. teachers' union of 'using students like drug mules' in school elections." April 19, 2010 [updated October 13, 2011].

Hennelly, Bob. *New Jersey Public Record*: "Dems Slam Christie Over Spending in NJ Budget Battle." June 13, 2012.

Hester, Thomas Sr. *Newjerseynewsroom.Com*: "Ousted education chief Schundler blames Christie and Bagger for Race to the Top missteps that led to his firing." September 1, 2010.

   Newjerseynewsroom.Com: Sen. Weinberg accuses Gov. Christie of insensitivity toward battered women." April 14, 2011.

Horowitz, Jason. *New York Observer*: "Prosecutor Makes a Meal of N.J. Senate Race." October 16, 2006.

Horton, Scott. *Harper's Magazine*: "Manure for the Garden State." August 19, 2009.

Huffington Post: "Chris Christie Cuts Down Town Hall Questioner" (Video). December 7, 2011.

Hunger, Matt. *Jersey City Independent*: "L. Harvey Smith on trial, Day Eleven: Closing Statements." February 6, 2013.

Huntsu. *Blue Jersey News Blog:* "Chris Christie: Caught in The U.S. Attorney Web of Lies." August 3, 2007.

Ingle, Bob. *Asbury Park Press*: "CPAC snub makes a winner of Christie." March 2, 2013.

Isherwood, Daryl R. PolitickerNJ: "Hanna and Christie co-authored deferred prosecution paper." December 10, 2012.

    NJ.Com: "Christie speaks about his rift with Tom Kean Sr." December 2, 2013.

    NJ.Com: "U.S. Attorney subpoenas Christie campaign and GOP State Committee over bridge scandal." January 23, 2014.

Jackson, Herb. *Bergen Record*: "N.J. Gov. Chris Christie defends cuts, promotes tax cap in Rutherford." May 25, 2010.

Jersey Journal Editorial Board. *Jersey Journal*: "Accusations against GOP nominee need full scrutiny." June 19, 2012.

Johnson, Brent. *Star-Ledger*: "Chris Christie holds early lead for 2016 Republican presidential nod, new poll shows." November 29, 2013.

Jordan, Bob. *Asbury Park Press*: "Christie on the road again seeking donations." March 6, 2013.

    Asbury Park Press: "GOP defends choice of AshBritt, despite cost." March 8, 2013.

    Asbury Park Press: "Watchdog: Christie's political connections to the Sandy 'cleanup network." February 27, 2013.

    Asbury Park Press: "'Bridgegate' documents show fight over ending of lane closures." January 11, 2014. [John Schoonjongen cowriter]

Katz, Mark. *Philadelphia Inquirer*: "Democrats begin to question Christie's strength: Sandy." March 8, 2013.

    Philadelphia Inquirer: "Christie's town halls a formula that works." March 10, 2011.

Kiel, Paul. *TPM Muckraker*: "Feds Probing Dem Sen. Relationship to Former Aide." November 1, 2007.

Kozinski, Alex. Chief Judge, United States Court Of Appeals For The Ninth Circuit. *Dissent Opinion: United States of America v. Kenneth R. Olsen.* December 10, 2013.

Kocieniewski, David. *New York Times*: "A Governor Unindicted, but Implicated." July 9, 2004.

    New York Times: "Showdown Looming Over McGreevey Fund-Raising Inquiry." March 16, 2006.

    New York Times: "Usually on Attack, U.S. Attorney in Newark Finds Himself on Defensive." February 13, 2008.

New York Times: "In Testy Exchange in Congress, Christie Defends His Record as a Prosecutor." June 26, 2009.

Kornacki, Steve. *Salon*: "What Chris Christie is really afraid of." March 4, 2011.
New York Observer: "See Chris Christie Skate." August 13, 2009.

Kosimar, Lucy. *Kosimar Scoop Blog*: "Former U.S. Attorney Chris Christie, GOP Candidate for NJ Governor, gets $ from IDT, NJ telcom investigated by Justice Dept. for bribing Haitian officials." October 22, 2009.

Kreig, Andrew. Justice Integrity Project: "Court Slaps Feds Again For Christie-Era NJ Prosecutions." February 2011.

KTBB.com [News-Talk-Sports on the Web]. "Decision 2012 [News & Opinion on the Road to the White House]: NJ Governor Chris Christie stumps for Romney in NH." January 10, 2012 [video link].

Kucinich, Jackie. *USA Today:* "Chris Christie supports Mitt Romney for president." October 12, 2011.

Larsen, Eric. *Asbury Park Press*: Dwek tells of meeting with Van Pelt, Ocean County GOP Chief." May 6, 2010.

Asbury Park Press: "Watchdog report: AshBritt didn't pad travel fees in cleanup." May 2, 2013.

Lautenberg, Frank, United States Senator: Letter to Department of Justice. October 21, 2009.

Limbaugh, Rush. *Rush Limbaugh Show*: Monologue: Analysis of Chris Christie's Speech. September 28, 2011.

Linhorst, Michael & Melissa Hayes. *Bergen Record*: "Lottery hopeful ratchets up lobbying, spending $180,000 and seeking help from Christie allies." March 11, 2013.

Lovett, Kenneth. *Daily News*: "N.J. Gov. Chris Christie: Not my fault that Mitt Romney lost!" November 7, 2012.

Maddow, Rachel. MSNBC: "Dubious traffic jam shows signs of politics." December 9, 2013.

Main Justice. *Main Justice*: Post Tagged "U.S. Attorney's Office for the District of New Jersey." January 8, 2010 through January 14, 2011.

Manzo for Mayor: Political Advertisement, *Jersey Journal*. May 11, 2009.

Margolin, Josh. *Star-Ledger*: "Arrests shine spotlight on an unknown crime fighter." August 1, 2009.

Margolin, Josh & Carl Campanile. *New York Post*: "One for the Gipper." September 28, 2011.

Margolin, Josh & Beth DeFalco. *New York Post*: "Christie chose NJ over Mitt's VP role due to fears that they'd lose: sources." August 27, 2012.

Martel, Frances. *Mediaite:* "NJ Governor Confronts Reporter Over His 'Confrontational Tone." May 14, 2010 [story and video].

Martin, John. *Star-Ledger*: "Congressman criticizes monitoring deal for Ashcroft." November 21, 2007.

Star-Ledger: "$52 M-plus payday for Christie's old boss." November 20, 2007.

McCarthy, Craig. *Bergen Record*: "Governor Christie's brother invested in real estate near PATH station in Harrison." January 29, 2014.

McGregor Jena. *Washington Post*: "On Leadership: In superstorm Sandy, Gov. Chris Christie praises Obama's crisis leadership." October 30, 2012.

Medina, Jennifer. *New York Times*: "The Caucus: After Speech, Christie Revels in Pleas to Run." September 28, 2011.

Megerian, Chris. *Star-Ledger*: "Democratic Lawmakers Seek Probe Of Alleged Offer To Keep GOP Candidate From Race." May 8, 2009.

Star-Ledger: "Merkt Says Christie Ally Offered Him Job In Campaign To Stay Out Of GOP Gubernatorial Race." May 7, 2009.

Method, Jason. *Asbury Park Press*: "Sweeney Says Relationship With Christie Has Changed." July 6, 2011.

Mikle, Jeanne. *Asbury Park Press*: "Dwek Gets Six Years In Prison, $22.8 Million Restitution." October 18, 2012

Mooney, Bill. PolitickerNJ: "Labor, Lautenberg, State Lawmakers Rally Against Christie, Public Sector Cuts; Governor's Office Dismisses Methodology Of 'Dubious' Study." October 3, 2012. PolitickerNJ: "Wisniewski: 'We may subpoena Baroni, Wildstein.'" December 9, 2013.

Moran, Tom. *Star-Ledger*: "Moran Column: In Christie vs. Buono, It's The Champ." February 27, 2013

Star-Ledger: "Cory Booker Ducks Fight With Gov. Christie." December 21, 2012.

Star-Ledger: "Five Things The Rest Of America Doesn't Know About Chris Christie." August 19, 2012.

Star-Ledger: "Gov. Christie's Magic Still Strong Despite N.J.'S Miserable Economy." January 9, 2013.

Star-Ledger: "In A War Of Wills, Supreme Court Nominee Kwon Was A Casualty." March 23, 2012.

Star-Ledger: "Will Christie Seek A Second Term?" November 4, 2012.

Star-Ledger: "Chris Christie Faces The Wrath Of A Scorned Friend." February 2, 2014.

Morford, Craig S. Acting Deputy Attorney General, United States Department Of Justice. Letter dated March 7, 2008.

Morrill, Jim. *News & Observer*: "NJ Gov. Christie Goes On Attack For McCrory." September 13, 2012 [modified on September 21, 2012].

Mueller, Mark. *Star-Ledger*: "Feds Tell Sen. Menendez 2006 Probe Now Closed." October 23, 2011.

Star-Ledger: "In Super Bowl 2014 Spotlight, Chris Christie Muddles Through Bridge Scandal Fallout." February 2, 2014 [Jenna Portnoy co-writer].

Mullen, Shannon. *Asbury Park Press*: "Christie Defends Wife's Charity; Donor Critical Of Delays." March 12, 2013.

Asbury Park Press: "Watchdog: Hurricane Sandy New Jersey Relief Fund Has Raised $32M, Doled Out $." March 12, 2013.

Nessen Stephen, Stephen Reader, Sarah Kate Kramer & Sarah P. Reynolds. WNYC-FM: *It's A Free Country* news blog: "Endorsement Report Cards: How Palin, Bloomberg and Christie's Picks Fared." December 7, 2012.

New Jersey Election Law Enforcement Commission [contribution reports]: Chris Christie 2009 gubernatorial campaign contributions from staff of the United States Attorney's Office for the District of New Jersey.

New Jersey Election Law Enforcement Commission contribution recording: Chang H. Kwong. August 11, 2009.

New York Times Editorial Board: "Money for Nothing." April 16, 2005.

"Why This Scandal Matters." May 21, 2007.

"The Bully Was a Dupe." January 8, 2014.

"Rampant Prosecutorial Misconduct." January 4, 2014.

Newport, Frank. *Gallup:* "Politics: Americans say Reagan is the Greatest U.S. President." February 18, 2011.

Office Of The Inspector General Report: *The Federal Bureau of Investigation's Compliance with the Attorney General's Investigative Guidelines.* September 2005 [pages 7-9, 103, 104, 106].

O'Brien, Michael. NBC News: "Christie Acknowledges Federal Subpoena." February 4, 2014.

O'Neill, Erin. *Star-Ledger*: "Amid Federal Probe Into N.J.'S Sandy Ads, Jersey Shore Mayors Weigh In On Campaign." January 13, 2014.

Pakman, David & TMZ YouTube: "Governor Christie: Nothing Left Unsaid – Christie Blows Up at Heckler While Eating Ice Cream."

Palmeri, Tara & Beth DeFalco. *New York Post:* "Christie reveals secret stomach surgery to lose weight." May 7, 2013.

Peña, Richard Pérez. *New York Times*: "New Tangle In Battle Over Court In Trenton." January 3, 2011.

New York Times: "Christie and Democrats Agree to Truce Over Court Seat." May 2, 2011.

Peterson, Hayley. *Dailymail.Com*: "Is this why Chris Christie was so loving toward Obama? New Jersey Governor was Romney's FIRST choice as VP and was bitter when Mitt Romney suddenly changed his mind." November 3, 2012

Pizarro, Max. PolitickerNJ:/ "'We're going to win big;' Christie Revels In Laborers Endorsement." December 18, 2012.

PolitickerNJ: "Congressman Calls For Federal Investigation Of Christie." August 18, 2009.

PolitickerNJ: "Long Branch Mayor Schneider Formally Backs Christie." June 17, 2013.

PolitickerNJ: "Marra Defends His Office's Response To Corzine Campaign's FOIA Requests." August 12, 2009.

PolitickerNJ Editor: "Marra says complaint is 'wholly trumped up'." August 25, 2009.

PolitickerNJ Staff: "Quinnipiac: Christie best GOP candidate against Clinton." / July 22, 2013.

Portnoy, Jenna. *Star-Ledger:* "Christie thanks Obama for federal resources, rebukes shore stragglers." October 28, 2012.

Star-Ledger: "'This is Bono': Christie's wife receives a celebrity voice message." April 24, 2013.

Star-Ledger: "A 2016 presidential preview? Mitt Romney invites Chris Christie to speak to major donors." April 27, 2013.

Star-Ledger: "A 2016 presidential preview? Mitt Romney invites Chris Christie to speak to major donors." April 27, 2013.

Star-Ledger: "Chris Christie tells Barbara Walters he isn't too overweight to run for president." December 12, 2012.

Star-Ledger: "Chris Christie the favorite among 2016 Republican presidential candidate, poll shows." December 18, 2012.

Star-Ledger: "Christie begins re-election campaign with endorsement from major labor union." December 19, 2012.

Star-Ledger: "Christie gives hospital executives an inside look at life during Sandy." January 26, 2012.

Star-Ledger: "Christie looks ahead to big victory in 2013, reflects on how Sandy changed him." January 6, 2013.

Star-Ledger: "Christie says tax cut will be focus of re-election campaign." April 18, 2013.

Star-Ledger: "Christie shares doughnut with David Letterman on late-night talk show." February 4, 2013.

Star-Ledger: "Christie unveils $32.9B N.J. budget that expends Medicaid, covers pension payment." February 26, 2013.

Star-Ledger: "Christie weight worries former White House doctor." February 6, 2013.

Star-Ledger: "Christie's cameo on 'The Michael J. Fox Show' may be too much for N.J. voters." July 21, 2013.

Star-Ledger: "Former Navy SEAL booted from Gov. Christie town hall after heated exchange." March 9, 2012.

Star-Ledger: "Gov. Christie prods Dems to hold hearing on judicial nominee Joseph Oxley." October 23, 2012.

Star-Ledger: "Gov. Christie says foreclosure aid fell short." October 2, 2012.

Star-Ledger: "Head of lobbying firm hired by AshBritt will host Christie fundraiser." February 7, 2013.

Star-Ledger: "Senate candidate endorsed by Christie says pregnancy from rape 'something that God intended.'" October 25, 2012

.Star-Ledger: "Top spot for Gov. Christie could be GOP Convention keynote speech; allows room for future in White House, N.J." June 17, 2012.

Star-Ledger: "Christie's ambitious fundraising schedule takes him to New York City and across country." February 20, 2013.

Star-Ledger: "Christie's quiet decision for Lap-Band surgery explodes into public eye." May 8, 2013.

Star-Ledger: "Gov. Chris Christie compares Democrats to vampires at town hall." June 19, 2012.

Star-Ledger: "Chris Christie cruises: coasts to second term with big win over Barbara Buono." November 6, 2013.

Star-Ledger: "Chris Christie's Port Authority appointee Davis Samson's judgment defended amid scandals." January 30, 2014.

Star-Ledger: "Chris Christie ramps up travel plans as scandals continue." February 4, 2014.

Star-Ledger: "In Super Bowl 2014 spotlight, Chris Christie muddles through bridge scandal fallout." February 2, 2014 [Mark Mueller cowriter].

Powell, Michael. *New York Times*: "The Quashing of a Case Against a Christie Ally." October 10, 2013.

Reilly, Molte. *Huffington Post*: "Chris Christie Blows Up At Jersey Shore Heckler." July 6, 2012.

Renshaw, Jarrett & Chris Baxter. *Star-Ledger*: "Firm offered cheaper rates to clean up after Sandy, but Christie stuck with AshBritt." February 28, 2013.

Renshaw, Jarrett. *Star-Ledger*: "Buono's money woes threaten campaign, cause a change of mind." May 5, 2013.

Star-Ledger: "FEMA 'blessed' Christie's decision to award no-bid contract, AshBritt head says." March 9, 2013.

Star-Ledger: "Florida cleanup firm's political ties sweep across N.J." February 15, 2013.

Star-Ledger: "Gov. Christie tells Wall Street that N.J.'s surplus may be lower." September 15, 2012.

Star-Ledger: "Hedge fund's risky ties to Revel casino shine light on N.J.'s investing habits." September 10, 2012.

Star-Ledger: "N.J. takes another financial hit as Standard & Poor's lowers state's credit outlook." September 19, 2012.

Star-Ledger: "N.J. unemployment rate rises to 9.9 percent, highest in 3 decades." September 20, 2012.

Star-Ledger: "Politically connected Florida firm gets Sandy cleanup contract." January 13, 2013.

Star-Ledger: "Top Republican on U.S. Senate oversight panel questions N.J. Sandy debris removal costs." March 20, 2013.

Rispoli, Michael. *Star-Ledger:* "Gov. Corzine wants GOP challenger Chris Christie to explain Rove talks." August 13, 2009.

Star-Ledger: "Karl Rove and Christie discussed N.J. governor run while serving as U.S. Attorney." August 12, 2009.

Rizzo Salvado. *Star-Ledger:* "Gov. Christie pushes Sen. Sweeney's tax cut plan in speech to AARP." June 7, 2012.

Star-Ledger: "Gov. Christie signs $31.7B budget with spending cuts." June 29, 2012.

Star-Ledger: "Justice Albin warns of political threat to N.J. judges' independence." May 17, 2013.

Star-Ledger: "Report: N.J. will be hard-pressed to fund pensions, education in coming years." December 13, 2012.

Star-Ledger: "Former prosecutor accuses Christie administration of corruption in NJ court." January 29, 2014.

Robillard, Kevin. *Politico:* Hurricane Sandy 2012: Chris Christie heaps praise on Obama." October 30, 2012.

Roth, Zachary. TPMMuckraker blog: "Did Christie Politicize U.S. Attorney's Office?" October 20, 2009.

Rucker, Philip. *Washington Post:* "Romney donors unload campaign staffers, Christie." November 8, 2012.

Rutgers Eagleton Institute Of Politics [press release accompanying polling results]. "Christie Re-election Support Soars In Sandy Aftermath, Rutgers-Eagleton Poll Finds." November 27, 2012.

Ryan, Thomas P. *Times Of Trenton* "N.J. Gov. Chris Christie's foul-tempered, foul-mouthed ways show disrespect [guest opinion column]. July 21, 2012.

Salon, David. *New York Daily News:* "Corruption arrests in N.J. hurt Corzine election bid, thrill GOP." July 25 2009.

Santiago, Katherine. *Star-Ledger:* "Acting U.S. Attorney Ralph Marra faces internal ethics probe." August 18, 2009.

Saulny, Susan: *New York Times:* "The Caucus: Christie Stumps for Romney at Iowa Event." December 7, 2011.

Schoonejongen, John: *Asbury Park Press:* "Capitol Quickies: Lautenberg criticizes Dems for cooperating with Christie." September 6, 2012.

Asbury Park Press: "'Bridgegate' documents show fight over ending of lane closures." January 11, 2014 [Bob Jordan cowriter].

Serrano, Ken & Michael Symons. *Bergen Record:* "Hurricane-force blast by Gov. Christie." January 2, 2013.

Shenon, Philip. *New York Times:* "Ashcroft deal Brings Scrutiny in Justice Dept." January 19, 2008.

Sherman, Gabriel. *New Jersey Monthly*: "New Jersey Nasty." October 19, 2009.

Sherman, Ted & Josh Margolin. *The Jersey Sting*: St. Martin's Press New York, 2011. Pp. 36-37, 70-71, 80-81, 84-95, 100-101, 118-119, 168-173, 250-251, 254-257, 259, 325-326.

Sherman, Ted. *Star-Ledger*: "FBI informant Solomon Dwek gets 6 years in prison for role in $50M fraud scheme." October 18, 2012.

> *Star-Ledger*: "Infamous federal informant Solomon Dwek is sentenced to 6 years, must pay $22.8M." October 19, 2012.

> *Star-Ledger*: "FBI informant Solomon Dwek headed back to prison after his bail is revoked." June 28, 2011.

> *Star-Ledger*: "Infamous federal informant Solomon Dwek is sentenced to 6 years, must pay $22.8M." October 19, 2012.

> *Star-Ledger*: "Corruption probe informant Solomon Dwek back behind bars after lying to the FBI." June 29, 2011.

> *Star-Ledger*: "FBI informant Solomon Dwek is mentally ill, his attorney says." October 8, 2012.

> *Star-Ledger*: "Bridgegate fallout: Chris Christie apologizes in wake of bridge scandal, fires top aide." January 9, 2014 [Steve Strunsky cowriter].

Shiner, Meredith. *Politico*: "Chris Christie: No vice presidential run in 2012." October 20, 2010.

Singiser, Steve: *Daily Kos* News Blog: "NJ – Gov: Are "Christie's" U.S. Attorney's Stonewalling the Corzine Campaign?" August 22, 2009.

Smothers, Ronald. New York Times: "Lurid Charges Hit Top Donor to New Jersey Governor." July 14, 2004.

> *New York Times*: "Rabbi Convicted of Sexual Abuse Is Freed Bail Pending Appeal." October 12, 2012.

Spoto, MaryAnn. *Star-Ledger*: "Chris Christie says no to N.J. gay marriage bill, would agree to strengthen civil union law." February 18, 2012.

> *Star-Ledger*: "N.J. Superior Court judges beware: Gov. Christie may be after you." May 7, 2012.

> *Star-Ledger* Editorial Board: "Brett Schundler had to go; education commissioner was out of sync with his boss." August 27, 2010.

> *Star-Ledger*: "Christie's self-serving stunt." June 5, 2013.

> *Star-Ledger*: "Chris Christie's subpoena on Senator Menendez during an election was a mistake." October 24, 2011.

> *Star-Ledger*: "In Gov. Christie's latest rant against Dems, a clue to his future." September 30, 2012.

> *Star-Ledger*: "Federal Sandy relief dollars inflate Christie's ego: Editorial." May 19, 2013.

> *Star-Ledger*: "Gov. Chris Christie compromises independent judiciary by denying tenure to Justice John Wallace." May 4, 2010.

Star-Ledger: "N.J. Gov. Chris Christie's new bullying target: Sen. Richard Codey's family, friends." December 15, 2011.*Star-Ledger*: "Christie's officials are hiding something in Bridge-gate." December 5, 2013.

Star-Ledger: "GWB scandal: Republicans wrong to try to stop legislative probe." January 22, 2014.

Star-Ledger: "Chris Christie should resign if bombshell proves true." Editorial / January 31, 2014.

Star-Ledger: "Christie used Sandy money as political slush fund, evidence shows." January 29, 2014.

Star-Ledger Staff: "N.J. Gov. Christie kills Hudson River tunnel project, citing taxpayers woes." October 8, 2010.

Star-Ledger: "Former head of N.J. community affairs quietly cleared of wrongdoing after two-year investigation." October 7, 2011.

Star-Ledger: Chris Christie's 2013 budget: Full text of the governor's speech. February 26, 2013.

Star-Ledger: "Federal prosecutor Ralph Marra joins N.J. Sports and Exposition Authority as top lawyer." February 18, 2010.

Star-Ledger: "Gov. Christie nominates two for state Supreme Court, including gay African-American mayor." January 23, 2012.

Star-Ledger: "Gov. Christie's helicopter rides raise ire of Democratic lawmaker." June 1, 2011.

Star-Ledger: "New Jerseyans make the most out of blizzard of 2010." December 28, 2010.

Star-Ledger: "Christie-Buono race draws record low turnout for N.J. governor's election." November 7, 2013.

Star-Ledger: "Hoboken mayor stands firm as Christie's office refutes claim over Sandy aid." January 20, 2014 [Kelly Heyboer & Ryan Hutchins cowriter].

State And Federal Laws & Guidelines

Attorney General's Guidelines Regarding the Use of FBI Confidential Human Sources. [pp. 30-40]

FBI Domestic Investigations and Operations Guidelines [excerpts]

The New Jersey Court Rules of Professional Conduct *New Jersey, RPC 8.4.* [Misconduct]

United States Attorneys' Manual [Criminal Resource Manual 2404].

(USAM) USAM 1-4.410 [restrictions on all Employees].

(USAM) USAM 3-27-260, USAM 9-27.260, USAM 3-27-260 [Recusals], USAM 9-27.260. [Initiating and Declining Charges-Impermissible Considerations]

The United States Code of Federal Regulations, 5 USC 7323 [Political activity prohibitions].

28 USC 528.

28 USC 530B [Ethical standards for attorneys for the Government]

Statehouse Bureau Staff. *Star-Ledger:* "Calling opponents 'numbnuts.' Christie refuses to back down from gay marriage comments." January 31, 2012.

> *Star-Ledger*: "Christie refuses to reimburse N.J. for traveling by helicopter to see son's baseball game." June 1, 2011.

> *Star-Ledger*: "Democrats line up to blast Gov. Christie for helicopter ride to baseball game." June 2, 2011.

> *Star-Ledger*: "Full text of Chris Christie's 2013 State of the State address." January 8, 2013.

> *Star-Ledger*: "Full text of Gov. Christie's keynote speech." August 28, 2012.

> *Star-Ledger*: "Gov. Chris Christie fires schools chief Bret Schundler." August 27, 2010 [updated on October 13, 2011].

Steinberg, Alan. *PoltickerNJ:* "Corzine is Not Corrupt – But The Corruption Scandal Dooms His Campaign." July 23, 2009.

Stile, Charles. *Bergen Record*: "A body blow to Corzine's reelection." September 7, 2009.

> *Bergen Record*: "Christie's gun plan plays it safe politically." April 23, 2013.

> *Bergen Record*: "Governor Kean cools on Chris Christie." November 12, 2013.

Stirling, Stephen. *Star-Ledger*: "Hoboken development at center of latest Christie allegations was rejected by city." January 18, 2014.

Strunsky, Steve: *Star-Ledger:* "Failed Christie court nominee gets Port Authority job." July 27, 2012.

> *Star-Ledger*: "Port Authority official resigning over GWB lane closure controversy." December 8, 2013.

> *Star-Ledger*: "Bridgegate fallout: Chris Christie apologizes in wake of bridge scandal, fires top aide." January 9, 2014 [Ted Sherman cowriter].

> *Star-Ledger*: "Chris Christie bridge scandal: Documents show Port Authority chairman blasting executive director." January 10, 2014.

Sullivan, Al. *The Hudson Reporter*: "Lunch hour for 'Buddy.'" March 20, 2011.

Symons, Michael. *Asbury Park Press*: "Capitol Quickies: Sweeney says Christie 'prayed a lot and got lucky' Sandy hit, then apologizes." January 7, 2013.

> *Asbury Park Press*: "Gov. nominates Holmdel man for Supreme Court." December 11, 2012.

> *Asbury Park Press*: "Gov. nominates Holmdel man for Supreme Court." December 11, 2012.

> *Asbury Park Press*: "Analysis: Christie's address walked political line." February 26, 2013.

Tat, Linh. *Bergen Record*: "EMS responses by GWB lane closures in what Fort Lee mayor calls 'absolute power corruption.'" January 8, 2014.

Terkel, Amanda. *Huffington Post*: "Chris Christie Administration in a Jam Over Charges of Using Busiest U.S. Bridge in Political Payback." December 10, 2013.

> *Huffington Post*: "Chris Christie's Top Aide Linked To Traffic Jam Payback Against Democratic Mayor." January 8, 2014.

Huffington Post: "Chris Christie Denies Knowledge of Bridge Payback Scheme." January 8, 2014.

Torres, Agustin. *Jersey Journal*: [Political Insider] "It's a chilly Massachusetts wind blowing on Menendez." January 23, 2010.

  Jersey Journal: [Political Insider] "Menendez will feel heat from new Gov." November 5, 2009.

  Jersey Journal: "Political Insider: Credit Manzo's unwillingness to go along." May 19, 2010.

Townsquare News Network: "Town Halls Become Hallmark of Chris Christie's Tenure." April 10, 2012.

United States Department of Justice Court Documents: Solomon Dwek Forensic Evaluation by Jerome Rubin, Ph.D. / issued August 10, 2011.

  −FBI 302 / Alfonso Santoro debriefing September 23, 2009 by SA Waldie & Brogan.

  −FBI 302 / Dennis Jaslow debriefing August 5, 2009.

  −FBI 302 / Jack M. Shaw debriefing July 22 & 27, 2009.

  −FBI 302 / Ronald A. Manzo debriefing by SA S. McCarthy / January 5, 2012.

  −FBI 302 / Solomon Dwek debriefing August 8, 2006 by SA William B. Waldie.

  −FBI Otherwise Illegal Activity Authorization: Case 270D-NK-114696 / February 23, 2007, May 15, 2007, August 6, 2007, November 21, 2007, February 12, 2008, August 8, 2008.

United States House of Representatives [Judiciary Committee Majority Staff]: Allegations of Selective Prosecution in Our Federal Criminal Justice System. Prepared for Chairman John Conyers, Jr. April 17, 2008.

United States Supreme Court: Robert L. McCormick, Petitioner v. United States 500 U.S. 257, 111 S.Ct. 1807, 114 L.Ed.2d 307 No. 89-1918. / Argued Jan. 8, 1991. Decided May 23, 1991.

University Of Notre Dame Archives: Knute Rockne's "Win One for the Gipper" Speech.

USA v Alfonso L. Santoro: Information pleading. December 3, 2009.

USA v Michael Manzo, Dennis Jaslow and Joseph Castagna: criminal complaint executed July 23, 2009.

USA v. Anthony Suarez Trial Transcript: Volume 6 October 8, 2010 [6.1–6.157].

  Volume 12 October 19, 2010 [12.190-12.200].

  Volume 4 October 8, 2010 [2.193-2.196] 5.150-5.201.

  Volume 5 October 7, 2010 5.38-5.45, 5.50-5.121.

  Volume 6 October 8, 2010 [6.158-6.169 & excerpts from evidentiary hearing].

USA v. Daniel Van Pelt Trial Transcripts: Pp. 228-234.

  Criminal Complaint executed July 23, 2009.

  USA v. Louis Manzo [select court documents]:

Second Superseding Indictment returned July 8, 2011 [excerpts] p. 13.

District Court Opinion dismissing charges May 18, 2010 [excerpts] p. 18.

District Court Opinion dismissing charges February 17, 2012 [excerpts] p. 58.

Transcripts of Proceedings: March 23, 2010 [excerpts] p. 60.

Opposition brief [Hyde Amendment petition]: April 16, 2012.

USDOJ District Of New Jersey U.S. Attorney's Office: Press Release. July 23, 2009 [bidrig0723.rel].

Video Café: "Chris Christie urges reporters to 'take the bat' to 76-year-old widow." April 14, 2011.

Vos Iz Neis? News blog, Copying the *Asbury Park Press*: "Dwek Accuses Long Branch City Prosecutor Fixed Traffic For The Jewish Community." October 9, 2010.

Ward, Jon. *Huffington Post*: "Chris Christie Denied Mitt Romney Request To Appear At Campaign Event Days Ahead Of 2012 Election." November 6, 2012.

Wikipedia: Compilation of Polling Results for 2009 N.J. Gubernatorial Election. Compilation of Polling Results for 2013 N.J. Gubernatorial Election.

Wing, Nick. *Huffington Post*: "Chris Christie Called Obama To Congratulate Him, Offered Mitt Romney Condolences Over E-mail." November 8, 2012.

Young, Elise. *Bergen Record*: "Christie urges media to 'take the bat' to Senator Weinberg on pension issue." April 13, 2011.

Zegas, Alan L. Letter to the NY/NJ Port Authority Re: David Wildstein legal fees. January 31, 2014

Zernike, Kate & David M. Halbfinger. *New York Times*: "Christie Decides on October Vote for New Senator." June 4, 2013.

New York Times: Legislative Panel Rejects 2nd Christie Pick for State Supreme Court." May 31, 2011.

New York Times: "Top Christie Staff Sought to Disrupt Traffic as Revenge." January 8, 2014.

New York Times: "Christie Linked to Knowledge of Shut Lanes." January 31, 2014.

Index

Y

Z

About the Author

Louis Manzo grew up in the West Side Ward of Jersey City, New Jersey. He is the son of Alexander and Mary Manzo, and the brother of Allen, Ronald and Judy. Louis was raised as a devout Roman Catholic and went to Catholic schools through High School – Saint Aloysius Grammar School and Hudson Catholic High School. He describes it as a "great childhood." Lou's closest friends still remain the kids he grew up with in his old Jersey City neighborhood.

Lou enjoyed playing plenty of sports in his youth – his Dad was an outstanding high school athlete and became a huge advocate for the baseball and football teams that Lou played on from little league through high school. In high school, Lou was honored to serve as co-captain of the school's football team.

Attending Jersey City State College, Lou earned a Bachelor of Science Degree in Health Education. He also devoted some of his time to coaching the same high school and grammar youth sports that he had participated in during his youth.

Fresh out of college, Lou was intending to teach health science. In fact, he was offered a teaching contract to serve in the high school where he had done his student teaching. Suddenly, his intended career path took a detour. There was a shortage of licensed health personnel in the Jersey City Health Department and his high school health teacher happened to be the Assistant Health Officer there. He recruited Lou to continue his schooling and take an internship with the department.

Within a year, Lou passed the State licensing exam and began a career in public health. In nine years, he had worked his way up to Chief of the Department. It should have been an enjoyable job, but it just so happened that Jersey City was on the cusp of its major Hudson River waterfront transformation – old railroad yards and dilapidated piers into luxury condominiums, back offices for Wall

Street, and a major shopping mall. An assortment of developers were anxious to get the massive project rapidly constructed.

Time was money. In the blink of an eye, the "Gold Coast" was born. Unfortunately, one of the calloused trademarks of rapid development is cutting corners, and the problems this practice caused ended up on the doorstep of the health department that Lou officiated. The department dealt with everything from displaced waterfront rodent populations invading neighborhoods, occupational hazards associated with the development, to developers dumping hazardous waste into the Hudson River.

At this same time Manzo's office was monitoring clusters of cancer, along with respiratory and skin disorders in pockets of Jersey City neighborhoods. His investigation determined that a hazardous waste known as hexavalent chromium – a carcinogen– was responsible. *Does Erin Brockovich ring a bell?* The investigation uncovered the fact that three chrome manufacturing companies, which were once located and affiliated with businesses in Jersey City, had been selling off the slag residue from the manufacturing process to building contractors for use as foundation fill.

The slag was pure hazardous waste and the companies, fully aware of the dangers posed by the hexavalent chromium, were avoiding costly disposal fees and at the same time profiting from getting rid of the waste. The health department found contamination on more than 300 Sites throughout the city. On one site, where a department store had been constructed, the chromium had buckled up the pavement and cracked the building's walls and foundation, causing it to crumble.

The most common human victims were children – kids who played outdoors in the contaminated dirt. They ingested the chromium through their skin pores and respiratory tracts. One of the sites turned out to be a public elementary school: Jersey City's PS # 15. Teachers and staff reported that the green slime oozing out of the walls of the lunchroom had been doing so for years. The school board would simply have the walls scrubbed and washed down every so often, but never did anything more – they didn't know any better.

Manzo's office discovered that the State Health Department had been aware of the situation for more than a year. They took samples and never apprised Jersey City school or government officials about the goings on. Manzo dispatched investigators to the State Health Department, who swiped the files right out from under their noses. It proved the State officials knew it was hexavalent chromium and just walked away.

Manzo blew his stack and, to the chagrin of the school board and the development community, he ordered the school closed. School Superintendent Franklin Williams called him "a modern day Paul Revere. Someone willing to run with the lamp and tell us the truth." This finally galvanized massive federal and state resources to remediate the contaminated sights and initiate a health study for Jersey City residents.

That truth did not sit well with others. Trying to sell waterfront condominiums to out-of-towners while the chromium story was playing out on the six o'clock news was like spitting into the wind. The development community had just about had enough of Manzo – he was bad for sales. They finally mustered enough political clout to force his hand and Manzo moved on.

That happenstance led to Manzo's entry into politics. He decided to step onto the political turf of Hudson County to level the playing field. This time the cause was stopping the construction of a pollution-spewing County incinerator project that Manzo had been fighting against in his previous health department position.

Manzo put his name on the ballot as an independent candidate in a primary election for County Freeholder. He was taking on one of the most powerful political organizations in the country – the Hudson County Democratic Party. The party never had a candidate lose in a primary election, but there was a first time for everything, and in what the local newspaper called a "stunning upset," Manzo won the primary election for Freeholder.

A few days after his primary victory, the Chair of the Democratic Party came calling with a $10,000 contribution for the general election. Manzo asked him if the Party would publicize his platform against the incinerator. The answer was an emphatic, "No." Lou tore up the check and handed the chairman back the pieces. It made for a nice news story.

Manzo's first bill as a Freeholder called for a moratorium on the construction of the incinerator. The legislation was voted down 8-1. The Chair of the Freeholder Board appointed him to head the Board's environmental committee to research the matter. He then assigned the two Freeholders who were the incinerator's staunchest supporters to Manzo's committee. Manzo held a series of meetings every month for two years, while the County prepared the permits for the incinerator. He even invited the proponents and builders of the incinerator to participate at each meeting. The evidence his committee collected was overwhelmingly in support of the position that Manzo had advocated in opposing the incinerator. The committee reported to the full board with a several-hundred-page document that he had authored. The full Board of Freeholders reconsidered the original bill to kill the incinerator project, and this time it was unanimously approved.

Manzo next tempted fate by running for mayor of Jersey City. He was attacking the development communities' use of tax abatements as incentives to build on the most valuable land in Jersey City. They were essentially asking working-class resident to support the tax breaks being handed out by the politicians they had helped to elect. The development community threw everything they had behind candidates other than Manzo. Anyone was palatable to them but him. He ran for mayor three times – once in a special elections – but could never overcome the developers' money or the clout of the local political organization.

Manzo then opened an insurance company and was fortunate to build a business that netted him a substantial income. He ran once again for mayor, now better able to self-finance the bulk of his campaign. Despite spending serious money, Manzo was still never able to overcome the development clique that saw him as the devil. But he did manage to help elect Jersey City's first African American mayor in 2001, former United States Marshall Glenn Cunningham. Manzo supported him in the runoff election, after Lou had placed a close third in the initial round of balloting.

Glenn Cunningham and Lou Manzo were good friends for many years. In 2003, now Mayor, Cunningham asked Lou to run with him for the State legislature and represent the district as an Assemblyman. They both won. Mayor Cunningham's sudden and shocking death in 2004 caused Manzo's entry into the special election to fill his term. Again, his battles with developers would be Manzo's undoing.

As an Assemblyman, Manzo came to the aid of a downtown Jersey City community that was trying to convert an old abandoned elevated railroad embankment into a greenway and an elevated city park in an area much in need of open space. A developer had somehow surreptitiously acquired the embankment property through very questionable means and was intending to construct massive high-rise condominiums on the site. Manzo asked the Office of Legislative Services to investigate the land transfer. They discovered that the railroad had failed to give the City first option to acquire the property, as required by law, and the developer's claim on the property was voided. The developer went ballistic and threw money into the election against Manzo's candidacy. Battling the entrenched party organization along with the developer was too much to overcome. Manzo lost by a whisker.

Manzo continued to serve out a second term in the legislature, his most effective public office. His record as a state legislator was fruitful. He sat on the Environment & Solid Waste, Health & Senior Services, and Commerce Committees. Manzo was a co-prime sponsor of what is considered New Jersey's most monumental and landmark environmental law: The Highland's Preservation Act. The law conserved for perpetuity the state's reservoirs and the lands and grounds surrounding them.

Manzo also prime-sponsored the bill that enabled abandoned industrial properties to be cleaned up by using existing spill fund resources –The New Jersey Brownfield Legislation Act. In 2004, When the State attempted to curtail vital programs for New Jersey's elderly – PAAD & Senior Gold – Manzo initiated and assisted the legislative battle that saved and preserved them.

In 2006, when the Special Joint-Legislative Session on Property Tax Reform was called, Manzo was appointed to one of the coveted committee positions. There he initiated and co-prime sponsored a bill that produced the largest property tax rebate in NJ history.

He was also a proud co-sponsor of the legislation that enhanced one of the State's most effective anticrime laws – Operation Cease Fire. He also sponsored the law that made it illegal to recruit minors into a street gangs.

When Governor Corzine attempted to sell the New Jersey Turnpike, Manzo became one of the leading and most outspoken assembly members to challenge the governor. His and the efforts of other legislators were credited with cancelling the attempted sale. Manzo also wrote the first legislative bill to bring a casino to the New Jersey Meadowlands for the purpose of creating thousands of jobs and shoring up the region's economy. The bill did not clear committee, but serves as the blueprint for legislative efforts to make this a reality today.

After an unsuccessful run for Senate in 2007, Manzo served out his term and left the state legislature in 2008. At his own expense, he kept his former district office open and founded a public advocacy office. He was still intent on serving and helping constituents to overcome government problems.

In July of 2009 Manzo's life and Chris Christie's ambitions became painfully intertwined. Manzo was falsely arrested as part of the Bid Rig III sting. The charges were dismissed and he was completely exonerated in February of 2012.

Acknowledgements

A champion is someone who gets up when he can't.

– World Heavyweight Champion, Prizefighter Jack Dempsey

First and foremost, I thank God, my savior, Jesus Christ, for his benevolence in sending me the cast of people that he has along the way of my life's journey. Thank you to my family – Mom, Judy, Ron, Rose, Steve, Alan, Mary-Alexis, Stephen, and so many other family relations for the blanket of support they all provided. To the many dear friends – too numerous to name – who extended their best wishes and provided encouraging support for my predicament

My former legislative staff and office volunteers showed why they were the best in the world – helping me to put together a strategy for survival. Mark, Barbara, Rick, Donna, Daryl, Gerry, Dan, Gene, Freddie, Betty, Kathy, Bob, Erma, Roberto, Phil, and Kevin. Most especially Patty Lynch, who became my right arm for a while.

To the world's greatest attorney and a tremendous Guardian Angel, the very gutsy John D. Lynch. He not only put up with hundreds of phone calls and thousands of e-mails – he answered every one. He always made sure that I knew I was never going it all alone. A special thanks to John's office staff as well, especially Kathy, who inspired me with confidence, and to the able co-counsels and friends in my case, Sam DeLuca, George Tate, and Paulette Pitt.

My thanks to many in the media who covered our side of the story, asked questions, and didn't swallow everything that the prosecutors tried to spoon-feed the press, especially the *Jersey Journal* staff and Editor Agustin Torres; *Associated Press* and correspondent Dave Porter; the *Hudson Reporter's* Al Sullivan and the *Star-Ledger's* Bob Braun; many of the New Jersey news blogs who covered our court crusade as well. Thank you Pat O'Melia for facilitating my press conference, and Mike Ransom for the in-depth cable television interview that you produced.

Thank you to those who provided a public forum for speaking out against the injustices that I and my Bid Rig III fellow defendants suffered. Justice Integrity Project and its Director, Andrew Kreig were an invaluable resource for all of those falsely prosecuted. Andrew was another enormous source of strength. Daoud-David Williams and Jersey City's Community Action Series provided a platform for exposing the truth about the Bid Rig III prosecution scandal as well. Once I had prevailed in my legal battle, I decided to tell the story of this ordeal.

The Book

My foray into writing about the complexity of this corrupt government sting resulted in countless pages of reflections and information, but something seemed to be missing. Jeff Schultz of New York Creative Management saw the potential and introduced me to Judy Katz. Judy, an established writer, editor and connoisseur of the literary landscape, is someone who I am now honored to call a friend.

Without Judy Katz this book would not have come to fruition. She refocused the project to shine the harsh light of reality on the career of Governor Christie, who at the time was poised to become a presidential contender, with the exclusive inside account of Bid Rig III and my experience as a part but not the main focus of that history. It meant two more years of research, writing, and hard work, but it paid off. Under Judy's careful guidance, the new book came to life and she crafted a knockout book proposal to market it as well. Whenever there was a problem, Judy became a modern day Unsinkable Molly Brown, always keeping the project afloat and its spirit alive. For Judy's help I am eternally indebted.

Again, my gratitude to my Mom, who helped to support my efforts during that time. And thanks to my longtime friend, Moon, who became my New York guide during the shaping of the book and someone to bounce things off – he lived the nightmare of July 23rd, also falsely accused.

My special thanks to Kris Millegan, the publisher, who had the guts to shine light on this controversial work and bring it forth to the public. Kris has been bravely bringing inconvenient and uncomfortable truths to light for years. TrineDay became a perfect fit. My thanks to Kelly Ray, the TrineDay editor who helped to trim and shape this work to read even better.

A thanks to our talented website designer, Tony Iatridis, for the great job and look he gave the book's webpage.

Finally, my thanks to journalists Josh Margolin and Ted Sherman for their fantastic work on their book, *The Jersey Sting*, which I strongly recommend as a companion to this book. In it they provided exclusive commentary from the prosecutors who ran the Bid Rig III Sting, which was crucial to connecting and backing up the timeline of events that are an essential part of *Ruthless Ambition.*

How did Chris Christie happen? In this book, you will see how a system out of control can breed a man out of control. For his victims, there is a measure of solace in his downfall. For the public-at-large, one can only hope there is a lesson learned.

Louis Manzo
Belmar & Jersey City, New Jersey
2014